THE
IPSWICH
WITCH

THE
IPSWICH
WITCH

Mary Lackland and
the Suffolk Witch Hunts

David L. Jones

The
History
Press

First published 2015
Reprinted, 2019
The History Press
97 St George's Place, Cheltenham,
Gloucestershire, GL50 3QB
www.thehistorypress.co.uk

British Library Cataloguing in Publication Data.
A catalogue record for this book is available from the British Library.

ISBN 978 0 7524 8052 7

Typesetting and origination by The History Press
Printed in Great Britain by TJ International Ltd, Padstow, Cornwall.

CONTENTS

I would like to acknowledge;
my teacher
the emotional support and interest of
Jean Platten-Jones
Catherine Darling
and the professional support over many years of the staff of the
Ipswich branch of the Suffolk Record Office and the Ipswich Museum.

I

Two Deaths in Ipswich

In late August 1645, the streets and markets of Ipswich were surely much quieter than normal. Only those who had pressing reasons for staying would have remained in the town rather than make the short journey eastward to Rushmere Heath outside the walls. For on this day justice was to be done; one woman, Alice Denham, was to be hanged, and another, Mary Lackland, was to be burnt. (Mary Lackland's name was variously spelt as Lakland, Lakeland or Lacklond. Consistency in spelling was not a seventeenth-century habit, but for ease I have used Lackland throughout.) Alice Denham's case was never reported in any detail, and it is not possible to chart her story, but Mary Lackland's case can be investigated.

It had been around 100 years since the last execution by burning had been carried out in the town. Then, the burnings had been for heresy but now the executions were for the dreaded crime of witchcraft, causing interest not only within Ipswich but spread throughout the land by pamphlets. Though no one could have known it – and there is good reason to believe that some had planned the opposite – this was the last time that anyone was to be executed for witchcraft in Ipswich.

Any public execution was something of a ceremony, which the whole community was expected to attend, and each had their different parts to play: the child was to learn about the punishment of sin; the potential evildoer to be overawed by the terrible majesty of the law; the respectable were there to endorse it by their presence; the clergy to point out the moral lesson; and the governors to see their judgement carried out and to preserve order. Ideally, a public execution was a religious drama of confession and repentance, with the clergy praying for the victim's soul. This gave a role to the condemned themselves. As the penitent sinner they were supposed to warn others not to follow them, and to be grateful for those ministers who had led them to repentance and given them hope of divine forgiveness, assuring them of a place in heaven.

But on this day, had the women confessed and begged for forgiveness? There is good reason to think that at least one of them would have had no confidence in the minister and would have seen nothing to repent. The two women would have made the journey from the town prison, through the streets and then the lanes to the stake, standing in a slow-moving tumbrel or cart. It is unlikely to have travelled at more than a walking pace as it needed to accommodate the halberd-carriers on foot. It would have taken something like an hour and a half, or more.

As they passed through the town and into the surrounding countryside, they would have seen signs of the harvest – a time of worry, work and finally of celebration, of laden wagons gathered in the barn and of harvest home feasts. But this was part of the rhythm of a world that was passing them by, from which they were becoming more separate by the minute. Were the women in shock? Did they frantically go over in their minds what had they done to deserve this, and would God forgive them for whatever they had done wrong? Did they wonder why they, of all the accused, had to suffer? Or did they know exactly why it had suited people to choose them for this death?

Perhaps they still hoped for some last-minute reprieve.

Given the notoriety of this case, we can imagine more crowds than usual and the presence of the local East Suffolk gentry from their estates, with their costumes and horses and servants, all adding notes of colour against the otherwise dark tones of the townspeople.

Rushmere Heath, the execution site for Ipswich where Anne Bedingfield was also burnt for the murder of her husband in 1763. (Author's collection)

At the centre, seated on horseback, would have been the two Bailiffs of Ipswich – Puplett and Pemberton – resplendent in their fur-trimmed scarlet gowns of office; and grouped around them, other leading local councillors, chamberlains, clavigers, wardens of Christ's Hospital and so on, in their gowns of murray (a slightly less gaudy shade of red). In attendance on them would be the various town sergeants in their blue jackets and with the town's heraldic badge on their arms in silver, carrying their maces; and possibly the town's bellmen, ready to ring for silence.

Close by, in cap and gown of black and white surplices, would be the clergy of the town, led by the town lecturer, Mr Lawrence, all no doubt clasping their Bibles. Respectable merchants would be dressed in black, and the poor in leather jackets and undyed linen, some in the distinctive clothes of their occupations, including mariners in thrum caps and slop skirts. The children and other inmates of Christ's Hospital would have made up the rest of the crowd, kept in order by some of their fellows who had been pressed into service and issued with javelins or halberds for the occasion. The stylised engravings in *Foxe's Book of Martyrs* give a good impression of the scene.

And at the heart, the focus of this crowd was the scaffold and the stake. The stake was a substantial post, taller than a person and firmly fixed in the ground, to which the victim was chained, while bunches of faggots were piled up around her, ready to be set alight. The engravings in *Foxe's Book of Martyrs* show the victims buried to the waist with bundles of faggots, or sometimes straw – or else they have been stood inside a tar barrel. If the fire was built up high enough the victim could inhale hot gases immediately, causing them to suffocate before they actually burned alive. Even such an awful death could be worsened if the smoke blew away from the person so that they burned rather than asphyxiated, or if the fire was sulky and slow. The fiercer the fire, the quicker the death.

Since Mary Lackland was sentenced for petty treason (the crime of killing her husband, whether with a knife, by poison or by witchcraft) and not heresy, the executioner should have strangled her with a cord once she was tied to the stake and before the fire was lit. This was, however, a very rare procedure, and we simply don't know whether it was carried out and, if it was, whether it was carried out efficiently – nerves on the part of the executioner could sometimes lead to a botched job.

How are we to imagine the crowd? As a brutalised group of thugs of the sort depicted on northern European paintings of martyrdoms and crucifixions, baying for blood? Or stunned, perhaps silent and sullen, some praying or singing psalms? As we shall see, there are reasons for thinking that a few possibly did see one of the women as a martyr, that some had severe reservations about the case that may have troubled them later and, indeed, that another small group were doing their best to forget that they knew very well that the poor woman was innocent of the crimes she had been charged with, and that they had deliberately chosen to destroy her. The solemn governors of Ipswich would have done all they could to preserve order and avoid the brutal fairground nature of an eighteenth-century Newgate hanging. The drunkenness, disorder, and the criminal gamely defiant to the last would have been the reverse of their intentions. Perhaps they did not succeed completely.

The Protestant women burnt for heresy 100 years earlier had often made a heroic choice to suffer and die a martyr's death, rather than recant. However, these two women were dying knowing that they could not have done what they were accused of, and they may have had no belief or cause to sustain them. One thing of which we can be certain is that as Alice Denham and Mary Lackland approached their ends, as they looked around at the faces of the neighbours – the people they had known since childhood, their friends and their enemies, their daughters and families – wherever they looked there was no way out. Something terrible was about to happen to them. Then the sentence of the court – *incendant ad cineres* (may she be burnt to ashes) – was carried out.

As we look at this event and its background, some things – like the cost (£3 3s 3d) – are clearly recorded, with an intimate sense of detail and concreteness; but much is unrecorded and uncertain. The little that we know for certain lies in the borough records. We know also what was said to have happened from a contemporary pamphlet. But, of course, what is said to have happened and what did actually happen are two different things.

The only things we can be sure of are what Mary was accused of, and some of the stages of the case. So we should start with the bare bones; the execution of a convicted witch was the end of a long process, which had to pass through a series of stages first and could be blocked at any one of them:

1   There had to be in existence a belief in witchcraft as an explanation for why bad things happened to good people.
2   There had to be some kind of actual quarrel or dispute amongst ordinary people, usually villagers or the urban poor, that led to accusations of witchcraft. (I can think of no case in which two landowners or wealthy merchants accused each other in this way.)
3   The local authorities had to decide to take up the case, usually the local Justice of the Peace who was lord of the manor, along with the local clergyman.
4   The case had to go forward to the assizes or sessions of the peace, which would be held at some distance from the village.
5   A jury had to convict the accused and then the sentence had to be carried out.

It is clear that many accusations which had passed the third and fourth stages and became formal trials failed to gain convictions. Indeed, it seems as if the majority of trials, once put to a jury from outside the immediate locality of the accusation, led to acquittals. Very few cases, however, led to pardons *after* conviction.

Before the trial Mary would have been kept in the town gaol, a squat, medieval stone box-like building immediately next to the imposing west gate of the town. Conditions in such places were notorious, and there is no reason to think that those in Ipswich were any better than those elsewhere. Outside the prison we know that one prisoner was chained up, but allowed to beg on behalf of all the prisoners who had no one to pay for their food. If we are to believe one source from around this time, there were thirty-eight people held in the Ipswich gaol accused of witchcraft.

The pamphlet, *The True Informer for the 23 of July*, describes the situation in Ipswich as follows:

> That there are at least 38 Witches imprisoned in that town: all of which (except one) by the testimony of the town-Searchers, confesse that they have one or two paps on which the Devill sucks: divers of them voluntarily, and without any forcing or compulsion, freely declare [a stock phrase of the lobby in favour of trials], That they have mad a Covenant with the Devill, to forsake ----- It is further certified thence; that there are divers women apprehended upon suspition from day to day, which if they should all be found guilty, there is scarce a village in those parts free.

The Ipswich trial would have been held in the Moot Hall before the two bailiffs and the other justices. This was a rather grand brick building with a Dutch gable and projecting window looking out over the Cornhill, and attached to what had originally been the medieval church of St Mildred before it was reused by the borough. It was reached by an external staircase that ran up from the stocks and the conduit house. From the borough records, we learn that the staircase was painted in different colours; the hall was painted with the town's arms and the royal arms; that it contained a long table, presumably behind which the justices sat; there was an elaborate carpet to decorate the table and two elaborately carved muniment chests, which still survive; and to make the place more inspiring, the armour and weapons of the town watch, newly repaired and polished. (There is a useful inventory included in John Webb's book *The Town Finances of Elizabethan Ipswich*.)

The bench was made up of very experienced men who had held all kinds of civic offices at the top of their society. On this occasion, they would have been the two bailiffs, Richard Pupplet and Joseph Pemberton, and the other justices, William Cage and John Brandling. Though they were not to know it,

Ipswich Town (or Moot) Hall, the scene of Lackland's trial. (Suffolk Record Office)

Pemberton and Cage were never to hold a senior office again. Also in the courtroom would have been the town recorder, Nathaniel Bacon, and the town lecturer, Matthew Lawrence. The year before, on 11 April 1644, Richard Grimston had been elected one of the attorneys of this court in the room of his father (Bacon's *Annalls of Ipswche*). They were all connected with each other in a complex web of interests – political, religious, shared administrative duties, and so on.

The trial itself was very different from any procedure with which we are familiar. At least some of the proceedings took place in Latin or Law French, and were, therefore, completely incomprehensible to the majority of those present. The accused were not allowed lawyers. Apparently they should, in theory, have been able to call witnesses but could neither compel them to attend, nor make them take the oath. The prosecution could (but usually didn't) have counsel, could compel witnesses and could make them take the oath.

Everything rested with the judge, or in this case with the justices. The legal authority, Coke, explained that the reason for not allowing defence counsel was 'first, that the testimony and the proofs of the offence ought to be so clear and manifest as there can be no defence to it; secondly the Court ought to be instead of counsel for the prisoner'. In other words, the judge was supposed to act as the defence lawyer. This might have been acceptable with an assize court at which career judges from outside the area presided, but in the Ipswich Court, where the justices in cases like this were drawn from the tight little group of oligarchs that had brought the case in the first place, it was little more than a very bad joke.

Trials in any court in those days could be very quick indeed. At the Bury witch trials, the grand jury dealt with ninety cases in a day. Juries consisted of twelve men, owning the equivalent of property worth £4 a year. The laws of Ipswich provided that jury men should be selected from a panel of people called for jury service by spinning a knife. Those to whom the knife pointed were to serve. Presumably, the aim was to prevent packing a jury with people favourable to one side or another. Because jury service was often unpopular, it was apparently quite common for people to pay illegal substitutes to take their places on juries.

Juries often heard a batch of cases before retiring to deliberate on them. They would frequently not have a private secure jury room but deliberated in open court, so that anyone who wished to listen would have known who supported a conviction or an acquittal. As there is no record of a separate jury room in the Ipswich Moot Hall, this may have been the case here.

The cases were actually tried on 2 August 1645, and to the first two accused were added Rose Parker, Margery Sutton and Alice Daye, and a couple, James and Mary Emerson. The charges and verdicts were recorded as follows:

Margery, wife of James Sutton, for felony and witcherye Ignoramus [unproven] to find sureties for good behaviour.

Rose Parker, wife of Christofer Parker, for witchcraft and murder of John Cole, plea not guilty, found not guilty for feeding of imps.

Alice Daye, widow, for felony and witchcraft, plea not guilty, outcome unknown.

Alice Denham, widow, for felony and witchcraft, for feeding of imps, pleads not guilty, found guilty, therefore hanged.

Jacobus [James] Emerson and Maria [Mary] his wife for witchcraft and sending lice upon **Robert and Mary Wade**, plea not guilty, proved guilty and sentenced to 1 years' imprisonment and four times standing on the pillory.

Maria Emerson, wife of James Emerson, for witchcraft and sending lice upon Joan Seeley, pleads not guilty, proved not guilty.

Jacobus Emerson for felony witchcraft and murder of Richard Braye, pleads not guilty, found not guilty.

Mary Lackland for witchcraft and murder of William Lawrence, plea not guilty, found guilty.

For witchcraft and murder of Elizabeth Alldham, plea not guilty, found guilty.

For witchcraft and murder of Sarah Clarke, plea not guilty, found guilty.

For casting away Henry Reades shipp and murdering the said Read and divers persons unknown, plea not guilty, found guilty.

For felony and witchcraft and wasting the body of John Beale, plea not guilty, found guilty.

For felony and witchcraft and wasting the body of Thomas Holgrave, plea not guilty, found guilty.

For felony and witchcraft and nourishing of evil spirits, plea not guilty, found guilty.

For felony and witchcraft and traitorously murdering of John Lackland her husband, *plitavit non culpa, sed culpa, Incendet ad cineres* [plea not guilty, but guilty, let her be burnt to ashes].

The case was then rushed into publication in a pamphlet, *The Laws against Witches and Conjurations*, by printers in London, to add to the considerable amount of

The site of Mother Lackland's house in St Clement's. (Author's collection)

witchcraft literature already being produced for an eager public. This is the only Ipswich trial to have been published. In detail, there are differences between the actual record and the much fuller pamphlet; notably that the pamphlet insists on her confession. In fact, it is a refrain added to each separate charge, while in the legal record she is recorded as confessing to nothing.

The trial lists her victims as: William Lawrence, Elizabeth Alldham, Sarah Clarke, Henry Reade and the unknown crew of his ship, Thomas Holgrave, John Beale, and John Lackland. The pamphlet lists them as: Mr Lawrence and his child, Mrs Jenings' maid, John Beale and burning his new ship, and John Lackland. It is, of course, quite possible that Sarah Clarke or Elizabeth Alldham is hiding behind the description 'Mrs Jenings' maid'. The pamphlet describes events as follows:

The said Mother Lackland hath been a Professour of Religion, a constant hearer of the Word for these many years, and yet a Witch (as she confessed) for the space of near twenty years. The Devil came to her first, between sleeping and waking, and spake to her in a hollow voice, telling her that if she would serve him she should want nothing. After often solicitation she consented to him, then he stroke his claw (as she confessed) into her hands, and with her blood wrote the covenants. Then he furnished her with three imps, two little dogs and a mole (as she confessed), which she employed in her services. Her husband she bewitched (as she confessed) wherby he lay in great misery for a time and at last dyed. Then she sent one of her dogs to Mr Lawrence in Ipswich to torment him and take away his life; she sent one of them also to his child, to torment it, and take away the life of it, which was done upon them both; and all this was because he asked her for twelve shillings that she owed him and for no other cause.

She further confessed that she sent her mole to a maid of one Mrs Jenings of Ipswich, to torment her, and take away her life, which was done accordingly and this for no other cause but for that said maid would not lend her a needle that she desired to borrow of her, and that she was earnest with her for a shilling that she owed the said maid.

Then she further confessed she sent one of her imps to one Mr Beale of Ipswich who had formerly been a suitor to her grandchild and because he would not have her she sent and burnt a new ship, that had never been at sea, that he was to go master of; and sent also to torment him and take away his life; but he is yet living, but in very great misery, and it is vainly conceived by the doctors and chirugeons that have him in hand that he consumes and rots and that half his body is rotten upon him as he is living. But since her death there is one thing that is very remarkable and to be taken notice of: That upon the very day that she was burned, a bunch of flesh, something after the form of a dog, that grew upon the thigh of the said Mr Beale, ever since the time that she first sent her imp to him, being very hard, but could never be made to break by all the means that could be used, break of itself without any means using. And another sore that at the same time she sent her imp to him rose upon the side of his belly, in the form of a fistula which ran and could not be braked for all the means that could be used, presently also began to heale and there is great hopes that he will suddenly recover again, for his sores heal apace. He was in this misery for the space of a yeare and a halfe, and was forced to go with his head and his knees together, his misery was so great.

This 'confession' was published, along with the Act Against Witchcraft of James I, and some useful hints for discovering witches:

Now for as much as witches are the most cruell, revengefull and bloody of all others: the justices of the peace may not always expect direct evidence, seeing all their works are workes of darknesse, and no witnesses present with them to accuse them.

These tips were drawn from the trial of witches in Lancaster in 1612, and from Richard Bernard's *Guide to Grand-Jury Men* (1627).

A survey of all of the evidence shows us that the first and second stages of witchcraft accusations, those contained within the local community itself, seem to have been present in the Middle Ages and to have lasted well into the later nineteenth century. What the evidence also shows, is that the third and fourth stages, those connected with bringing formal cases, were not continuous but took place in clusters at various periods.

Witchcraft trials were not common in Ipswich. I estimate that around eleven people were accused, and there were few convictions throughout the whole period. A number of smaller places in Essex had seen more: for example, Hatfield Peverel saw twenty-five cases from 1566–1589; Stisted, twenty-three from 1581–1643 and St Osyth, twenty-one from 1582–1645. The most obvious such cluster are the 1645 cases that immediately followed the period of Archbishop Laud and Bishop Wren of Norwich, during which no cases at all seem to have been brought, and which in Suffolk is followed by a similar lack of cases, until a second flurry just after the Restoration.

This burning, like the previous heresy burnings, was not a common event. It was unique and, like them, marked a watershed in belief and practice. It did not take place in a vacuum, but is clearly related to the largest ever outbreak of witch trials in England – those associated with the activities of the famous Matthew Hopkins, the famous 'Witchfinder General' and his associate John Stearne. These two are never mentioned as being directly involved in the Ipswich trials, which therefore have not become so famous, but the Ipswich trials were backed by the interest group behind Hopkins at exactly the same time. Ipswich valued its separate legal jurisdiction to the rest of the county, and its council preferred to do the same thing in its own way. After this unprecedented campaign of witch hunting, nothing similar happened again.

To make some sense of this brutal occasion, we have to enter the world; walk its streets; learn what it believed and how it ran community life; understand its hopes and fears, its divisions and tensions; listen to its people and try and comprehend them. Paraphrasing the words of advice given to justices of the peace quoted above, it is fair to say:

> The historian may not always expect direct evidence, seeing all their works are workes of darknesse, and no witnesses present with them to accuse them

It will become rapidly clear that this remark not only applies to witches but even more to witchfinders, their backers and the justices of the peace before which they appeared.

As the evidence will show, the participants were confused and moreover they sought to confuse others. Yet, in this fog it is possible to see certain shapes loom up indistinctly, there are currents and eddies in the fog, there are forces hidden within it, even if we never see them clearly. We will find our expectations turned inside out.

Ipswich: The Setting

Ipswich has always been the market town and administrative centre of East Suffolk. Its position, about 7 miles from the coast and the estuary of the River Orwell, means that it has always had a port as well as a market. During the period of the witch trials it was comparatively much more important than it is at present. Textiles and the coastal coal trade, as well as the usual crafts and shops of a market town, helped to keep it prosperous.

The town was invisibly linked to a network of contacts and trade which, even at this early date, had become global. Trade across the North Sea with the Low Countries was constant. There was a significant Dutch colony in Ipswich during the reign of Henry VII, and troops led by members of the local Withipole family had campaigned for years on the Continent. Political and religious refugees from Suffolk took shelter in the Netherlands whenever necessary, Samuel Ward amongst them. Ipswich men had a warehouse in Elbing (Eblag) just outside Danzig (Gdansk) on the Baltic.

Men from Ipswich, led by Thomas Cavendish of Trimley and navigated by Thomas Eldred of Ipswich, had sailed around the world, the second group of English to have made the voyage. Local merchants were trading in North Africa and the Turkish Empire, and taking part in campaigns against pirates from Algiers.

This part of Suffolk, Ipswich and its hinterland, as well as the Harwich area on the other side of the river in Essex, had provided many of the backers of the first Virginia voyages. Bartholomew Gosnold, Edward Maria Wingfield, Richard Hakluyt and Captain Christopher Newport all played leading roles, and all came from a small region around the banks of the Orwell. The second and third governors of Virginia, Sicklemore and Scrivener bore the names of families who had supplied Ipswich with leading councillors and bailiffs (Sicklemore was also known as John Ratliffe, under which name he was governor). This probably accounts for why the Borough of Ipswich bought shares in the Virginia venture, which in time they passed on to the Ipswich town lecturer, Samuel Ward. Ward was organising the emigration of Suffolk people to New England. These ventures had been promoted by firstly the Earl of Essex, and then by Robert Rich, Earl of Warwick.

On any bright day in the seventeenth century, a visitor standing on the well-known beauty spot at Stoke Hills would have seen the whole of the town of Ipswich stretched out to the north before him, cradled in a bowl of land surrounded by hills. This view was captured by John Speed's sketch map of 1610, and by the later engravings and paintings of Buck, Clevelly and Frost.

To the south and west, the town was bordered by the estuary of the Orwell, with its fish weirs and oyster beds, then by the Gipping and the streams of the two water mills at Handford and Stoke Bridge. Water meadows gently led up to the gardens of the town. The green of the meadows contrasted with the white of the many blankets stretched out on tenterhooks, a testament to the town's textile industry (and a detail preserved on Speed's sketch map). Even from a distance, one could see that the centre of the town was green with gardens and orchards.

The northern side of the town contained most of the markets and shopping streets, while the southern river frontage contained the wharves and the maritime trades. The river was crossed by Stoke Bridge, which was a wooden bridge consisting of two sections like the modern Tower Bridge, which could be lifted by cranes for shipping, and were painted and gilded with the town and

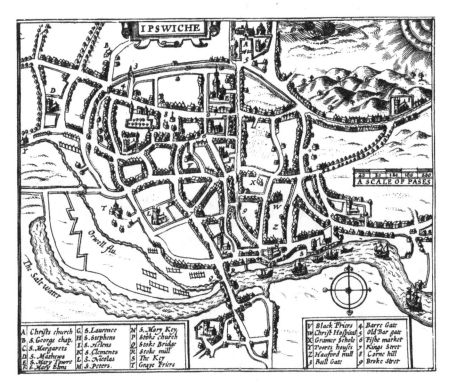

John Speed's 1610 Ipswich map. (Ipswich Museum)

royal arms. Alongside the bridge was a ford and there was a smaller footbridge at Handford Road.

Ships were moored along the quayside, and at the point where the river turns to the south the hulls of the ships under construction drawn up on the banks were a common sight, reflecting the important maritime interests of the town. From the reign of Elizabeth I, Ipswich had been identified as the largest producer of sail cloth in the country. It was also a major supplier of rope, and the region produced the majority of supplies for the navy – including an extremely hard, Parmesan-like cheese called 'Suffolk Bang'. Trinity House certificates show that in this period, Ipswich built more ships than any town except London. A little later, during the Restoration, Suffolk was seen as having inexhaustible oak forests for ship building. Ipswich was also the home port for the sailing fleet that ran the coastal coal trade from Newcastle to London.

To the north and the east, the town was enclosed by the green ramparts of its earthen walls, on top of which was a wooden palisade looming over the smaller houses. In front of the rampart were the well-maintained ditches, access to which was controlled by stiles and gates. Householders could climb to the top of 'their' section of wall, and had a key to their little section of the ditch beyond. These ramparts were pierced by the grand Westgate, with its stone base and brick upper floors, soon to be ornamented with its own clock. Visitors entering by this gate were reminded of the brutal realities of life when passing by a chained-up prisoner, who would be stationed there to beg on behalf of all the penniless prisoners held in the gate.

Westgate. (Ipswich Museum)

A south-west prospect of Ipswich. This detail shows the town's waterfront from Stoke Hills at the base of Stoke Windmill, looking across at St Clement's Parish. (Samuel and Nathaniel Buck, 1774, Suffolk Record Office)

Next was the Northgate, and at the other end of the town the new bar gates at the end of Carr Street. At this time, the gates and walls, which had lost something of their practical use, were busily being refurbished to meet the threats of the Civil War.

Apart from the stone and flint churches, Blackfriars Monastery, and the West gate and North gate, there were five or six brick buildings in the town. Three of these were quite elaborate. The most imposing was Seckford Place in Westgate Street, with its turrets and cupolas. Christchurch Mansion was a little less grand, but was beautifully surrounded by its own park, and then was finally the smaller New Place in Gyppeswyck Park. One church, St Mary Elms, was also partially brick. The Moot Hall, the second storey of the Westgate, and Pykenhams gateway were also brick. The use of brick and even the design of some of the buildings reflected the town's strong links with northern Europe.

All the remaining buildings were timber-framed houses of typical Suffolk form, although the borough had insisted, as a fire precaution, that all were to have tiled, rather than thatched, roofs. A few were the town houses of great landowners; there were mansions belonging to the Wingfields, the

Corner post with monstrous padlocked woman, from No. 10 Lower Orwell Street, by John Shewell Corder. The original post is now in the Ipswich Museum. (Ipswich Museum)

Withipoles, the Seckfords, the Duke of Suffolk, Sir Thomas Rushe and Lord Curson. Somewhere between Northgate and Carr Street lay the mansion of Sir Harbottle Grimston the Elder.

Most, however, were the homes of the town's oligarchy of rich merchants and traders. They represented a major, but surprisingly little-studied, art form, for the principal beams of these houses were richly carved and sometimes painted. Their upper storeys were supported by massive oak corner posts carved with monumental figures and emblems that, for their variety and striking designs, recall

Tudor totem poles. Inside, they were plastered and covered in mural paintings, or lined with painted 'steyned' cloths which served as poor men's tapestries. The images on all these artworks were drawn from Christian angels and bishops, plant designs, figures of workmen, political and heraldic imagery, classical gods and heroes, but also – and as time progressed, more and more frequently – with images of bisexual creatures, heavily bearded but with big breasts and nipples and animal legs, emerging from foliage: half-men and half-women; half-human and half-animal; half-animal and half-plant. Carvings of screaming grotesque women with animal legs, imprisoned in gibbets, appeared on the outside of buildings. There is, I think, no clear contemporary statement that these carvings represented witches, nor is there any clear explanation of why they were carved on houses, but the fact remains that such images coincide with the witch fear.

The principal shopping streets of the town ran from the Westgate to the Cornhill, and from thence along Tavern Street and Carr Street, and along the Buttermarket and Dial Lane. These, and the more prestigious residential streets, had been progressively paved since the reign of Elizabeth I. They were designed with a central channel for refuse, and the owners of the houses were each responsible for the stretch of road along their frontage and out to the channel. The paving stones were probably stone setts: larger stones laid edgeways.

The council was concerned about carts, and forbade any carts used within the town to be shod with iron tyres in order to prevent them from damaging the roads and lanes. Cart drivers were ordered to drive with one wheel on either side of the channel in the middle of the road – in part, as a protection for

Cornhill, showing the square and Moot Hall. (Ipswich Museum)

children playing in the streets. Anyone blocking the roads with rubbish; leaving piles of timber or other materials in the streets; with holes in the roadway outside their house or leaving cellar trapdoors opened; setting up the posts of inn signs; extending their property with a new bay window or study; or shoring it up with timbers in the streets, could expect to be reported by the ever-watchful 'headboroughs' and ordered to make repairs, fined or made to pay extra rent for their additions. Further improvements were introduced in 1614, when the town began to lay water pipes along main streets.

Streets in the town centre were often extremely narrow, and with stalls running down each side it must have been difficult even for shoppers on foot to make their way through the crowds. The main streets were 'pedestrianised' on market days and posts were set up at either end from the Westgate to the New Bar Gates to prevent anyone trying to get a cart through.

Most buying and selling was done directly from the houses of the tradesmen. The shutters on the windows of groundfloor rooms were often hinged horizontally along the top of the window so that, when propped open, they sheltered the stalls of boards on trestles set up underneath them. By James I's reign, some shopkeepers were making their stalls more elaborate and permanent, and setting up glass windows – much to the concern of the headboroughs. One house might contain several shops, each consisting of a single small room rented from the wealthy merchant who had had the house built.

From amongst the mass of houses, the towers of twelve churches rose up. Almost as prominently, windmills with their sails turning in the breeze could be seen on the tops of most of the surrounding hills. The violent religious changes of the Reformation had left their visible mark on the town, as the two Austin priories of Christchurch and St Peter and Paul, along with the priories of Whitefriars, Greyfriars and Blackfriars, still stood but were either converted to other functions or left as substantial ruins.

It is easy to see why local authors, like Nathaniel Bacon in the 1640s, described Ipswich as 'the glory of the parts about.' Evelyn, in 1677, wrote in his diary that 'it is for building cleanness and good order, one of the best towns in England' and also noted, 'There is not any beggar asks alms in the whole place, a thing very extraordinary, so ordered by the prudence of the magistrates.'

Ipswich is particularly well provided with a wealth of contemporary documents. From these, the picture that emerges of the town is one of an obsessively controlled and recorded community, far from the squalor, beggary and chaos beloved of the historical film-maker. However, away from the principal streets, there would have been areas with farmyard smells and heaps of muck, and certainly the tanners' and curriers' lanes and the dyers' pits cannot have smelt too pleasant.

This world pulsed according to its own slow rhythms. The weekly cycle ran something as follows: Monday, the Cloth Hall was open; Tuesday, wagons left

An earlier style of corner post. It shows a blacksmith at work, rather than the monsters which later became popular. The corner post is one of the few still in its original position, at the corner of Northgate Street and Oak lane. (Suffolk Record Office)

from the Waggon & Horse Inn in the Buttermarket for London; on Wednesday, a general market was held, the Cloth Hall was open and a compulsory lecture was held at St Mary Tower church; Thursday had no special features; on Friday, the Cloth Hall was open again and another lecture was held; on Saturday the main food market was held on the Cornhill, with small stalls selling oysters or nuts; and on the Sabbath there were the regular church services, and in addition the three hour lecture in St Mary Tower church.

The yearly cycle still included some of the older religious festivals such as Christmas and Hocktide, but Corpus Christi survived only as a guild feast for wealthy merchants. In addition, there were the secular annual ceremonies of opening the markets, the training of the town militia, the four Sessions of the Peace, and the distinctively Puritan ceremonies of November the Fifth (the annual symbolical burning of evil in the form of the Pope and Cardinals), and Crownation Day (the celebration of the coronation of Elizabeth I, a festival which irritated the Stuarts, who would have preferred their own coronations to be celebrated).

The town held two fairs a year, and other aspects of commercial life were seasonal too. The collier ships tended to sail together to Newcastle and back; merchants timed their visits to Bordeaux to coincide with the new vintage, and went together to Antwerp for the cloth fairs.

It is easy to imagine what it sounded like, for each of the various trades had its own distinctive series of sounds. The rattle of looms, the hammering of metalworkers on anvils, the creaking of wheels, the ringing sound of caulking mallets (the heads of which were designed to resonate) from the shipyards, and the warm sound of stones grinding together in the mills.

The boundaries of Ipswich were not delimited by the walls and the fields immediately surrounding them. Ipswich projected a further 7 miles or so eastwards, along the river down to the mouth of the Orwell, including some of the land at Felixstowe and part of the town of Harwich. Its charter gave it control over the Orwell, and the Admiralty rights for the river belonged to the town. At this time travel by road was slow and difficult, and the best route north from London was along the coast by ship. So, the Stuart 'motorway' to the capital from Ipswich passed down the Orwell by 'hoy' (a ferry boat powered by oar and sail) to Harwich to take a place on a coastal ship.

Harwich was the nearest town to Ipswich, and they were linked to each other in a variety of ways. Every year, when the bailiffs of Ipswich travelled around the bounds of their authority, they went down the Orwell by boat and landed and walked through part of Harwich to remind everyone that King John had given them control over the whole of the port of Orwell. From Harwich it was also possible to take a boat up the Stour to Brantham and Manningtree or to Sudbury. At present, road and rail transport makes Harwich a distant, remote spot from Ipswich, but until the early nineteenth century the two towns were closely linked.

Houses had already begun to spread out from the walls, especially along the dockside to the east, where the town had spread through the parish of St Clement's. This was where Mary Lackland lived. The riverside and port of area of Ipswich was divided between three parishes: St Peter's, St Mary Key and St Clement's. St Clement is the patron saint of sailors, and this was the maritime quarter and the one that had suffered the most from Buckingham's wars, and whose sailors had been most active in the rioting against Bishop Wren. Here lived the crews and captains of the coal trade.

St Clement's was a relatively new area of Ipswich just outside the circle of the old town wall. Past the old wall down to the Orwell ran the stream called the Wash. At its lower end were public toilets which the stream cleared out into the river. To the north, it was bounded by Ropers Lane (later the Rope Walk) and to the south by the river. To the east it spread out into the countryside. Through it ran the road to the south-east of the town, then known as St Clement's Street, and now known as Fore Street. This road led to the estuary villages and finally to the Landguard Fort opposite Harwich.

St Clement's waterfront, from a panoramic painting by John Cleveley (1712–1777). (Ipswich Museum)

We can learn more about St Clement's from a detailed study of two maps of Ipswich: that of John Speed, published in 1610, not strictly surveyed and using a pictorial approach, and the far more accurate survey made by Ogilby in 1668 and published in 1678. These two maps, the differences between them, and the borough records together reveal that Mary Lackland was living in the middle of a property development boom, and what amounted to a large open air industrial area intermingled with housing.

Between 1610 and 1678 the whole river front of the Orwell had been turned into wharves, and a shipyard with two slipways had been built. Three rope walks had been set up in the parish. There was a gunpowder factory, poor women were issued with spinning wheels, and merchants' houses were full of looms. The Ipswich probate inventories show that Henry Piper had nine looms, and that Thomas Hawkins, who specialised in weaving sailcloth for sails, had seven looms. There was also a huge claypit for brick and tile, as well as timber yards, so house builders did not have far to look for materials.

Along the river frontage, fine new houses had been built, probably in the reign of Elizabeth I. These properties consisted of the house of the merchant, provision for an office and, in some cases, a shop, running parallel with the street frontages. A number seem to have had a large carriage entrance, which led to a square courtyard with first-floor galleries over an open colonnade which could be used to provide cover and stabling for teams of pack horses. Running back at right angles to the street, there was accommodation for apprentices; rooms fitted out with looms; and warehouses to store goods ready for shipping or for goods brought into the town by water. These led down to moorings alongside the quayside waterfront.

Two good examples still survive, and more are known from later drawings, photographs and surviving decorative timbers. The properties now known as 'Isaac Lord's', the 'Neptune' and the former '98 Fore Street' had all received elaborate new frontages in the 1630s, of which the demolished No. 98 was the most elaborate, decorated with bearded men with prominent breasts and cloven goats' feet.

Behind these grand properties, with their desirable waterfront locations, was the main street, St Clement's Street. On the other side of the road, especially behind the street front, were much smaller properties, many rented out and quite densely packed, between the main street and the churchyard of St Clement's. These houses were often let to people connected with the maritime trades.

The borough documents called 'Enrolments' or 'Entries upon the Rolls' recorded purchases of land within the Borough of Ipswich. Each plot is defined by its relationship to the plots that surrounded it, and frequently an individual's profession is recorded too. They show, therefore, those parts of town where development was going on and where properties were changing hands fast. They do not provide a complete or organised picture, for example they do not record ownership where no change occurred, and they don't appear to include transfer as a result of marriage or inheritance, except as notes. Nevertheless, taken jointly they can be used to build up a picture of a neighbourhood in detail, almost providing a street directory of occupations and of families. This is what they tell us of St Clement's:

Open ground was being filled in and the former Cold Dunghills of the town were being built over. Much of the land, when it had been open fields, had belonged to the former Dominican priory, Blackfriars, and was called Abbots or Friars Close. This land had first come into the hands of a Nicholas Freeman and was then sold to Thomas Tye, a gentleman of Clopton, and Richard Bull, a shipwright of Harwich. They, in turn, had sold off the land in smaller parcels to individuals who had subdivided it again into tenements which were being let to poorer people.

In this way, the north side of New Street had been developed. There was land (later shown as an orchard in 1678) belonging to John Ward, and Luke Jowers, a turner; then a passageway giving access to the fields behind the houses of W. Hammond, a mariner; Richard Cole, a shipwright; and the last house which Tobias Dawes, a carpenter, had sold to J. Plover, a sailor.

The south side of New Street had been developed by Richard Kettle Snr, a chapman (later on in the same document described as a maltster), and Richard

Pilaster showing a demonic figure from the facade of No. 98 Fore Street, St Clement's, Ipswich, c. 1638. (Ipswich Museum)

Kettle Jnr, a maltster. Richard Kettle Snr became a bankrupt and ran away to avoid his debts. This forced sales to Samuel Lane of Washbrook, yeoman; Richard Grymeston (or Grimston) of Ipswich, gentleman; James Smithe of Ipswich, maltster; J. Wilbie, maltster, and T. Jenings of Wherstead, yeoman. Eight people, including R. Kettle Jnr, were living in the rented houses. (Enrolments 1636–1637. 21. 16 September 1637.)

Next to the church was a pound in which stray animals were kept until they could be collected by their owners.

St Clement's Church Lane ran down at right angles to New Street to meet St Clement's Street. Halfway down on the west side of the street was a warehouse for coal, and on the corner was land belong to Mary Lackland's husband, John. His western neighbour was William Gravenor, tailor, who later sold part of his land that would become a house rented to Edward Button, sailor. The house and land at the back, running along the churchway that separated the houses from the parish churchyard, belonged to Selfden Hoye, a mariner who had a share in the coal warehouse.

The principal inn was called the Cocke, and stood at the corner of the street. There was another called the Ship. The house belonging to Thomas Eldred was in this section of the street. Thomas Eldred was the navigator who voyaged with Captain Thomas Cavendish, the second Englishman to travel around the world, and who had brought back an enslaved African who died at Little Wenham in 1618. Eldred's house was also decorated with fine carvings, painted frescoes of antique work in which strange half-humans cavort and a mantlepiece with a picture of his ship, himself and the world (these are now in Christchurch Mansion).

A survey of the poor, carried out in Ipswich in 1597, gives a detailed picture of the poor of St Clement's. Although decades had now passed, and the individuals named were all dead by this time, it is likely that it still gives us an insight into the life of the poor. It shows that St Clement's had the second largest number of poor (St Matthews – seventy-four, St Clement's – thirty-nine, St Nicholas – thirty-two, Stoke – sixteen, St Mary Elms – twelve, St Mary Tower – five, St Mary Key – five, St Lawrence – three). Many of the St Clement's poor were widows, as follows:

Mother Ingram, aged 80, who lived by spinning and carding, received 7d.

Agnes Curtis, aged 66, who was lame, had no trade and received 3d.

Mother Forde, aged 70, earnt 8d for picking oakum and received 4d.

Mother Bunche, widow, aged 70, earnt 8d for picking oakum and received nothing.

The Widow Ward, aged 44, who had two small children, earnt nothing and received nothing.

Widow Ellen Howldernose, aged 34, with two small children, earnt nothing and received nothing, but it was felt she should be provided with a spinning wheel and cards and taught how to use them.

Widow Susan Blage, aged 40, knitted and received 6d in relief.

Widow Abell Arnold, aged 50, earnt 6d by picking oakum and had two children, one at school and one earning by knitting. She received 2d relief.

Widow Eme Daye, aged 46, earned by knitting and had three children, one at sea, one knitted and the other was unemployed. She received nothing but should be given two wheels and cards.

Widow Thomysinge Nowell, aged 52, picked oakum, earned 4d, had two children who knitted but should be given spinning wheels and taught.

Widow Margaret Powell, aged 50, dressed hemp and had a daughter.

Widow Agnes Rytchman, lame, 66 years old, 'some small relief will suffice', received 8d.

Widow Fynne, aged 70, was a woman's keeper with one child of 14 who was idle.

So, a large number of the poor were widows who made a living by picking oakum or knitting. Picking oakum involved unpicking rope so that it could be used by ships' caulkers, who hammered it into the seams of a ship to help make it

Carving from a house in Carr Street, believed to be part of a courtyard colonnade. The evil witch is captured in an iron cage similar to those in which the bodies of the hanged were exhibited. (Ipswich Museum)

watertight. However, the borough was keen to make sure that poor women were taught to spin. It is clear just how dependant they were on Christ's Hospital, which provided them with work and some financial support. This is what it meant to be a widow in St Clement's. Widow Lackland's life, fifty years later, would not have been very much different.

Christ's Hospital was a close neighbour of the Lacklands, as the following set of property transactions show. Closer towards the walled town stood the house, rented property and lands of Daniel Snowe, a salt refiner who, in 1630, became the treasurer and one of the wardens of Christ's Hospital. In 1635 he became a portman, and was well on his way to the top of the borough oligarchy. However, in 1636 Nathaniel Bacon records that:

Mr Daniel Snowe, upon his earnest offer and request in regard of weakness of body shall be discharged off and from office of Portman, immediately from and after he shall have conveyed his house in Clements, purchased of Peter ffisher and Samuel Lane, to ffeoffees for the educating and apparelling of poore children in Chr: Hospitall.

And on 13 July 1636:

Mr Puplett, Mr Aldus, Mr Tyler, Mr ffisher, Wm. Sparrow, Robt. Duncon, Willm. Hayles, Tho; Ives Jun: shall be feoffees of Danll. Snows house, to p'mitt

Brown's Courtyard looking out on to Fore Street. A nineteenth-century view of an elaborately decorated Ipswich merchant house fallen into ruin. The corner post is in Ipswich Museum. (Suffolk Record Office)

the governors of Chr: Hospitall from time to time to take the p'fits thereof, to maintaine the house, and wth the rmt. To educate, maintaine, and binde out apprentice soe many of the poore children of this Town as the same will reache unto.

The transaction was duly entered in the Enrolments, which give some more details of the property (Enrolments, 1635–1636.12):

Daniel Snowe of Ipswich salt fyner and wife Abigail p Richard Pupplett of Ipswich gent, J. Aldus of Ipswich gent, W. Tyler of Ipswich mercer, P. Fisher of Ipswich mercer, W. Sparrowe of Ipswich grocer, R. Donnkon of Ipswich tanner W. Hailes son of Richard Hailes of Ipswich mercer, T. Ives junior son of T. Ives of Ipswich mercer, tenement in occupation J. Benjamin in parish of St Clement Ipswich since in occupation of T. Nuttman and tenements in occupation of Beatrice Bacon widow J. Bice and – Glede widow between messuage of Samuel Grene and messuage of T. Scott clerk on N and tenement now or late R. Longley in occupation R. Lakeland and messuage late T. Cocke on South as trustees for governors of Christs Hospital Ipswich for the education of children in said Hospital 15 July 1636. Enrolled 16 Juily 1636.

This is written in the usual compressed style of the Enrolments, and means that Daniel Snowe and his wife Abigail (who had to register her agreement to the transaction because, in Ipswich, the widow would otherwise be entitled to the use of the property during her lifetime) have passed to the leaders of the town council (whose names of Puplett, etc, are listed), a large tenement which is now rented to T. Nuttman and was previously rented to J. Benjamin, and three smaller tenements rented to Beatrice Bacon, widow; J. Bice, widow; and the Widow Glede. North of the property, which Daniel Snow was renting out, were the two tenements of Samuel Grene and T. Scott, clerk. South of this property was a tenement belonging to R. Longley, who had let it to R. Lakeland (a relative of Mary Lackland, the accused witch), and a house owned and lived in by T. Cocke.

This bit of land was at a point where the street ran north–south and not east–west. From another Enrolment (Enrolments 1644–1645. 3), the north and west head of T. Cocke's property was the way from Cold Dunghills to the church of St Clement's. The widow Abigail Snow lived in a house that she purchased from her daughter and her husband, which also was on the south side of this way.

This was the world of Mary Lackland.

3

THE HOLY CITY OF IPSWICH
AND ITS ENEMIES

The task of town government was seen as a religious duty, a struggle to create a godly community. Forty years later, in 1682, John Bunyan caught this idea exactly, in his book *The Holy War*.

Now there was in this gallant country of Universe a fair and delicate town, a corporation called Mansoul; a town for its building so curious, for its situation so commodious, for its privileges so advantageous (I mean with reference to its origin) that I may say if it, as was said before of the continent in which its is place, there is not its equal under heaven.

Bunyan goes on to describe the house kept ready for its Lord Shaddai, and the town's gates: Eye gate, Ear gate and so on. This situation was, of course, too good to continue and the town was taken over by agents of Shaddai's enemy, Diabolus. Diabolus put in two of his own creatures, Lord Lustings as mayor, and Mr Forget-Good as recorder:

Besides these Diabolus made several burgesses and aldermen in Mansoul such as out of whom the town might when it needed chose them officers, governors, and magistrates. And these are the names of the chief of them: Mr Incredulity, Mr Haughty, Mr Swearing, Mr Whoring, Mr Hard Heart, Mr Pitiless, Mr Fury, Mr No-Truth, Mr Stand-to-Lies, Mr False-Peace, Mr Drunkeness, Mr Cheating, Mr Atheism – thirteen in all. Mr Incredulity is the eldest, and Mr Atheism the youngest of the company. There was also an election of common councilmen and others, as, bailiffs, sergeants, constables and others; but all of them like to those afore-named, being either fathers, brothers, cousins or nephews to them, whose names for brevity's sake, I omit to mention.

During this time, Lord Innocence had been murdered, Lord WillbeWill had thrown in his lot with Diabolus' men, Mayor Understanding was in house arrest and Recorder Conscience was half mad. Town politics was a very serious business – a religious obligation.

In Ipswich, twice a week the two bailiffs in their scarlet gowns and fur tippets, followed by the twelve portmen in their murray gowns and tippets, and the rest of the common council preceded by the mace bearers, would process through the town the short distance from the Moot Hall to the church of St Mary Tower, called by the bell that they had repaired. They had been doing this since 1576, paying a fine of 16s 8d for the use of Christ's Hospital if they turned up incorrectly dressed. Passing into the porch under the newly installed sundial, they took their seats in the new pews set up for them, as the mace bearers placed the silver maces into the wrought-iron mace holders they had paid to fix on the columns. In the case of the bailiffs, at least they had new cushions made for them. The powerful and important would enter their own family pews, and the rest of the congregation would take up their places as custom dictated – men to one side, women to the other. The church might

Title page to John Bunyan's *Holy War* showing the town and corporation of Mansoul surrounded by the forces of evil. (British Library)

have lost the statues of the saints, but it had gained the new funeral monuments of the merchants whose descendants sat in the corporation seats.

They had come to hear the town lecturer preach (whom they paid). It was his duty to preach two three-hour sermons every week, on Wednesdays and Fridays. The children of Christ's Hospital were marshalled on to stools in the aisles, kept well away from the council, who had had the former chapel of St Catherine converted into their private corporate pew with special places for the recorder and the bailiffs. This had been done in 1579:

[Assembly Book 30 Sept, 21 Eliz. 1579.]
It is agreed that there shall be no children from henceforth sett on the chapell where the Portmen do sytt in St Mary at Tower and that the mydell dore be shett upp and a convenient place therto be made for the recorder to sett in and also then a convenient dore be made where the Portmene do enter the said Chapell and that the treasurer make these dores and seats at the town's charge and that the 24 of the town shall have the use of the seat already made afore the said chapel from the chancel doore to the arch wher Mr Bayliffs sitt and that convenient places be made where no seat now is.

This was the age when spoken and written English became a major art form: the age of the King James Bible, Foxe's Book of Martyrs, Milton and Bunyan.

Sermons were a major performing art, written down and circulated. Connoisseurs of sermons could recall ministers who would reduce a church crammed full of listeners to tears by acting out a dialogue between the minister and God himself, in which God threatened to take away and hide the Bible because no one really took it seriously, while the minister begged for one last chance. Another could terrify a church by imitating the roars of pain and groans of the damned in hell. Mary Lackland was described as an eager listener to sermons.

Sermons were supposed to guide the lecturer's flock, including especially the council, for they bore the heavy task of ensuring that Ipswich followed the heavenly blueprint contained in the Bible and interpreted for them by the lecturer. He was by far the best paid town official, chosen with the utmost care, given a free house, with access to a fine theological library and treated with the greatest deference. Ipswich had either the first or second earliest public library in England (depending on whether one takes the date of the will that established the library, or the date on which the library actually was established) and it still survives.

When the lecturer had incurred some extra expenses in 1577, the council named several 'persuaders' to go into the various wards of the town and ask everybody to make a contribution towards the expense. Everyone, that is, except the portmen and the common council.

The three heads of the Ipswich community. Tobias Blosse, the bailiff and head of the merchant oligarchy, Samuel Ward the town lecturer and head of the Puritan movement in Ipswich, and Nathaniel Bacon, town recorder and chief legal advisor to the town, as well as author of the first history of Ipswich. (Ipswich Museum)

In St Mary Tower, Samuel Ward had thundered to the council of Ipswich, in a sermon quickly printed and published as *Jethro's Justice of the Peace*:

A Justice must have manhood which our straight buttoned, carpet and effeminate gentry wanting, cannot endure to hold out a forenoon or afternoon sitting without a tobacco bayte, or a game at bowls, or some such breathing to refresh their bodies and minds.

It is incredible to those who know it not, what strength great men will put to (especially if once interested) for the upholding of a rotten alehouse, countenancing of a disordered retainer, etc., the resistance whereof requires it not some spirit.

I mean such as hold religion a disparagement to the gentry and fear nothing more than to have a name that they fear God, who think when they have gotten an office, they may swear by authority, oppress by licence, drink and swill without control. What shall I say of such? Are these gods and children of the most high or the characters of his most holy image? Devils are they rather, than deputies for Him, Imps of his kingdom, far better becoming an ale bench than a shire bench.

Such as the country calls capon-justices: as also such mercenary lawyers as sell both their tongues and their silences, their clients causes and their own consciences, who only keep life in the law so long as there is money in the purse. And when this golden stream ceaseth, the mill stands still, and the case is altered: such extorting officers of Justice as invent pullies and winches for extraordinary fees, to the miserable undoing of poor suiters: such false perjured sheriffs stewards of liberties and their deputies as for money falsifie their charges: such corrupted jurates and witnesses of the post, which are as hammers and swords and sharp arrows in their brethren s hearts: such Cheese-bailiffs and lamb-bailiffs as vex the poor countryman with unjust summons to the assizes and sessions, with the rest of that rabble.

Justice like the statue in Daniel.

The head of gold.

The shoulders of silver.

The legs and feet or iron and clay or mire. Indeed the very mire and dirt of the country, the bailiffs, stewards of small liberties, bum-bailiffs, gaolers etc. If Beelzebub wanted officers, he need no worse than some of these: what mysteries have they to vex the poor countryman with false arrests? And by virtue of the statute tying every freeholder of forty shillings per annum to attend the assizes, but I list not to stire this sediment of the country too unsavoury to be raked up in a sermon.

Ward's listeners on the council, the bailiffs who were themselves magistrates, cannot have been dozing in their seats at this point. The first part of this quotation might perhaps have had them nodding in agreement. They were no gentry, effeminate or otherwise. However, they knew who the closest gentleman to Samuel Ward actually was. It was Sir William Withipole, whose manor of Christchurch included all of Ipswich town to the north of Tavern Street, in which, in keeping with the name, were several taverns. Withipole, rumoured to be a closet Catholic, was not popular with the town's rulers. His family and the town council had been squabbling over control of the water supply for decades. As it happens, Christchurch Mansion had a bowling green.

However, the real bailiffs must surely have felt a little uncomfortable with his attacks on corrupt bailiffs purchasable with cheese or a lamb. The poor in his audience surely were beginning to listen with interest.

This insistence on the political dimension of religion, the sacred nature of town politics, continued perhaps less fiercely but just as strongly in the lectures of a contemporary lecturer, Ward's successor Matthew Lawrence.

The Use and Practice of Faith was delivered in the public lectures at Ipswich by 'the late eminent and faithful servant of his Lord Mr Matthew Lawrence' and printed in 1657 (p.438):

> Art thou to choose a magistrate or inferior officer? Dost thou enquire whether such a man be thy Friend or thy kinsman or thy customer or one that hath bespoke thy voice? And dost thou never enquire, How Just he is and faithful to men or how religious in his carriage to God? Do not judge Gods messengers as busie bodies in other men's matters, whilst they give magistrates their charge from God and people their charge also in the choice of magistrates – I shall not descend to particulars, only in general: be sure to discharge your oaths, and a good conscience therein, both as freemen of this town, and as freemen of Jesus Christ; keep to your charter and you shall not do amiss – I need not tell you (unless it be in the way of acknowledgement) the great charges you are and have been at, for a long time, in maintaining the public ordinance twice in the week, upon your ordinary days. I hath heard it hath been one of the most Ancient Lectures in the Kingdom. But I fear, if you well observe one another in this particular, though there are many constant and willing auditors, yet there are some that hear me this day upon this civil occasion, whose faces you saw not here of many days before; no I am afraid, many a week together. For my part I do not see how such as are faithful to their heavenly Charter and have to do in Election of officers, can shew any countenance to such persons as do usually discountenance and slight the Public ordinance. If they judge the ordinance not worthy of their presence, one thinks others should judge them not worthy of public trust.

In other words, 'do not elect those who haven't turned up at my lectures!'

God was believed to directly send misfortune, disease, war and famine to punish, not only individuals, but whole communities that were corporately guilty for permitting the unpunished existence of the sinner in their midst. Sin was therefore, not only a social nuisance and a moral failing, it was a very real practical risk to all concerned. Samuel Ward, in his most famous sermon, *Woe to Drunkards*, listed example after example of instances known to him where God had punished drunkenness by some terrible accident:

An Alewife in Kesgrave neare to Ipswich, who would needs force three serving men (that had been drinking in her house, and were taking their leaves) to stay and drinke the three Outs, first that is Wit out of the head, Money out of the purse, Ale out of the pot, as she was coming towards them with the pot in her hand, was suddenly taken speechlesse and sicke, her tongue swoln in her mouth, never recovered speech the third day after dyed. This Sir Anthony Felton the next gentleman and Justice, with divers other eye-witnesses of her in sicknesse related to mee; whereupon I went to the house with two or three witnesses inquired the truth of it.

(pp.531–532)

Two servants of a Brewer in Ipswich drinking for a rumpe of a Turkie, struggling in their drinke for it, fell into scalding Caldron backwards: wherof the one dyed presently, the other lingeringly and painfully: since my coming to Ipswich.

(p.532)

A Bayliffe of Hadly upon the Lord's Day being drunke at Melford, would needs to get upon his Mare to ride through the street, affirming (as the report goes) that his mare would carry him to the Devil; his mare cast him off, and broke his neck instantly. Reported by sundry sufficient witnesses.

(p.534)

Ward listed carefully, similar instances known to have happened in the following places in Suffolk: Kesgrave, Ipswich, Barnwell, Bromeswell, Bungay, Hadleigh, Haslingfield, Melford, and 'Somewhere in Suffolk'; in Essex: Harwich, Near Maldon, Tillingham and in Norfolk Aylsham; and events in London at Bread Street, Chancery Lane, Tenby in Pembroke, and Northampton.

The government of Ipswich was in the hands of the two bailiffs, twelve portmen, the twenty-four councillors and around 150 freemen. The Borough of Ipswich was the supreme legal authority in Ipswich, in charge of the administration of justice. It is difficult to draw an accurate plan of the borough constitution, because in this period there were two competing models of how it should work.

In the first, control was meant to be in the hands of all male heads of households, by voting in General Courts. Men became freemen in three ways: through inheritance from a freeman father (not residence, and so Ipswich voters could live in towns up and down the east coast or even further afield); by serving an apprenticeship to a freeman (only a freeman could open a shop in Ipswich); or as a gift from the town in return for a service (usually by making a cash payment). On becoming a freeman, one was supposed to come into General Court with one's father's sword and swear to protect the town's laws and liberties. A high proportion of the male population were freemen. The General Court of Freemen voted each year for a two-tier working group of elected officers, the Assembly, composed of the twenty-four and the twelve.

In the second, control was in the hands of twelve self-selecting portmen. The Assembly was made up of the twenty-four self-selected from the freemen and the twelve portmen self-selected from the twenty-four. The Assembly produced a single candidate list to be rubber stamped each year by the votes of the General Court. The Freemen also elected two burgesses (MPs) to the House of Commons.

There was a normal career path to bailiff. Usually a person had to first take on those unpaid duties which were awkward and time-consuming. In fact, by this period the initial post of guildholder was so unpopular that nearly everyone paid a fine to the borough rather than carry out the duty of organising the Guild Feast. In reality, this had become an entrance fee. Then, they could gradually take on unpaid posts which were both more important and which offered more opportunities for self-enrichment, for example by being awarded leases of meadows, farms and woodlands owned by the borough, or being awarded contracts to supply Christ's Hospital or carry out borough building contracts.

In the 1640s, the General Court regained more power only to progressively lose it again to the Assembly after 1647.

Ipswich, perhaps uniquely for an English town, was able to adopt the Presbyterian model of church and town government. The right to appoint priests to various churches in the town had belonged to the prior of Christchurch Priory before the Reformation. When the priory was dissolved, its lands changed hands a couple of times before passing to the Withipoles and becoming Christchurch Mansion. For extended periods of time, the Withipole owner of the mansion was a minor and, therefore, it had become unclear who now had the right to appoint ministers to these town centre churches. Under the innocent title of 'An Act to Pave the Streets of Ipswich' the town managed to get Parliament to agree that the town council had this right. The borough also believed it had the right to appoint its own lecturer, the highest religious authority in the town, and the grammar school master.

The lecturers were not simply sermonising about some theoretical project. They had determined to make Ipswich into a 'holy city' full of the sober hard-working devout. The town council paid them to suggest policy, and so that's what they did. One of their very first acts was to protect the poor from themselves by outlawing the stuffing of hose with wool in 1570. Perhaps they thought that, rather than the poor insulating their legs with wool or hair, they should keep warm by working faster! Typically, this was not just an extravagant luxury but a sin against Almighty God:

Whereas the common and meaner sort of people in this Towne are growne to excess of apparell, especially in theire hose, to the ruine, decay and impoverishment. of the Towne against the com'andmt. of the Scriptures: in contempt of the lawes, to the increase of wickednesse and sinne, where through they fall into the greate displeasure of Allmty. God: Its therfore ordered, determined and agreed, by the whole concent of the Bayliffs, Burgesses, and Commonalty assembled, that noe inhabitant of this Towne using any mystery or occupacon wth.in this Towne, theire apprentices, servants, or journy men, shall use about their hose, any stuffing wth. haire, wooll, or other stuffing therein laid, bolstred, or interlined, other then one single lining of cotton, and one other like woollen or linnen lining, uppon paine of IMPRISONMT. by the Bayliffs.

In 1590, the rules for attending church and for keeping the Sabbath were tightened up still further. Modernised, they read:

The inhabitants of this town shall upon every Sabbath go to their churches carefully and reverently as by the law they are bound to do and upon the Sabbath day all men of this town shall cease from their labour and no man shall set open his shop windows upon the Sabbath day and all carriers and labourers shall not use their carriage nor other labour upon that day.

Such poor persons as do receive any alms money of this town shall come for it unto their several parish churches and there receive the same. and such poor persons as do not usually resort unto the church upon the Sabbath day in service time and there stay all or the most part of the service time shall lose his alms for that week without lawful cause.

All the ministers within the town shall routinely teach the youth of their parishes the catechism upon the Sabbath day in the afternoon

All the inhabitants of this town on every holy day in service time and during the time of sermon preaching shall cease from all open working and shall not those times set open their shops.

This was extended on 12 November 1599 to order that:

Inhabitants that shall open their shop windows upon the Sabbath days, to the intent of making sale, the goods proffered for sale shall be forfeited, unless such as they be as are in case of necessity of life, and the parties working in their shops or selling wares shall be committed to prison by the bailiffs.

And on 6 December 1599:

No waggoner or common carrier shall return with his wagons or carriage or shall labour or travail within this town upon the Sabbath.

In 1644, the keeping of the Sabbath was enforced even more strictly. Amongst the things now forbidden, not only on a Sunday but on any of the increasing number of 'fast days' called in times of trouble, were: idle and needless sitting in doorways; walking along the river front or in the fields; unnecessary rowing of boats; washing oneself or horse riding. In order to control children and apprentices, it was ordered that their parents or masters should be fined a shilling for any infringement of the rules by their charges:

1644 Order of the Great Court:

For as much as the Lords day nowe is and of late hath been much prophaned within the towne by usinge diverse pastimes and recreations Children sportinge and playinge in the Streetes And a great part of the Day after the publique Worship of God ended wastefully and vainely spent in idle and needles sittinge at doores Walkinge at the Key in the ffieldes and other publique places to the great dishonour of God and the increasinge of that guilt which lies upon this Nation for Sabbaoth breaking. Nowe for the better sanctyfyinge of that day and the more strict and due observinge of the ffastdayes And to the intent that after the publike Service of God ened each ffamily apart may spend the remainder of these dayes in the exercise of Religious duties It is Ordered and agreed That all persons inhabitintinge withine this towne that after the Twentieth day of March next shall prophane the Lords daye by sportinge or playinge at any games Walkinge at the keye in the ffeildes or other publique places in or neere this towne by unncessary Roweing in Boates Washinge themselves in the Sommer time: Rydeing of Horses out further than to the neerest water and leapinge runninge or otherwise sportinge with the said Horses and all Masters and parents that shall suffer their apprentices Servants or children to Committ any of the said Offences or to bee playeinge and idleinge in the streets upon the Lords Day or ffast Dayes shall for the first offence forfeit 12d.

The proofe whereof shall be eyther view of one of the bayliffs, or Portmen, or justices, or of the Common Councill, or proof of two witnesses before the Bayliffs etc.

In 1644, the butchers petitioned the council to move the meat market from Saturday to Friday, the better to preserve the Lord's Day from profanation. Reading between the lines, it appears that the problem was that there was so much work to be done after the market that it tended to go on into the next day. The objections to the move are interesting, because it shows with what seriousness the whole issue of the Sabbath was taken, and the complicated nature of the problems that it threw up.

Essentially the work schedule of the whole town had to be organised to make it possible for one day to be set aside from all work. All household chores needed to be doubled up on a Saturday so that they did not need to be done on a Sunday; no major task could be organised on a Monday that required preparation the day before; the week's schedule had to allow time for the sermons during the week as well. The council had to discuss the following points:

> Saturday market is held by prescription, and the country as much interested therein as the town.
>
> The whole Saturday market would be destroyed if the meat market was moved.
>
> If the country butchers come to keep the Friday market they will still keep [attend] a Saturday market.
>
> Meat from Friday will not keep until Sabbath day or Monday so it [a Friday market] will bring on a Monday market again [and a Monday market will need to be prepared for on the Sabbath].
>
> The town butchers would sell meat in their houses [not in the market] late into Saturday night. [They will, therefore, not properly do all the work needed to avoid working on the Sabbath.]
>
> The poor people receive not their wages until Saturday.
>
> It will hinder them that come to town to meet the carriages from London which arrive on Saturday.
>
> London and other places have Saturday markets.
>
> If butchers don't come to the Saturday market they will sell more at home and this will harm the market.
>
> If butchers keep market at home, besides the trouble in sending meat down, it will make meat dearer.
>
> If a Friday market is set up then the Thursday market will be set by.

Every so often there was a crackdown to make sure that the rules were being kept. The amounts that had to be given as sureties for the good behaviour of offenders were quite substantial for the time, and showed that the council really meant business. In 1608, Peter Brett (shearman) and Robert Brett (carpenter) were fined the heavy sum of £10 each for playing 'slide grott' in their house on the Sabbath. John Cutberd was indicted on 26 June 1626 for profaning the name of God several times He was fined 6s to the use of the poor.

Edward Melsoppe was indicted for playing at bowls and was fined 3d on 1 December 1638. In 1644, Richard Lowe had to come up with a total of £10 paid by himself and two others, to guarantee his good behaviour for the future after having been caught playing the fiddle on the fast day at night. Even the work ethic was no excuse – Steven Neave had to find a surety of £30 to guarantee his future good behaviour for preparing a vat of woad dye on the fast day in September 1645.

It is obvious that such crimes could only have been brought to light through the public-spirited activity of neighbourly informers. Yet this picture of town government and church, united by a common vision to create a devout, well-ordered society on earth – a vision supported by compulsory twice weekly attendance at sermons, enforced by punishments on individual backsliders – was something of an illusion. Far from being a consensus, there were conflicts on all sides, common council against portmen, town council and its Admiralty Courts against Harwich and landowners with properties along the banks of the Orwell.

The bishops and the Crown did not accept that the council could appoint parish clergy, and they demanded the right to license any lecturer or grammar school master that the corporation wanted to employ. They sought to silence Lecturer Ward through the courts.

The only role for the town council in this model was to bow its head respectfully, feast the officials of the bishop when they turned up in Ipswich, presenting them with barrels of wine and marzipan cakes and silver cups, and to ask if His Grace had any special tasks for them, such as once again redecorating and reorganising the churches of the town in line with the latest theological fashion of the king and bishops.

When Dr Nathaniel Brent inspected the town as Visitor to Archbishop of Canterbury Laud in 1635, he was met by the twelve and twenty-four, and presented with a banquet worth £4 12s, and two gallons of white and claret wine. While in 1638, the town gave the bishop a cup of silver gilt costing £15 8s, inscribed to 'Richard Lord Bishop of Norwich. Reverend father in God.' In 1636, the council was ordered to remove all the seats it had set up in the chancel and to rail in the altar.

Lecturer Ward is said to have believed and preached that the Crown was plotting to bring back Catholicism. Charge and counter-charge flew backwards and forwards. After Ward's arrest and imprisonment, through which he was loyally supported by the council, the borough was accused of organising riots against Bishop Wren.

The town council and the lecturer might control most of St Mary Tower church but the south aisle was the seat of the Bishop of Norwich's Consistory Court, where his visitors sat in judgement upon the people. Worse than that, they sat on the council itself and ordered the council as to how it should organise the churches of Ipswich.

Councillors could look across at where one of their members, described by the bishop's men as the 'schismatical shoemaker' Ferdinando Adams, church warden of St Mary Tower, had written boldly, high on the walls of the south aisle in black paint against the whitewash, a text from Mark XI: 17: 'Is it not written My house shall be called of all nations a house of prayer but ye have made it a den of thieves.' A quotation which made the bishop's lawyers furious.

The bishop attempted to order the town council to remove the quote. In 1636, the town council led armed riots against the bishop's officials and attempted to bar them from the church. The council had to defend itself against charges that it had attempted to hunt and kill the bishop, their 'Reverend Father in God'. When William Prynne was charged with authorship of the pamphlet 'News from Ipswich' recounting events there, he was fined £5,000, had his ears cut off and his cheeks branded with the letters 'SL' (seditious libeller).

Two decades before the Civil War, relations between the rulers of Ipswich, the Crown and its bishops had pretty much broken down. In 1634, Laud's Commissioner Dade brought eleven charges against Samuel Ward in the Star Chamber. One of Dade's charges against Ward was that he was working up people's fears about a return to Catholicism, in order to organise emigration to New England. Ward, he said, was joined by Mr Dalton, pastor of Woolverstone, and another enthusiast for emigration. Dade's information led to the halting of two ships due to sail from Ipswich around 10 March 1634, by order of the Privy Council, each with about eighty emigrants aboard. Ward was found guilty on all counts. Thought to be especially damning were his statements that 'The Church of England was ready to ring the changes' and 'Religion and the gospel stood on tiptoes ready to be gone'. Ward's supporters in Ipswich were to countercharge that Dade had expressed pleasure when an emigrant ship to New England had sunk.

When Wren, in turn, was charged in 1640 it was alleged that his persecution had caused 3,000 to flee East Anglia, and head to New England. Wren's answer was that poor wages had caused the flight.

Sometimes, Ipswich must have felt a very different place to the beautiful view from Stoke Hills on a sunny day – threatened and cut off, and claustrophobic within its earthen ramparts, with its gates shut. As night drew on after a day of fasting, in which people had been encouraged to stay indoors, leaving the streets to run the gauntlet of carved wooden monsters that decorated the houses in which noise was intended to be kept to a minimum, many in Ipswich would be scared. They were encouraged by their spiritual leaders to wonder what hidden sins of theirs were bringing the wrath of God down upon the town.

In fact, it was threatened on every side, from careless sinners bringing down the wrath of God, to pirates, Catholics and other enemies within. Catholics were not just political opponents, to the Ipswich lecturers they were also agents of the Devil. Ward's famous cartoon on the proposed 'Spanish Marriage' shows the pope, monks and cardinals feasting with the Devil, and a demon leading Guy Fawkes to the Houses of Parliament. Even their own king (or at least his wicked advisers who had bewitched him with their spells) and his bishops were suspect. Enemies in the open and in secret surrounded Ipswich, raising tension and paranoia in the town. Authorities and populace alike were in a state of hypervigilance.

Ward's frontispiece for his sermon *Balme from Gilead* … Pope, cardinal, bishop, monk and Devil try to shake the immoveable world. (Suffolk Record Office)

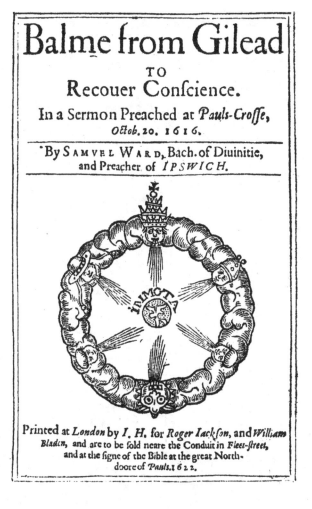

Balme from Gilead
TO
Recouer Confcience.

In a Sermon Preached at *Pauls-Croffe*,
Octob. 20. 1616.

By SAMVEL WARD, Bach. of Diuinitie,
and Preacher of *IPSWICH.*

Printed at *London* by *I. H.* for *Roger Iackfon,* and *William Bladen,* and are to be fold neare the Conduit in *Fleet-ftreet,* and at the figne of the Bible at the great North-doore of *Pauls.*1622.

Every summer the town faced the risk of plague, generally introduced from London by travellers. To the Puritan lecturers of Ipswich there was no doubt that the plague was a divine punishment upon the town, and they demanded that everyone search their hearts to see in what way they had angered God. Fear of the plague and of God's vengeance was a whip with which they did not fail to terrify their audiences:

Marke this you that dwell at ease and swimme in wealth in London. Your consciences that lie still like sleepy majesties; in plague times and sweating sickness, they flie in the throate – Marke then you that have Mils of businesse in your heads, whole West Minster Hals, Bursses, Exchanges and East-Indies (as I fear many of you have whilst I am speaking to your conscience) that making hast to be rich, overlay your braines with affaires, are so busie in

God punishes sinners directly in the 'Fatal Vespers', Ward's cartoon of the death of
ninety English Catholics when a secret chapel collapsed in the French ambassador's
house in Black Friars, London, in 1623. (Suffolk Record Office)

A diagram of the cosmos and the spiritual world by Samuel Ward of Ipswich, complete with terrestrial and celestial globes. The equivalent of John Gauden's diagram. It shows the search for a logical and coherent world order amongst intellectuals with different religious ideas and politics. (Suffolk Record Office)

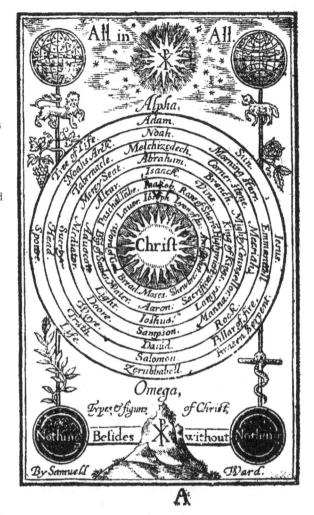

your Counting-house and bookes; and that upon this very day, that you never have once in a weeke or yeere, an houres space to conferre with your pore Consciences – There be three dayes especially, the day of Sicknesse, of death, of Judgement; in which Comfort is worth a world, and then all worldy comforts and comforters, like run-away servants and drunken Seruing-men are to seeke when one hath most use and neede of them,--- In these times you shall see the merry and jolly worldling hang the head like a Bul-rush and the Ruffians brags lagge like a starcht Ruffe in a storme

How doe Achitophel and Judas dye the death of cowardly Harts and Hares, pursued with the full cry of their sinnes, which make them dead in the nest before they dye; then a kingdome for a good Conscience. Then send (as in the Sweating sicknesse and the Plague) for Mr Minister Conscience.

(*Balme from Gilead to Recouer Conscience*, Samuel Ward, 1616.)

A
COALE FROM
THE ALTAR TO
KINDLE THE HO-
ly fire of *Zeale.*

In a Sermon preached at a generall
Vifitation at Ipfwich.

By S A M : W A R D Preacher of *Ipfwich.*

The fixth Edition corrected and amended.
Θιῷ χ̦ ὑμῖν.

LONDON,
Printed for *Iohn Grifmond,* and are to bee
fold in *Ivie Lane* at the Signe of the
Gunne. 1 6 3 5.

A Coale from the Altar,
another of Samuel
Ward's sermon designs.
(Suffolk Record Office)

Writing about plague had become a definite topic of its own. The London-based dramatist and pamphleteer, Thomas Dekker, wrote at least three plague pamphlets. One has the lengthy title, *A Rod for Run-awayes. God's tokens of his feareful judgements, sundry wayes pronounced upon this city and on severall persons, both flying from it and staying in it.* The frontispiece shows runaways turned back by armed citizens from entering, with the words, 'I follow (death) We fly (Londoners) Keepe out (locals).' Dekker 371:

Where if you look into the fields, look into the streets, look into the taverns, look into the ale houses, they are all merry, jocund; no plague frights them, no

Samuel Ward's design
for *Woe to Drunkards*,
demonstrating how
all misfortunes are the
direct punishment of
God on sinners. (Suffolk
Record Office)

WOE TO DRVNKARDS.

A Sermon by S A M·V E L W A R D
Preacher of *Ipſwich*.

LONDON,
Printed for *Ichn Griſmond*, and are to bee
ſold in *Ivie Lane* at the Signe of the
Gunne. 1 6 3 5.

prayers stir them up, no fast ties them to obedience. In the fields they are (in times of divine celebration) walking, talking, laughing, toying, and sporting together; in the streets blaspheming, selling, buying, swearing; in taverns and ale houses drinking, roaring and surfeting. In these and many other places God's holy day is their work day, the king's fasting day their day of riot.

(Quoted in Lake, The Antichrist's Lewd Hat, p.369.)

There was good reason to be terrified. A few days after being infected, a victim developed a rash and there was pain all over the body. The victim began to feel tired and lethargic, but the pain made it difficult to sleep. The temperature

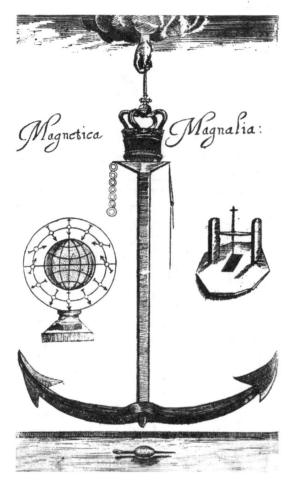

Samuel Ward's design for
The Wonders of the Lodestone,
a book of sermons and
scientific experiments using
compass needles. (Suffolk
Record Office)

of the body increased and this affected the brain and the nerves. Speech deteriorated and the victims became less and less intelligible. As the disease took more of a hold, the victim took on the physical appearance of a drunk with stumbling movement and gait. The victim then became delirious. After about six days, the lymphatic glands became swollen and inflamed. In the groin, neck and armpit areas of the body this led to buboes – large and highly painful swellings. These buboes caused bleeding underneath the skin, which turned the buboes and surrounding areas blue or purple. In some cases, red spots appeared on the buboes as death approached. The average time of death from the first symptom was four to seven days. It is thought that 50–75 per cent of those who caught the disease died.

In 1579, the town council ordered that the churchwardens of every parish should have a copy of the printed book of the orders of Her Majesty's Privy Council on how to behave during a plague. This set the basic pattern of response, refined and tightened with each subsequent attack. The headmaster of Ipswich School was told to send away his pupils. The main response was to keep everyone in an infected house shut in, until they either died or recovered.

It was obvious that the poor would not sit and simply starve in their houses if they could not go out to get food, and so some provision had to be made for them. The constables of each of the four wards of the town were to identify 'every sick person of poor estate sick of the disease not able to relieve themselves' and to decide what meat, drink and medicine ('potecarye diet') they should be provided with. Each household was to be provided with a load of wood to ensure that a fire could be light to thoroughly dry the house, because damp was believed to be a cause of the disease. The constables were to find and enrol with the bailiffs suitable women to look after and keep within doors the sick, and £20 was set aside to cover the cost: 'No children shall henceforth go begging. Those accustomed to do so where need and want shall compel them to keep within their houses such upon notice being brought to the constables and shall be relieved by the discretion of the Bailiffs.'

In 1584 grim quarantine measures were taken against the inhabitants of Lady Lane: the lane was to be barred up at both ends. All the animals of the people living in the lane were to be killed. The appointed women were to examine everyone and make an official list of the sick. The sick were to be shut into their houses and 'not suffered to wander or go abroad', and provided with diet, wood and potercarye. Every ancient person was to be allowed 18d weekly, and every young person 12d in two instalments, and someone honest should be appointed to buy them victuals on their behalf with the money daily. No one was to be buried until the body had been inspected by the appointed women. The bedding and clothes of the dead were to be burnt and wood and broom burnt in the lane (to purify the air). It was also agreed to shut up the footpath from St Nicholas church to the Friar's Bridge because infection had established in the little house upon the Friar's Wall.

Actions in 1589 were much the same. The house called 'Poltnye' in Brook Street, where the plague had begun and which had several different rooms with different exits, was to be shut up. Lanes next to infected houses were to be closed. People living next to the infected house were to be removed elsewhere. These orders were passed by a deputy for the senior bailiff, John Knapp, who presumably had left the town for a safer place.

So the next thing to do, in later outbreaks, was to make sure that no one tried to avoid their duty or escaped the common financial burden of these arrangements:

Any of the Portmen or 24 who remove from fear of infection to pay double his weekly payment so long as he is out of the town.

(Assembly Book, 7 Oct, 1 James I.)

Opinion of Counsel to be obtained as to whether outdwellers holding tenements or houses in the town are liable to be charged payments assessed upon the inhabitants for the maintenace of infected persons.

(Assembly Book, 30 Nov, 1 James I.)

Ministers who neglected their churches could be imprisoned. Headboroughs who did not carry out their duties to provide men to watch and ward, or to find a deputy, were to be fined 5s a day, as were the constables themselves if they didn't turn up.

A more courageous role was played by a Mr Lufkin, who is mentioned twice in the Assembly Book by a grateful town:

Whereas Lufkin hath tended and visited certain poor people and ministered sundry drinks and medecines to them at the Town's charge a certain time past it is ordered he shall be discharged presently of the said service and moreover shall have 10s over and above his allowance.

Mr Lufkin to have a further sum of 10s in consideration of his travail and charges about the curing of the infected of this town.

The councillors had their own duties. There was a certain grim logic to their arrangements, as the oldest members were to risk their lives first:

Every day two men of the best sort to be appointed to ward at the pest house one at one end therof for the keeping of the infected persons therein. The warders to be elected daily. The most ancient of the company of the 24 to be the first chosen and so on in age order.

(Assembly Book, 16 Oct 1604, 2 James I.)

Soon it was decided to remove the sick to special plague houses where they could be looked after and kept secure. In turn, successive sites were looked at: Mr Seckford's stables; the Rope House in Rope Walk; and finally a temporary boarded structure that was set up as needed on Rushmere Heath. They also took over and renovated the fallen-down ruins of the old medieval leper hospital of St Leonards at the end of Wherstead Road in Stoke. Frysell, who was the Guider of the Hospital, was to be responsible for looking after six poor impotent diseased people besides himself, his family and household.

During the 1604 outbreak, the quarantine rules were tightened further, not only to keep the plague confined within an area of the town but also to keep it out of the town to begin with:

No carrier by land or water nor any masters of hoyes or other vessels shall offend concerning the bringing of any passengers goods or wares from

London or receive any Londoners to lodge in their houses under a penalty of 20 days imprisonment. The water-bailiff shall not permit any hoye or other vessel coming from London to come or be unloden without permission of the Bailiffs under like penalty.

There shall be warding by the head-boroughs on Saturday and till further notice at Stoke Bridge and Hanford bridge warding of one bridge one day with three other inhabitants at least and likewise at the other bridge.

(Assembly Book, 1 Aug 1604, 1 James I.)

This led to trouble for the brothers who ran a business hauling goods to London by stage waggon. Their business could not operate. A leading figure, John Sturgeon, told the waggoner Richard Lane: 'Colchester men did not go to London.' Lane told Sturgeon he lied and bade him to 'wipe his mouth'. The result: 'John Lane waggoner, committed to gaol for refusing to come before the Bailiffs, he not to bring passengers or wares from London.'

The process of isolation was a grim one, and was more or less an inevitable sentence of death on the other family members shut up with the infected person. It was necessary to keep watch over the houses to prevent desperate people attempting to break out and run away. The constable of each ward was supposed to appoint watchmen one by one to watch infected houses 'AND KEEP THEM IN'.

The next step was to discover who had the plague, for people were understandably reluctant to report themselves. Searchers John Cole and William Fosdike were appointed, whose dangerous job it was to inspect the sick and the bodies of the dead for signs of plague. They received 16d a day and free food. To mark them out and give warning to others, they were ordered to carry white wands, or rods, in their hands. Cole and Fosdike buried the dead in 'coarse sowtage', and Cole's wife received an additional 6d a week to inspect the dead.

In 1604, they first raised the money to pay for two searchers, as charged in the Subsidy Book. Every man was taxed on land to pay 3d in the pound, and on goods 2d in the pound. John Kirke was appointed to provide those shut up in their houses with food and drink, and Anne Spalding was to serve those who couldn't care for themselves. Cole, Fosdike and their wives served all that year and into January, when it was hoped that the epidemic might cease.

But Cole's family did not escape, for the churchwarden's accounts for St Mary Elms show that his wife and daughter fell sick and died:

1605 To Warner for carrying away Widow Cole and her daughter to the Rope House 2s 6d
More for carrying away the beds and other things to be ayered 2s 6d

Samuel Ward's most famous cartoon, for which he was imprisoned: 'The Double Deliverance' shows the Spanish Armada and the Gunpowder Plot with the Devil, the King of Spain and the Pope plotting the downfall of England. (© The Trustees of the British Museum)

But the loss of his wife did not release Cole from his task:

> To old Cole for searching of Gallant 8*d*.
> To a woman for laying of him forth and winding him 2*s*.
> For a yard of new cloth to lengthen his sheet 7*d*.
> For four men to carry him to church.

Attempts were made to genuinely care for the unfortunates locked and guarded in the sick house. The renter of the sick house was told to be kind to them, they were provided with fuel and food and the charitable supplied them with extra food and drink:

> A chalder of seacoal to be sent to the houses provided for the infected persons for their use and for Marie Hagtree that shall make ready the victuals for the infected persons.
>
> (Assembly Book, 14 May, 1 James I)

> Thomas Gabson shall have and occupy the sick house and lands; he to maintain and keep five such persons as the Bailiffs shall appoint, with meat, drink, lodging and washing and shall use etc and entreat the said persons well and discretely during the said time.
>
> (Assembly Book, 6 Sept 1604, 2 James I)

Extracts from St Nicholas parish churchwarden's accounts show further small details of care:

> 1604 to Widow Riggs at the Pest House for oil, sack and prunes some pence.
> 9 Sept 1605 3 James I beer given to those sick of the plague by direction of John Kirke.

Cole, the widowed searcher, having survived the 1604 outbreak, was still carrying on in 1609 at the next attack for the wage of 3*s* 4*d* a week (Assembly Book, 11 Oct 1609, 7 James I).

Going to church, fasting and praying, along with the use of special books with suitable prayers, were enjoined and strongly supported, on pain of summary imprisonment, by the bailiffs. But there was a tension between this attitude and the clear awareness that this was a contagious disease and so gatherings of people were dangerous, so the number of sermons was reduced and people could only attend their own parish church:

> From henceforth every minister in the town in his several parish church shall read Divine Service appointed for that day of 7 o'clock of the forenoon and

5 o'clock of the afternoon and the parishioners or one of his household of every parish at the least that are not infected shall resort thither to parish church and none other every day twice to hear Divine service and prayers and if the ministers shall neglect the reading of service as aforesaid or the parishioners or their household shall neglect their coming to church to hear service and prayers that then every of the said persons so offending shall be imprisoned by Mr Bailiffs.

(Assembly Book, 2 May, 1 James I.)

There was little else for the sick to do but die. And if they couldn't afford the funeral then their parishes would bear the costs of their shroud (1s 7d), digging the grave (1s) and sometimes for preparing the body. They also made small payments to help the bereaved husbands and children.

In 1604, forty-four people seem to have died of plague in St Matthew's parish, and the next year the churchwardens were flooded with the petitions of those who could not pay their church rates as a result of the deaths:

Item paid to Miles Rose sexton for burying of Edmond Bowle and of his household and children who died of the infection of the plague and for ringing of the bells for divers sick persons of the plague at sundry times 3s 4d.
Petitions [i.e. of people not paying rate]:
Of Thomas Brotherton's house who himself and all his children died of the infection of the plague 16d.
Of widow Clefton who herself and all her household died of the plague 12d.
Of Rowland Browne who died as aforesaid 4d.
Of Bennett who died of the sickness 6d.
Of widow Jeremy 2s for which these accomptants took a distress [seized goods for debt] being a pewter pot and a mortar.
Of the house late William Hebden which was shut up by the space of half a year 10d.
Of the house late John Bower infected (note six Brothertons and five Bennets died).

There were some strange parallels between an outbreak of plague and an outbreak of witchcraft: both were invisible; both spread from neighbour to neighbour; both saw those suspected shut up until the outcome; both saw groups of women employed to look for physical signs on the affected and both revealed, not simple sickness, but hidden sin.

Plague was a 'divine punishment', and war was a 'satanic plot'.

It is rarely appreciated that at this time, Suffolk and other parts of the East Coast were in the front line in a naval confrontation between England and the Catholic powers of France and Spain. Directly opposite Ipswich and Harwich, on the Continent, lay the Catholic Spanish Netherlands. There, from bases in Ostend, Nieuwpoort and especially Dunkirk, privateers licensed by Spain harassed all North Sea fishing, and trade with Holland and Zeeland. In order to counter this threat the Landguard Fort was to be built at Felixstowe, but this represented yet another burden on a hard-hit community. The man in charge of its building, the Earl of Warwick, was worried about the possibility of plotting by Suffolk Catholic supporters (recusants), and in his letters to the council included rumours of secret meetings at their houses.

Just how many Catholics or Catholic sympathisers might have been left in Suffolk, and just what their political loyalties were, is hard to know. Yet the Gunpowder Plot was still a recent memory, and was a semi-religious festival with evil, in the shape of paper popes and cardinals, burnt annually.

In 1626, at the end of Buckingham's botched raids on Cadiz and failed support of French Protestants at the Île de Rhé, the town was to calculate massive losses. Seizing twenty-four merchant ships of Ipswich for the Cadiz expedition had cost their owners at least £80–£100 per ship in lost trade; Ipswich sailors had only been paid 9s 4d a month by the Royal Navy, when they had been paid 25s a month by the merchant navy; the ship *Long Robert* had been lost with all hands at a cost of £1,200; two Ipswich ships had been seized by Dunkirkers; fifty-eight ships were trapped in the Orwell for fear of the Dunkirk pirates and so could not trade. Fishing in the North Sea and Iceland was at an end. Shipbuilding had collapsed and, although for thirty years twelve ships a year had been launched at Ipswich, none were being built at that time.

Ipswich was a hotbed of political confrontation between the town council, led by its lecturer, and the Crown. As the country descended into the violence of the Civil War, likewise, debates in the town council became ever more unruly. These incidents are carefully recorded in the various borough records: husbandmen, yeomen, tailors and starchmakers were beginning to speak out; contemptuous speeches and unbecoming conduct were complained of and 'scandalous verses' were circulated.

It was at this time that Sir William Withipole led the soldiers under his command into a fight at Martlesham Bridge, against soldiers under other officers. This disgraceful affair arose out of arguments over the Withipoles' Catholic links.

The paranoia about the enemy within continued, this time directed against foreign Protestants. Sometime in 1640/1641, Sydrack Toney wrote to the 10th Earl of Northumberland:

In these dangerous times I have presumed to make known to you the danger of home-bred mischiefs. Strangers in this kingdom have so provided themselves with arms, both here in London and other places, especially

Ipswich, Yarmouth and Norwich, where the French Walloons and Dutch are as many if not more than the natives and exercise military discipline once a fortnight, if occasion happen, they may easily become a greater encumbrance to us.

(Calender of State Papers Domestic 1641–1643, p.208.)

Toney was after a commission to seize these arms and to force foreigners to swear allegiance to Charles I. Two years later, it was secret Cavaliers that were the concern. According to the pamphlet *Certaine Informations* in 1643:

From Ipswich it is informed that to preserve the peace and quiet of that Towne and to prevent all combustions amongst themselves, the Mayor and Magistrates there raised the trayned band and such Volunteers as they could best confide in, and apprehended all the malevolents amongst them, both in and aboute the Towne amongst which they have now in custody four new Justices of the peace, who are extremely disaffected to the Parliament and in the search of their houses they found muskets and fowling pieces ready charged, so intent are these kinde of people to do mischiefe, that they had the meanes to effect it in readiness.

The first thing to be done in Ipswich was to put the existing defences of the town in order. This is itemised in a special book called *Mr Fysher's Accompt for the Fortifications and the Accompt of Joseph Pemberton of the Moneys received and laid out by him about the Fortifications* (Pemberton was one of the bailiffs of Ipswich who was to sit at Mary Lackland's trial and later watch her burn).

Orders were passed to stop-up all the little private ways through the earthen walls that had grown up, and to stop all the use of the ditches as tenting grounds for stretching newly woven cloths, and other civilian uses. A hundred muskets with bandoliers, rests and headpieces were bought for the town's use. Next, a military engineer was sent for from Colchester. A special sum of money was set up to enable the work to go ahead.

From the accounts, it is clear that not only were the old ramparts readied but new works lined out and dug. Iron-bound turnpikes were set up at the Westgate, Mr Ward's Corner, St Mathew's and in St Clement's, and the street was specially paved about them. These turnpikes were revolving spiked barriers made by fixing a revolving beam with projecting pike heads. This could be locked in place on a framework to close off a street against a surprise raid by cavalry or popular disorder. Down by Stoke Bridge the river was closed off by setting up eight pillars and a 'sweape' (presumably some kind of boom), and chains were set up to close the bridge. More chains and a post were set up by the Powder Mill. Waggons for taking away earth and bringing gravel, wheelbarrows and spades were all ordered for the excavations. It seems that, in

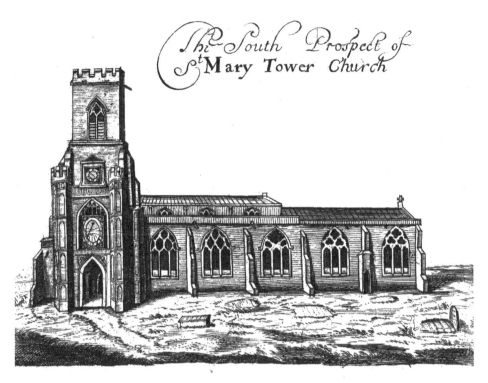

St Mary le Tower before Victorian restoration, where Ward preached and town and bishop came into conflict. (Ipswich Museum)

all, about twenty-two men laboured on the fortifications. The work went ahead as a genuine community project; the accounts speak of sons of influential men turning up to work for free and bringing their father's carts along with them, of free food and beer being distributed to the workers and all to the martial sound of John Brame beating his drum.

In London, the town purchased ten cannon, saker, along with 100 round shot and fifty mosle bar shot (designed to attack masts and rigging) and shipped them home. Allen Daye was paid for mending and repairing the weapons belonging to the town. Brown, the cutler, sharpened swords. Coals for their forges were taken from the stockpiles of fuel provided for the poor and sold to the armourers at a fixed rate, the money being used to buy firewood to replace the coal. The powder store at the hospital was put in order and eight barrels for keeping additional gunpowder and match for matchlocks were made.

All in all, about £356 12s 9d was spent on fortifying Ipswich.

Fear, paranoia and political and religious differences encouraged from the pulpit honeycombed Ipswich life throughout the whole period of the Elizabethan, Jacobean and Caroline witch trials. The bailiffs trying Katherine Dameron for witchcraft in the Moot Hall in 1640, were within earshot of Benjamin Brame, whom they had paid to play his drum in order to encourage the men building the defences around Ipswich. The same group of men trying Mary Lackland were also terrified of secret Royalist malignant plots, and they all feared the possibility of divine punishment. Ipswich was already at war when the Ipswich witch trials took place, and it was a very scared town.

Diabolus's attack on Mansoul was not only moral and religious, but practical and military.

4

UNDERCOVER RELIGION AND CUNNING MEN

At present it is frequently believed that witches were the female priestesses of the 'old religion' and, in some way, martyrs of their belief. Frankly, taken at face value there is no evidence for this. Yet nonetheless, there were experts in very ancient patterns of belief involved in the wider world of ideas about witchcraft. While the organised Christian churches, whether Catholic or Protestant, attempted to define and monopolise belief and religion, when we look at what people actually did there, there is another complete but overlapping dimension of popular, and even learned belief which had its own experts. These experts were on a spectrum running from the village 'cunning man' to the court 'wizard'. If any figure represented a continuity with an old pre-Christian religion it was these men, whose charms, angelology, alchemy and astrology can be shown to have originated in Late Classical antiquity. This world of popular belief seems to have always existed in some form. It was to prove very stable, and was to continue to exist well into the nineteenth century, when we find some of the most vivid accounts.

They, and their beliefs and practices, were above all concerned with providing religious, magical or spiritual help that would bring practical and emotional results to specific individuals with specific needs and problems. They were not principally concerned with moral issues, philosophical world views or the 'big' questions: they provided a service designed to offer solutions to problems. Unlike the churches, no one was compelled to use them or financially support them. They had clients rather than parishioners. The cunning men believed in the existence and evil of many kinds of beings that the scientific paradigm with which we explain the world does not accept as real. They believed in devils, ghosts, fairies and, elsewhere in Europe according to the region, in vampires, werewolves or trolls. They also believed in witches.

The witches of their beliefs did not exist any more than the other creatures. They could not have done, unless we are also prepared to believe in impish

A
BRIEFE
DESCRIPTION
OF THE NOTORIOVS
LIFE OF *IOHN LAMBE*,
otherwise called Doctor
LAMBE.

Together with his Ignominious
DEATH.

Printed in *Amsterdam.* 1 6 2 8.

John Lambe, Buckingham's infamous cunning man, killed by the mob. He is shown being stoned to death and literally 'getting the boot'. (British Library)

familiars in animal shapes that carried out evil curses in return for being suckled by their owners. Many villagers believed in witches, just as they believed in ghosts, but no villager could ever really have had the powers ascribed to a witch, or is likely to have thought of themselves that way.

Cunning men offered all sorts of ways to combat the malevolence of the witch, and so they spread the tales of the evils of the witch and the success of their anti-witchcraft charms. Some of those who believed themselves the victims of witchcraft in the trials had clearly sought their help. Who better for them to accuse, than the unpopular losers and eccentrics of village life?

The cunning men and healers were socially useful, and therefore unlikely to be attacked by the local community. Also, from their consultations they were in a position to know where missing objects might be found; or who was so desperate to win someone's love that they turned to magic; which of those loves ran counter to the rules of society; who had problems with pregnancies, or who was worried that their partner was unfaithful – they just knew too much. Such knowledge gives power.

Some of these people may well have been out-and-out criminals. It is easy to see how a 'cunning man' could come to know local villains, and arrange with them that he would 'magically' find the horse they had stolen all safe and sound in a distant field and receive a reward from the former owner for his skill. The two parties, cunning man and thief, could split the money paid out by the deluded owner. In addition, the reputation of the cunning man grew with every such successful operation, and he, of course, could easily misdirect people's suspicions away from the real culprits.

In this world view, the role of the witch was used 'to explain unfortunate events', as the anthropologist Evans-Pritchard famously put it in his study of witchcraft amongst the Azande: Why do your pigs fall sick? Why do you suffer from lice? Why do you have a disaster in the dairy or in baking or brewing? Why do your children die? The witch, the loser, so embittered by their own misfortune that they turn on their neighbours. This belief was, as we shall see, in direct conflict with the belief of the more educated and intellectual amongst the Puritans. Such popular belief has a history of its own. In the later medieval world much of this function was taken up by the cult of saints and, consequently, at this time legal cases of witchcraft were almost non-existent.

The popular Catholicism of the pre-Reformation church was itself far more concerned with magic, miracles and healing than the Protestants. The 'cult of saints', to put the matter one way, was prepared to get its hands dirty, to deal with the real, daily concerns of ordinary people. It was precisely this world view that the former prior of the Ipswich Carmelites, and later committed reformer, John Bale, had satirised in verse. The following speech was made by Idololatria Necromantia:

With blessing of Saint Germane
I will me so determine
That neither fox nor vermin
Shall do my chuckens harm
For geese, seek Saint Legard
For your ducks Saint Leonard
For horse take Moses's yard,
There is no better charm.
Take me a napkin folt
With the bias of a bolt
For the healing of a colt
No better thing can be.
For lamps and for bots
Take me Saint Wilfrid's knots;
And holy Saint Thomas's knots.
On my life I warrant ye
For the cough take Judas's ear
With the paring or a pear
And drink them without fear
If ye will have remedy –
Three sips are for the hickock
And six more for the chickock
This may my pretty pickock recover by and by.
If ye cannot sleep but slumber
Give oats unto Saint Uncumber
And beans in certain number
Unto Saint Blase and Saint Blythe.
Give onions to Saint Cutlake
And garlic to Saint Cyriac
If ye will shun the head ache
Ye shall have them at Queenhithe.
A dram of a sheeps turdle
And good saint Francis' girdle
With the am'let of an hurdle
Are wholesome for the pip.

                (John Bale, *A Comedy Concerning Three Laws.*)

She and her fellow demon, Sodomy, are called forth by Infidelity to attack mankind. Described as an old woman, she is also described as a good midwife, one able to protect children from sprites, to charm everything to go well or ill in the kitchen, and no beer making, bread making, poultry or anything else will go well unless she is pleased. In other words, something between a cunning woman and a witch.

The answer to the concerns of the ordinary believer in the pre-Reformation Church came down to this; it was a matter of finding the right saint at the right shrine and making the right offering. It was a world in which emotional and symbolic experiences and truths often took precedence over the everyday. A world, in fact, in which it was quite possible that the Shrine of Our Lady in Ipswich contained a crystal flask in which there was some of the Virgin's breast milk.

In 1516, a miracle took place in Ipswich at the Chapel of Our Lady. The story began in November in the previous year when the 12-year-old daughter of an important Essex nobleman began having fits, supposedly caused by demons. These lasted until March, when she had a vision of Our Lady of Ipswich and demanded to be taken to her shrine (it is typical that it had to be Our Lady of Ipswich, not just *any* statue of Our Lady). Since her father was Sir Roger Wentworth of Gosfield, news of her pilgrimage soon got out and became a public spectacle. Abbot Reve of Bury St Edmunds decided to walk to Ipswich to pray for her cure, with the additional promise that if she were to be cured he would repeat the pilgrimage in the same way every year. A crowd of 1,000 turned up to see if the expected cure would happen. The Virgin, speaking through the 12-year-old girl, summoned not only the bailiffs of Ipswich to attend but also Robert Lord Curzon, Count of the Holy Roman Empire. This was great power for even a noble child to wield.

The girl was cured, but promised to return to pray at the shrine in eleven days. Unfortunately her parents wanted to postpone the return until it had been possible to arrange for the attendance of all the most important local people. After this had dragged on well beyond the promised date, the girl was once more possessed and divine and satanic voices scolded her parents for the delay. Another trip to Ipswich was quickly arranged, and this time 4,000 people attended. Apparently all was going calmly, she attended and prayed at the shrine and made a nice little speech telling the crowd to have more faith.

In the middle of the night, however, the 'voice of Our Lady' once more summoned the bailiffs, the county JPs (now present) and the priest of the shrine to her hotel and began, through the child, to deliver a two-hour sermon, despite her mother trying to offer calming words which drove her into another fit. Curzon calmed her by thrusting forth his crucifix, but during the same eventful night, first her sisters, then her cousins and last of all her brother, also fell into fits and, after suitable ceremonies, were duly cured at the shrine. In following years, Queen Katherine of Aragon and Cardinal Wolsey paid visits to the shrine and the whole was duly recorded by Sir Thomas More in *Dialogues Concerning Heresies*, as evidence of miracles in modern times.

It is the literalness of divine intervention that is the most important aspect for us – troubled girl, demonic intervention, standard cure, shrine pilgrimage and prayer, failure to perform promise, divine punishment, demonic intervention, use of a crucifix, with everything all right in the end. Moreover, this world view was not especially that of the crowd but of the most educated and powerful in the region, indeed, in the land.

This ended with Reformation. The Reformation had created a new form of religion which distanced itself far more from the popular religion and concerns of the people than medieval Catholicism had.

To Puritan ministers, behaviour which a decade or so earlier would have been seen as orthodox piety was nothing but witchcraft. The rector of Blaxhall in Suffolk, Dr William Bullein, wrote in 1562 in his pamphlet entitled *Defence against all Sickness, Sornes and Woundes that dooe Daily assaulte Mankind*, that:

A false Witch called M. Line in a town of Suffolk called Perham which with a payre of Ebene beads and certain charmes had no small resort of foolysh women when theyr chyldren were syck. To thys lame Witch they resorted to have the Fairies charmed – through the prayers and the Ebene beads whych she sayd came from the holy land and were sanctifyed at Rome.---I knew in a towne called Kelshall in Suffolk a witch whose name was M. Didge who

An index page from Richard Argentine's book on magic showing entries for devils (*diabolus*) and demons (*daemonae*). (British Library)

with certain Aue Maries upon her Ebene beades and a waxe candle used this charme folowyng for S. Anthonies fyre having the sicke body before her, holding up her hande saying 'there came two Angels out of the North east one brought fyre the other brought frost, out fyre and in frost. In nomine patris etc.' I could reherse an C of sutch knackes of these holy gossips, the fyre take them all for they be God's enemyes.

(The East Anglian: Notes and Queries, Vol. XIII.)

More or less, exactly what Idololatria says in Bales' play:

> I never miss but palter
> Our Blessed lady's psalter
> Before Saint Saviour's altar.

Catholic writers, in the bitter paper war waged between Catholic and Protestant in the last years of Queen Elizabeth I, took pride in their superior power in dealing with practical healing issues, particularly in exorcism. Bishop Diego de Yepez recorded stories about the demonic possession of English Protestants: a Hampshire Catholic who had decided to 'conform' by attending his Anglican parish church was possessed by a devil; a possessed Oxford student who wanted to commit suicide, but was successfully exorcised by a Catholic priest and later 'conformed' and attended the Anglican church, whereupon he was repossessed and then succeeded in committing suicide.

John Foxe, author of the immensely influential Puritan classic, *Foxe's Book of Martyrs* (which refers to many Suffolk cases) tried to exorcise Mr Briggs, a possessed student of law. There were some signs of success, but then Briggs became worse than before and Foxe himself seemed possessed (Lake, *The Antichrist's Lewd Hat. Protestants, Papists and Players in Post-Reformation England*, p.252).

The Reformed religion did not provide the same kinds of services. So, where did the lovelorn, the sick, those looking for protection against danger, those looking for an explanation of their misfortune, or some kind of other direct benefit turn when they could no longer turn to the saints? In the sixteenth century this behaviour moved away from formal religion and rejoined the existing hidden world outside the Church.

As far as the Puritan ministers who were now lecturing from pulpits and paid by the town councils were concerned, all of these older beliefs, those of the Catholic priest and those of the cunning man were both equally delusional. They were deluded by the Devil, and were endangering their own and other people's souls, for all power resided only with God and only through faith in Him could any lasting blessing flow. Certainly not from the charms of curers or the mass of priests. It was possible that God had allowed a small proportion of

Bellarmine jug used as a witch bottle. (Ipswich Museum)

His power to be exercised by demons, but this was only so mankind could be tested, as Job had been tested. Would humanity turn from God if they thought they could get some worldly benefit elsewhere?

The more educated amongst the Puritans were men like the Essex Puritan minister George Gifford (1548–1600), who was lecturer at Maldon. Gifford wrote a pamphlet entitled *A Dialogue Concerning Witches and Witchcraftes* published in 1593. Gifford's position was that people did not suffer misfortunes as a result of the curses of witches, and that both cunning men and witches were equally deluded, indeed, that many people called witches were innocent victims of mob violence. Maldon was a town under the influence of the Rich family and, given the importance of the Riches in this story, this is significant.

He wrote his pamphlet in a dramatic theatrical format, as a discussion between Minister Daniel; a simple farmer, Samuel and his wife, who believed themselves bewitched; and a schoolmaster MB. The schoolmaster's is the voice that stands for those who would see the use of cunning men and women as only prudent. Gifford's Minister Daniel, of course, carries the day in the author's little play, but clearly not in reality. Samuel the farmer tells Daniel in these terms of his problem:

Others will me in time to seek help at the hands of some cunning man before I have any further harme. I would be glad to do for the best.

Daniel asks him: 'Have you any cunning man hereabout, that doth help?'
Samuel replies:

There is one, they say, here twenty mile off at TB that hath holp many. And this much I know, there was one of mine acquaintance but two mile hence, which had great losses—. He went to that same man and told him he suspected an old woman in that parish. And I think he told me that he showed him her in a Glass— and told him also what he should do. There is also a woman at RH five and twenty miles off that hath a great name and great resort there is daily unto to her

Daniel then finally tells his troubled friend:

The Devil has bewitched your mind with blindness and unbelief to draw you from God even to worship himself by seeking help at the hands of devils.

Daniel's point is that there are indeed devils, and that they continually surround mankind seeking their spiritual downfall. This is their real aim, and preventing yeast from turning mash into beer in the vat, or preventing cheese from setting or butter from rising in the churn, or killing hens and pigs is only a means to the end of destroying souls. People think devils are easily driven away when they do come:

> … as by burning some quick thing as hen or hog or beating and drawing blood upon the witch. Such people as can thus drive him away, or by thrusting a spit red hot into their cream are far from knowing the spiritual battle in which we are to war under the banner of Christ against the Devil. --- he may deal with their souls even as he listeth when they take him not present but upon such sending and where such hurt doth follow in their bodies or goods.

Gifford's English is a little hard to follow exactly here, so it can be paraphrased as follows:

> Those people who believe that they can drive the Devil away by burning some living animal such as a hen or a hog or by thrusting a red-hot spit into their cream do not understand the spiritual battle that we are called to fight under the banner of Christ. The Devil can do as he pleases with their souls if they believe devils are only present when witches send them to hurt their body or their goods.

Gifford sees clearly the contradiction between the informed, educated Puritan belief and unreflecting popular belief. In the first, all power is in the hands of God, and human sufferings and misfortunes are the methods that God uses to make humans aware of their own weakness and His power, to get them to reflect on their sins. This flatly contradicts the idea that ordinary women can compel devils to attack their human enemies, or even that any devil could ever harm anyone unless God so ordered.

In Gifford's version, the farmer who experiences some problem with his farming or faces some illness is actually guilty of an offence for which God is punishing him. The farmer is guilty, and making himself still more guilty by blaming witches rather than looking into himself. In the village view, the farmer is a wholly innocent victim of the wicked witches. Gifford sums up:

> The Devil only hurteth and that none can give him power neither man nor woman but only God and tell me whether or not the people be wonderfully carried awry in a rage. For when as they should consider, that the Devil is the Lord's executioner. And then finding that he hath any power given him to molest to hurt and vex them in their bodies or goods to know certainly it cometh from the Lord and then gather from thence (as the trueth is) that the Lord is displeased with them for their offences. And so seek unto him humbly craving pardon and deliverance from this enemy, seeking to be armed with the mighty power of faith to cast him forth and to resist him as the

Lord willeth. Here is no such matter, no looking so high among the people but running deeper into errour and sinne as if the witches did it and that it cometh from their anger and not from their own sins and infidelity, here is no repentance, no humbling themselves by fasting and prayer, but running for help unto devils using means which those devils by the cunning men and women appoint, scratching and clawing thirsting often after guiltless blood as raging against those whom they imagine to be witches, which many times are not, because they imagine that if there would be no such witches there would be no such plagues As if they had no foul sins or unbelief or that there remained not a just avenging God to punish, or as if he had not the devils still the executioners of his wrath.

Gifford's Puritan attack on the village belief in witchcraft is important, for it includes both the witches *and* their opponents in its sights, and in quite a sophisticated fashion highlights the way in which innocent old women were made the scapegoats for the hidden moral failings and uncertainties of their neighbours. The witchfinding mob is defined as being led astray by its own unthinking rage. The cunning man is led astray himself, and is used to lead others astray into false belief. Misfortunes of all sorts do not come about by the malignance of witches ordering devils to attack their enemies with petty misfortunes, they are in fact the just punishment of an all powerful God.

For the educated Protestant Christian of the day, Gifford's arguments should have been logically compelling. As a result, no good Puritan should have sought to deal with the possibility of witchcraft, or indeed any other kind of harm, other than by asking himself how he had offended God and by asking forgiveness in humble fasting and prayer. That is how logically they *should* have reacted. Actually, they mostly agreed with Gifford's schoolmaster MB, who argued: 'Does the word of God forbid us to take means, if I am sick shall I not take physic, if I am thirsty shall I not drink?'

MB agrees that Gifford has shown him how the Devil is really after his soul and not his pigs, but answers: 'I resist him [the Devil] in those greater [matters of the soul] may I not use those helps which drive him away in the lesser.' By this he means the methods of the cunning men.

Gifford talked the schoolmaster around in his pamphlet, but not in the reality of East Anglia. It is interesting that Gifford makes a schoolmaster the spokesperson for such an attitude. Were the schoolmaster and the minister in some senses competing to control the ideology of the smaller community of the parish?

In Ipswich the Marian headmaster of Ipswich school, Richard Argentine (1510/11–1568), was fascinated by the occult. Whether or not he in any way was directly involved in any form of complimentary religious activity is unknown, but he was interested enough to write a learned book on the subject, entitled *De Praestigiis et Incantionibus Daemonum et Necromanticorum* (On the Illusions and Spells of Demons and Necromancers).

Richard Argentine was a learned man but rather a shady one. According to his enemies, he came to Ipswich as a servant, presumably a private tutor in a prominent family. It is thought that he had become an usher at Ipswich School in 1537, and became headmaster in 1538 while still pursuing his academic studies, becoming a doctor of medicine at Cambridge in 1541. He was, therefore, present in Ipswich during the transfer of the minor monastic houses in order to fund Wolsey's glittering, but very short-lived college, and throughout the period of the suppression of the religious houses and the further Protestant policies of Edward VI. He would certainly have known John Bale.

During this time he was, to all appearances, a committed supporter of the Reformation. He was responsible for three English translations of Latin books by the leading Protestant figures of the Continent, Martin Luther Bernard Ochino and Ulrich Zwingli (all, by the way, printed in Ipswich by Anthony Scholoker).

However, when Queen Mary raised her standard at Framlingham and marched on London, Argentine suddenly became an enthusiastic supporter of the new regime and of the return of Catholicism. He was rewarded with a grant that made him permanent headmaster of the school, and he was made the priest of St Helen's, Ipswich; St Clement's, Ipswich; Whitton, Brantham; and East Bergholt. According to the hostile evidence of his opponents, he gloried in his new position, and could be seen always in his white ermine hood performing mass; carrying the pyx in processions; even re-instituting the Christmas ceremony of the Boy Bishop.

This was, of course, no more than might be expected of someone who had, arguably, simply rediscovered the faith of his childhood. However, according to Peter Moone, Foxe's Ipswich source, it was Argentine who led the persecution of local Protestants, seeking out Agnes Wardell, Peter Moone and his wife for examination at the risk of their lives. He was almost certainly responsible for drawing up lists of wanted men and women to feed the fires. When Mary's regime was collapsing, Argentine was positioning himself ready for another change of heart and had decided that he would have to leave Ipswich for London and Exeter. He was, for a time, under a cloud with the government of Elizabeth, but somehow scraped through and held on to both his Exeter and his Ipswich parishes up to his death.

It was at Exeter that he finished his book on the occult. Only a few copies survive, and the book has never been translated, largely because it appears to have been very closely based on the identically titled book by the Dutch doctor Johan Weyer, who had taken up a court position in the German duchy of Cleves. Weyer's book was called, in English translation, *On the Illusions of the Demons and on Spells and Poisons*. It was printed in 1563. Argentine's book was called *On the Illusions of the Demons and on Spells and Necromancy*. His book had sixteen chapters, all with intriguing titles, here are four:

3   Of those who consult Demons in crystals displaying different images and showing facts.
5   Of pacts and agreements between enchanters and demons.
9   Of those who observe a part of the heavens to divine the future and those who divine through the songs and flights of birds which sort of men the Jews called Hober.
13 Of Beelzebub the Prince of the court of demons.

Argentine's book was quoted by the Norwich doctor, Richard Burton, who referred to Argentine's belief in storm demons and also in those spirits attached to certain families that appeared to foretell a death.

Richard Burton was called as an expert witness in the trial of Lowestoft witches mentioned below. The Victorian writer Montague Summers also quoted Argentine in his book, *Werewolf*, in the untranslated Latin of the original. Argentine saw a medical element in the condition of the werewolf: it was the excessive amount of black bile in their system that made certain people particularly liable to possible possession by demons. Such people were driven to become Lycaons (a Greek king who had sacrificed his own children to Zeus, and who was turned into a wolf as a punishment, and at whose shrine every year someone was turned into a wolf for a period) or lycanthropes (werewolves), people who were melancholy, ferocious and monstrous. They could be helped by exorcists with sacred prayers and sprinkling of holy water, but their black bile also needed treating with hellebore.

Weyer had been unusual and courageous in his time for denouncing previous writings on witches. He described the women who had confessed to witchcraft as being mentally ill, a phrase he is credited with inventing. Weyer believed that witches and magicians had no real powers but were deluded, although he believed that these delusions came from the Devil. This 'medical' explanation of witchcraft was an influential view amongst the learned, but cut no ice with villagers.

In 1573 there is a very different kind of record to Argentine's learned interest, giving a glimpse of how in practice Elizabethan 'justice' worked in relation to formal magic rather than witchcraft in Suffolk. Sir Nicholas Bacon Snr to Sir Nicholas Bacon Jnr, on 18 March 1573:

Son, Sir Ambrose Jermyn hath written to me for a pardon to be obtained for one Morris who at the last assizes condemned for invocation of spirits as it seemeth by his writing by somewhat too straight [strict] a proceeding in law. And besides he writeth that the prisoner is become a very repentant and sorrowful man for his offence. Nevertheless I have forborne and mean to forbear to proceed in it until I hear from you, whether the county thinketh the man worthy death or no. And if you had been at the assizes [in Bury] as you should have been, if you had done well, you might have informed me of this of your own knowledge – if this man be of any wealth as I hear he is he should have his charge if he can get his pardon [this sentence is struck through].

Morris has apparently been convicted at the Bury assizes for raising spirits and is under sentence of death. One of the justices, Sir Ambrose Jermyn, has been persuaded somehow to write to the Lord Chancellor begging for a pardon for him. Bacon wants to know what public opinion in Suffolk is concerning Morris, but also just how rich he is and, if wealthy, he should have his charge, or in other words be made to pay Bacon, as well as Jermyn, for his pardon. Neither man seems particularly shocked at Morris's alleged crime, it was the opportunity to extort money which was interesting.

There is a legal record in Ipswich that shows how any unusual skill or exploit could be grounds for suspecting some kind of uncanny power. It refers to a case in which Robert Keble, a gentleman, was trying to get out of honouring a debt to Richard Howe arising from a bet over the time it would take Howe to go from Aldgate in London to Stowmarket in 1603:

[Rich Howe] ded goe and run on fote from Aldgate in City of London unto the parish church of Stowmarket within 20 hours together without intermission of further time without fraud or decept.

Deposition as to truth of performance. Query Did you see Richard Howe use any sinister or extraordinary means or practice for his case to further his travel in his journey otherwise than by going and running and did he perform the same bona fide without fraud or decept?

Griffen Warner of AshBocking clerk aet 64 years on 10 Nov 1603 said he knew Richard Howe and that Richard Howe 'did goe and rune on foote from Algate – unto the parish church of Stowmarket' within 20 hrs starting at 12 o'clock mid-day and arrived at Stowmarket next day at 1/2hr and more before 8 o'clock in the fornone and he knew this to be true as he Griffen Warner and one Richard Kinge of Stowmarket travelled with the said Richard all the way at that time and had some diet with them and timed the same by some clocks and dials. He travelled by his own strength and with a walking stick in his hand in his journey.

Richard Kinge of Stowmarket shoemaker aet 40 yrs deposed as above.

Keble had obviously suggested that Howe used some 'sinister or extraordinary means or practice' to speed him on his way, with the implication that the bet was therefore null and void. Clearly the possibility of some kind of magical aid to running races was plausible.

Another Ipswich case from the Sessions of the Peace, 1609, provides unusual legal evidence of one of the most common practices of the cunning man:

> We find that Robert Moore had divers goods stolen from him and after the sums were so stolen he went to Nathaniel Tennant in the indictment named to hear of the same again and gave him money whereupon the said Nathaniel did tell him he would help him to those goods again and did appoint him to meet him in the fields and so he did where the said Tennent told him that the planets would not then serve for they must be in the same place where they were when those goods were lost and afterwards he appointed him to meet him again And then he told him so far as he could find by his familiar the same were stolen away by John Hart or otherwise his familiar deceived him for he had holpen one Fayerweather to certain goods which were lost and that they were brought again by the party who had stolen the same from Ardlie. Whether he be guilty in the matter or no we pray the Judgement of the Court and if the Court shall adjudge him guilty upon that matter then we find him guilty.

Obviously Nathaniel Tennant was known to use both astrology and his familiar spirit to help people recover stolen property. He had successfully helped Fayreweather in the past to recover some goods, but was having less success with Moore's lost property. What is interesting is the uncertainty with which the court viewed the case – had either Nicholas Tennant the conjurer or Robert Moore committed any kind of crime by using magic in this way?

Presumably Moore was beginning to feel cheated of his money. Tennant does not appear as a convicted criminal and so apparently the matter was just dropped. Tennant may have been genuinely convinced that he could indeed discover lost property this way, but he could just as easily have been working a scam in which he had himself arranged with thieves to steal Moore's property (or at least knew them) only to miraculously recover it, dividing his fees with the thieves.

By the seventeenth century such beliefs had moved out of the underworld and shadows to become almost fashionable – the subject of intellectual enquiry and controversy, of legal action and legislation. Far from being a phenomenon of isolated villages, it was based in the larger towns, where they attracted clients from a wide area.

This period was not as obsessed by statistics as our own. Numbers in contemporary documents could often mean little more than 'I think there is a lot', but one particular source is interesting. Much of the medicine practised in the land was done by unlicensed individuals, to the intense annoyance of

A DECLARATION, 20

Of a strange and Wonderfull MONSTER:

Born in KIRKHAM Parifh in LANCASHIRE (the Childe
of Mrs. *Haughton,* a Popifh Gentlewoman) the face of it upon the breaft,
and without a head (after the mother had wifhed rather to bear a
Childe without a head then a Roundhead) and had curft the
PARLIAMNET.

Attefted by Mr. F L E E T W O O D , Minifter of the fame Parifh, under his own hand ; and Mrs. *Gattaker* the Mid-wife, and divers
other eye-witnefles : Whofe teftimony was brought up by a *Mem-*
ber of the Houfe of Commons.

Appointed to be printed according to Order : And defired to be publifhed in all the
Counties, Cities, Townes , and Parifhes in England : *Being the fame*
Copies that were prefented to the Parliament.

march 3   London, Printed by *Jane Coe.* 1646.   1645

'A declaration of a strange and wonderful monster', this image brings together ideas of God
directly punishing sinners, the evils of the Catholic Church, and the idea of 'monstrous'
births being supernatural. (British Library)

the physicians who often prosecuted them – Thomas Gale reported that over sixty women were curing illegally in London in the 1560s. 'These women,' he said:

> … be called wise women, or holy and good women, some of them be called witches, and useth to call upon certain spirits, and some of them useth plain bawdry, and telleth gentlewomen that cannot bear children how they may have children.--- as some for sore breasts, some for the stone and strangurie, some for pain of the teeth, some for scald heads, some for sore legs, some cunning in Mother Tomson's tub, and some to help maids when they have lost their maidenhead, when their bellies are grown too great, to make them small again, with a thousand more.

Full of indignation at these unlicensed practitioners, Gale reported that in 1562 alone he had seen over 300 people in St Thomas's and St Bartholomew's hospitals who had been injured, maimed and even killed by witch's charms and women practising herbal medicine. The very approximate estimate of the population of London around that time is 50,000–80,000. He was afraid that the surgeons were being blamed for these failed cures, but it was common knowledge that witches hurt people.

There was definitely an occult underworld in seventeenth-century England. This is, after all, the period in which Ben Jonson's play *The Alchemist* was written, in which two confidence men persuade a lawyer's clerk that the queen of the fairies has fallen in love with him. This was based on some well-known (at the time) real cases in which people had convinced others that they could arrange their marriage to the queen of the fairies, leading to court cases. The villains in these cases were Judith Phillips, the Wests (husband and wife) and the third case involved a lawyer in Dorset.

Experts in this world were 'cunning' in both the modern and the seventeenth-century sense. Moreover, they had patrons amongst the powerful. These practitioners were usually male and at the top of their profession, highly educated with very wealthy and powerful patrons and clients (Dee, Kelly, Ripley, Forman, Lambe and Lilley are some of the best known English examples).

Ipswich's own local gentry family, the Withipoles, were drawn into the world of court magicians. The astrologer and magician Simon Forman (1511–1611) was a leading 'cunning man'. His notebooks show that he was consulted about illnesses, pregnancies, stolen goods, career opportunities and marriage prospects. He was used by the highest nobility and involved in their various criminal actions, being accused by Chief Justice Coke of having provided the poisons used in the Thomas Overbury murder. These notebooks show that he met with and was consulted by Lady Frances Withipole.

Lady Frances Withipole had a minor part to play in one of the greatest scandals of the court, and one in which magicians were involved. Chief Justice Coke violently fell out with his wife, Lady Hatton, over the marriage of their daughter, Frances. Coke wanted to force his daughter into marriage with John Villiers, the raving mad brother of George Villiers, Duke of Buckingham. George was the royal favourite and so one of the most powerful men in the land. Coke himself had fallen from royal favour and was desperate to recover his fortune and influence.

Lady Hatton, Coke's wife, was first cousin to Frances Withipole and had used her influence to get her cousin's husband, Edmund Withipole, knighted and awarded the immensely valuable lease of Corfe Castle and its lands. So when Lady Hatton rescued her daughter from Coke, it was to the Withipole's town house that she took her and from which Coke's thugs took her back by force. The marriage took place after Frances Coke was whipped into submission in 1617. The young bride escaped with Sir Robert Howard, but unfortunately the first thing the runaways did was to turn to the magician Dr John Lambe for help. They did not know that Lambe was Buckingham's private magician and he immediately betrayed them to his master.

At that time, and for years afterwards, Buckingham was by far the most powerful man in the kingdom (excepting the king) and the especial hate object of the Puritans. Nowhere was he more hated than in Ipswich, where he had seized practically all of the town's shipping and pressganged many of the town's sailors to serve in his disastrous attempt to invade France at the Île de Rhé in 1627. Satirists of the time believed that Buckingham's mother, Compton, was a witch too – she was certainly a Catholic, which to them was next to witchcraft anyway – and that she and Lambe had bewitched the king to fall completely under Buckingham's spell. Lambe was stoned to death by a mob in London after he had been convicted of raping an 11-year-old girl but left free.

The religious leader of Ipswich, the town lecturer, Samuel Ward, was charged with preaching against the Duke of Buckingham just before John Felton of Playford (just outside Ipswich) assassinated the duke in 1628. Lambe and Buckingham's deaths were celebrated in satirical verse throughout the country:

> Where is thy devil, and thy doctor Lambe
> That purchased thee, with Charles so great a name
> What, are they gone unto the Stygian Lake (hell)
> And would thee so unkindly so forsake?
> —— O strange at first, to get so great promotion
> with Dis (Lord of hell) (I saith) it was for pure devotion
> Thou bear to Lucifer: then think of this
> That Felton, merits everlasting bliss,

Who caused thee, to gain that exaltation
And sent thee to such a place of recreation
There must thou use, thy magic and thy charms
Thy spells and figures could do little harm —

(www.earlystuartlibels.net)

Some of these events are reflected in a satirical play written by Ben Jonson in 1616, *The Devil is an Ass*. The play is heavy with references to contemporary court events – a mass of topical court allusions very difficult for us to fully decode, but which have to reflect contemporary rumour and gossip in some way to have been worth including in the play in the first place. Chief Justice Coke is mocked as Fitzdotterell. Lady Frances Withipole's son, Sir William Withipole, seems to be the model for the character Wittipoll, a pun meaning 'clever head'.

The Coke character in the play, Fitzdotterell, is depicted as desperate to recover the fortune he has lost and willing to do anything to get it back, pretty much like the real life Coke. Just like Coke, Fitzdotterell is a Norfolk landowner and just like Coke, one of his schemes to recover his money is to drain the fens, in fact he is called the Duke of the Drowned Lands. He is also depicted as being obsessed by magical rituals to call on devils. He complains that for fifty weeks he has been getting all of the most famous conjurers to try and call up the Devil:

They do now, name Brentnor, as before
They talked of Gresham , and of Doctor Forman
Franklin and Fiske and Savory (he was in too)
But theres not one of these, that ever could
Yet show a man the Devil, in true sort
They have their crystals, I do know and rings
And virgin parchment, and their dead men's skulls
Their raven wings, their lights and pentangles
With characters; I have seen all these.

Fitzdotterell then decides that the Devil will not come for conjuring, to be compelled to carry out tasks for wizards, but he will come to any who really calls on him, and that if the Devil did come he would make him welcome and offer him his wife's bed and even his wife. A very junior devil, Pug, then appears but is completely outmatched by the human evil around him and the corruption of human society.

The Wittipol character in the play is shown as the gallant lover of Fitzdotterell's wife. Fitzdotterell, who is depicted as being even greedier than he is jealous, allows Wittipol to speak to his wife. Wittipol is shown reminding

Mrs Fitzdotterell of how her husband has left her alone in her cold bed to go drawing circles and conjuring devils in Lincoln Inn Fields.

Whatever reality lay behind the innuendoes of the play, it was at least credible to both Jonson and his audience to depict a Withipole as deeply, though innocently, involved with a family in which the husband, the leading legal figure in the country, was involved with ritual magic. So intense were the rumours around Lady Hatton and the Cokes that they gave rise to a gruesome folk story in which the Devil first danced with and then abducted a Lady Hatton, leaving nothing but a bleeding heart behind, an event after which the current Bleeding Heart Yard in London is named.

Sir William Withipole, at the end of his life, had an elaborate astrological investigation drawn up for him by William Liley who was now the leading astrologer of England. Sir William desperately wanted advice for the future (he had been imprisoned, and his daughter had turned against him). However, Sir William did not know the hour of his birth, which was vital to cast an astrological chart. Liley worked backwards from what had actually happened already to Sir William to work out when he must have been born in order for these things to have happened. Then he was able to predict his future. Liley was also a witness to Withipole's contested will.

To sum up, scandal and allegations of the use of sorcery by the highest of the land reached out to touch the Withipoles the leading family in Ipswich; these and other occult scandals concerning the political enemies of the town would have been well known to the ruling elite of Ipswich. Sir William Withipole was closely linked to the greatest astrologer in the land.

Neither John Stearne nor Matthew Hopkins were particularly well-educated men compared with Puritan ministers, and their ideas are in some ways closer to the world of popular belief. In his *Confirmation and Discoverie of Witchcraft* John Stearne, Hopkins partner, makes a clear distinction between 'white', 'curing' or 'helpful' witches and 'hurting' or 'cursing' witches. He is prepared to admit that some of the first are self-deluded into not realising that the source of their power comes from the Devil. But nonetheless any healing power can only come from one of two sources: either from God, in which case it is natural and not due to the healer for the age of miracles is over, or unnatural and from the Devil.

Stearne is absolutely clear that all such people, even those who use Christian prayers are, in fact, nothing better than witches in league with the Devil. Admittedly the first sort are in secret covenant with the Devil and the second sort in open and deliberate covenant, but nevertheless both are equally condemned. From his writings it is clear that he would have loved to have seen all of them brought to trial and convicted. This rather long but extremely interesting quotation makes this abundantly clear, as well as listing some more standard techniques which were to have a very long lifespan as we shall see:

Some to set spells; Some Charms; Some to cure diseases several ways, either by words, or washing clothes, or anointing the Instrument which gave the wound to cure the wound; Some only by laying on of their hands; Some by using and saying superstitious words, or form of prayers, using good words to bad ends; Some by both; Some by herbs; Some to know where stolen goods are, either by raising the Devil, or Familiar Spirits; Some only by words, and so likewise the same for lost goods, or man or beast, and to bring them again; and so by such like ways and means do these work by: Yet many times they err, all of these: For the Devil cannot perform his promise at all times. So that it is not to be questioned, but all these sorts are in league with the Devil.

May not Spell-setters and Charmers be also added? For I cannot conceive any less, when the shall say that by words they can charm, set Spells, and help or cure mad Dogs, or any bitten by them, and such-like; though it be by their implicit league, (as some of them do) yet it is distrust of Gods providence, putting their confidence in their words, rather than in the living God, who's faith it is an abomination to him. And I have heard some of these, not long since, boast of Their doings therein, saying they had it from their parents, and were not their parents good Christians? And they do but use the words for good ends.

Hereto I might add the healing of a wound by anointing the instrument which gave the wound, Spell-setters, and Charmers, and such-like, who many of them are in express league as aforesaid: for the Devil contents himself sometimes, to wit, there where he well perceives the party will not be brought to the other, and lets them please themselves with hope of Gods mercy, employing them only about seeming-good things, for that in so doing they suppose they in not, nor are in danger of the Devil, nor under Gods wrath, as the others are, because they fall not so foully into the pit of destruction by express league, as the others do, and make an outward show of Religion as well as others.

For what can be said of those who only cure by laying on their hands, and using certain words or forms of prayers? Is it not done by this secret Compact, though ignorantly they think otherwise? For if the remedy is not natural, then it is supernatural, then either from God, and so has warrant from his Word, and is ordinary, not miraculous; for that work of God has ceased long since: or else is from the Devil, as works wrought by Spells and Charms, and such-like, forbidden by God. Yet these sorts of persons, finding their practices successful, are not against Satan, nor can lightly speak ill of his working power, because of their secret and implicit league they have with him, and especially because of the profit they find come to them thereby. And herein also does the Devil imitate Christ, who allowed some, which openly as yet did not follow him, to have power to call out devils, who were not, as he said, against him, nor could lightly speak ill of him, nor of his power, by reason of their

The Witch of Edmonton
A known true STORY.
Compofed into
A TRAGI-COMEDY
By divers well-efteemed Poets;
William Rowley, Thomas Dekker, John Ford, &c

Acted by the Princes Servants, often at the Cock-Pit in *Drury-Lane,*
once at Court, with fingular Applaufe.

Never printed till now.

London, *Printed by* J. Cottrel, *for* Edward Blackmore, *at the Angel in*
Paul's *Church-yard.* 1658.

The Witch of Edmonton. This image shows the ambivalent attitude of many people towards witchcraft; it is both supposedly true *and* a tragi-comedy, taking place amongst the ignorant village community, and amusing to court sophisticates. The demonic black dog asks, 'Have I found you cursing?' while the witch replies with a Catholic Latin prayer, 'Blessed be Thy holy name.' (British Library)

secret and implicit faith, and covenant with Christ; yet did it, because they found success in it.

So, likewise in the Scripture is found the cutting of hair, and burning it, the writing of words, and the blotting of them out again, and to give them unto one. Also the giving of a portion. So Satan teaches his to cut off hair and burn it; as the White-Witch will do to such as come to them, advising them to cut hair, or such-like, off the beast they suspect to be bewitched, and to write a Charm, and to blot it out, and then give it one; also to use potions; thus seeming, by their imitations, to have Scripture for their warrant. And so after this manner I might reckon up several other ways: as, the Lord had some which by cursing and threatening procured evil upon others, so Satan has such, which by cursing and threats procure mischiefs upon others, as you may plainly see by their Confessions.

However, whatever Stearne might say, there is no known case in which the accused is convicted for healing someone, curing cattle, detecting (other) witches or finding stolen goods by diabolic means. Certainly neither Hopkins nor Stearne were able to convict one. Spell setters, charmers, white witches and cunning men existed but were not persecuted.

Stearne's view of the reality of witches and their power to hurt the innocent was relatively unsophisticated, even unorthodox, by the standards of many more educated and fully trained Puritans. Hopkins and Stearne's use of the infamous trial by water was no part of due legal process or of formal Puritan (or Catholic) belief. Their belief in imps and familiars and their searching for marks, places them clearly within the world of popular belief.

5

A Witchfinder's Career Cut Short: Patrons and Enemies

In June or July of 1645, a presentable young man wrapped in a travelling cloak, with a broad-brimmed hat, shoulder-length black hair, and black clothes of good quality – contrasting dramatically with the simple white collar of his fine shirt and riding boots of which he was obviously proud – crossed over the River Stour from Essex into Suffolk. It is possible that his pet greyhound trotted along beside his horse. He had three horses with him, and formed part of a little company which included his colleague, John Stearne, and one or two middle-aged women. They were needed as 'searchers'. Quite probably, armed servants sent out by the local justices escorted him. He would have needed the servant escorts to lead him down the obscure lanes and pathways to the smaller villages on his path and to vouch for him as he travelled about the unsafe roads which were imperfectly patrolled by various paranoid authorities. The state of the country meant that some of the men would have been heavily armed.

At that moment, Matthew Hopkins, the self appointed 'Witchfinder General' had crossed over into Suffolk on the first stage of what was to be a gruelling 300-mile or more journey around the east of the county, Norfolk and Huntingdon. He was soon to part from his companion John Stearne, who set off for the west of the county. For most of the rest of that year and into the next he was on the road. About thirty years earlier, Robert Reyce had described the state of Suffolk roads in his *Breviary of Suffolk*. Reyce was normally a great enthusiast for Suffolk, but he had to work very hard to find anything good to say of the roads:

> What with the foulness of the ways, which in the clay woodland soil is ever increased especially in winter season, that the ordinary passage one from another during that time is made most difficult: yea the usual and most common roads, if they were not yearly repaired, and continued, by virtue of the several necessary statutes to that end made; they would in the winter season breed a loathsome weariness to the passenger.

However, he did feel that they were so bad that they might deter a foreign invasion:

> ... by that time the invaders meet with our dep miry soil, our narrow and foul lanes, our manifold enclosures, severed with so many deep ditches, hedges,, and store of wood bushes and trees, seeing the impassibleness of this Country-- albeit there were no other means of resistance, they will have just cause to repent their rashness.
>
> (p.12)

This was just the difficulty of the roads, but as the country fell apart in chaos and warfare the traveller could also expect to be stopped and questioned harshly by local officials with no trust of outsiders. Arthur Wilson, who was the steward of the immensely powerful Earl of Warwick, had a rough experience travelling through the Stour valley:

> With difficultie I pass'd through the litle villages of Essex where theire black bills [men armed with a black bill, a type of spear] and course examinations [rough questions] put us to divers demurs [many troubles]. And but they had [and if they had not had] some knowledge both of mee and the coach, I had not pass'd with safetie.
>
> (Arthur Wilson, q.v.)

Where we have evidence from official accounts such as those of Hopkins' visits to Aldeburgh, we can see that he stayed in the best inns and ensured that he got the best in food and drink that they could provide. After all, his clients were the ones paying, and they passed the cost straight on to the local ratepayers (a constant theme of Gaskill's book is the cost of the witch persecutions upon already stretched authorities). Sometimes we learn that he was received with a little civic pomp, as at King's Lynn, accompanied by a trooper and a drummer.

Rumour must have preceded him, and something of the eerie terrifying nature of his supposed specialised knowledge must have made him loom very large in the imagination of the inhabitants of Framlingham or Aldeburgh. Matthew Hopkins riding down the byways of East Suffolk to bring doom to witches is a familiar image. Much less well known is the reality that, as Hopkins pursued witches, he was himself being pursued by a cloud of rumour and concern that was in time to bring him down.

For a figure who looms so large in the popular imagination, really very little is definitely known about Hopkins, and what is known is marshalled very well by Malcolm Gaskill in his book *Witchfinders*. Yet the events, despite being retold many times, and despite their continuing resonance in modern thought, are really not very well understood, in a variety of ways. For all his grand title,

Hopkins was actually not a very important person, and made little impression on contemporary documents.

He was a younger son in a modestly successful clerical family, born about 1620. It seems likely that he was descended from John Hopkins, a Protestant minister of Great Waldringfield, who had fled abroad during the Marian persecutions to return later. This John Hopkins is known for working together with a man called Sternhold to create a rhyming version of the Psalms which could be set to music and sung. Hopkins contributed sixty psalms to the 1562 Psalter, which is more than any other contributor by a considerable margin. All of his psalms are in common metre, like Sternhold's, but they differ in that Sternhold only rhymed the second and fourth lines of his verses, while Hopkins would rhyme both the first and third, and the second and fourth lines. This metrical version was a great success, being reprinted 200 times in about 100 years as a separate book. It was very often published together with the *Book of Common Prayer* and the *Geneva Bible*. The singing of psalms became the chief musical expression of the devout Puritan. For centuries most English people would have been familiar with the tune and words of the 'old Hundredth', 'all people that on earth do dwell.' One of the many ironies of the witch trials that were to follow is that several of the condemned at Bury, the victims of Hopkins and Stearne, went to their death singing these psalms.

John Hopkins' son, and Matthew's father, was a James Hopkins who had secured a reasonable position as an Anglican minister of Puritan leanings at Great Wenham in Suffolk. James did not manage to progress up the ranks of the bishop's administration, nor did he secure any Puritan lectureships or wealthy Puritan private patrons. There is no hard evidence as to exactly how strict a Puritan he was. He certainly never clashed with his bishop so he cannot have been as determined as many of his colleagues. Nevertheless, he was obviously concerned about the direction matters were taking, for in 1633, when he was about 61, James decided to radically change his life. He wanted to emmigrate to New England, and wrote of his intentions to his friend John Winthrop, who had become the governor. Such a decision would have, of course, brought him firmly into the circle of Samuel Ward who was organising the emigration from Ipswich, even if he had not already been associated with him.

However, James Hopkins had left it too late. He became ill and died in 1634. His eldest son, another James, was still training for the clergy at Cambridge. His second son, Thomas, was to emigrate, and this left Matthew on his own. Matthew had attended neither Cambridge nor the Inns of Court. Therefore, Matthew Hopkins was in a very frustrating, even though materially comfortable, position: he could not easily progress far in a clerical career without a university education and could not easily progress in a legal career without having attended the Inns of Court.

Matthew Hopkins. (*The Discovery of Witches*)

Nevertheless, he was not destitute. His share of the will was 100 marks and he is believed to have entered into some kind of legal position in Ipswich. As his name does appear once as a witness on a legal conveyance, there seems no reason to doubt this tradition. Matthew Hopkins was a bright lad who would have to make his own way in the world. Once Matthew Hopkins had come into his money at 22, he moved to the town of Manningtree where he is said to have lived in South Street and owned the Thorn Inn at Mistley. In Manningtree was a man ten years or so his elder, called John Stearne, who came from Long Melford. Stearne was married and had just had a baby girl. From Long Melford he moved to Lawshall and from there he moved to Manningtree, where he apparently owned property. He and Hopkins became acquainted. Just before the time of Hopkin's arrival in 1638, the local landlord, Sir Harbottle Grimston, had sent four local women for trial in Colchester for the crime of witchcraft.

There is an intriguing, but not completely conclusive, piece of evidence that a young Matthew Hopkins was himself involved in a case of witchcraft connected with a failed courtship. The record is contained in a book of legal decisions recorded by Harbottle Grimston the Younger (more about this book is given below). The record of the case is as follows:

13 year of Charles I [1637/8] Ceely against Hopkins and his wife:
Whereas the wife, [Mrs Hopkins] dum sola fuit, [when she was still single] spoke of the plaintiff [Ceely] these words 'he is a witch, and a strong witch, and hath bewitched me and my aunt A.S. [the aunt of the said wife innuendo] therfore I will not marry him'. The defendant pleaded not guilty and it was found against her and damages given to forty pounds. It was claimed for the fined woman that no specific act of witchcraft was alleged but the claim that the aunt had been bewitched was enough.

If it could be shown that the Hopkins, whose new wife had broken off with Ceely for her present husband amidst all kinds of bitter accusations, was a member of Matthew Hopkins' family (one of his brothers, perhaps even a cousin), it would certainly add to our knowledge of the young Hopkins and give a further insight into the picture of the obsessive young man listening to the calls of witches across the winter wastes of the Stour estuary, confused perhaps in his mind with the cry of all the great flocks of water birds and waders. It may also indicate an earlier link between Hopkins and Grimston.

The accusations, trials, acquittals and further accusations linked to the 1638 charges dragged on into the 1640s. The constant rumours and hushed discussions regarding various women were coming to a head. They began to obsess the young Hopkins. He believed that he could hear witches calling to each other on Friday nights, every six weeks; that they had learned he had heard them and that they had sent a bearlike spirit to kill him. However, his prayers had driven the spirit away.

In 1645 Sir Harbottle Grimston and the local magistrate, Sir Thomas Bowes, were faced with another set of accusations concerning the widow Elizabeth Clarke. The accusations made by various inhabitants of the area were laid before the magistrates by John Stearne. Stearne also brought a 'confession' from Clarke in which other people were named. He walked out of the meeting with a written warrant 'for the searching of such persons as I shall nominate'. This warrant, of course, only held good for the Tendring hundred where Grimston and Bowes were magistrates.

According to Stearne, Hopkins started as his assistant. These initial accusations were in fact, not only the beginning but the most successful part of Hopkins and Stearne's collaboration. Both men were later accused of simply brutalising and browbeating witnesses to confess. Part of these charges involved the folk ordeal of swimming people to test if they were witches, in the way that was to survive into the late Victorian period. Both men later published denials of the use of undue force, but both did say that 'at the beginning' perhaps some practices had been used, but before they themselves had become directly involved in a case, or that swimming had indeed been used but only in cases before the time Sergeant Godbold had declared this illegal at Bury St Edmunds.

All of this strongly suggests that it was, therefore, these initial cases in which Hopkins and Stearne had been able to perfect and use the full range of their techniques. This involved shaming the accused by having them stripped and searched, a process amounting to sexual abuse in that the searchers were looking for physical marks usually hidden in the genitals, in a society dominated by ideas of modesty and shame. Another method involved throwing them bound into water, and then subjecting them to a series of interrogations based around a set of key questions while the accused was deprived of sleep and forced into a stress position.

All of these methods could all be described as legitimate parts of the investigation or looking for signs and evidence, not forcing a confession through torture which was not part of the English legal system. They also could be described as just that – torture.

What is also obvious, once one assembles the full range of sources, is that these first confessions are the most lurid. It is in these confessions that we hear of groups of witches meeting, of them seeking to recruit others, of the use of some kind of a 'bible' and communal rituals, combined with the nearly universal charges of signing a covenant and having sex with the Devil.

Neither Hopkins nor Stearne had any religious position. They had no legal authority. Neither was especially wealthy. No one has found any trace of them ever being appointed to a post under Parliament, or in the household of some mighty landowner. Despite the darkly grand title of Witchfinder General, Hopkins had no power or authority of his own; the title was his present to himself. Hopkins and Stearne were not agents of a state persecution organised from the centre by either the Crown, the bishops or Parliament and the organised Puritan movement. Hopkins was undoubtedly a very powerful and malignant catalyst for precipitating persecution and disaster, but, like traditional creatures of darkness, he first had to be given power by being invited in. The persecution was a movement from below, not above.

A witch could not be killed on the simple say so of an aggrieved farmer. For a witch to be executed in England the law required evidence that the witch had actually carried out specific crimes of witchcraft at specific times. Under

English law a confession forced by torture was invalid and a lot of witch trials ended in acquittals.

As far as I can establish, the history of Ipswich cases of witchcraft had been as follows:

DATE OF TRIAL	NAME OF ACCUSED	VERDICT	BISHOP OF NORWICH	TERM
1581	Emma Burradge	unknown	Edmund Freke	1575–1584
No trials held			Edmund Scambler	1585–1594
1600	Rose Dibnall	not guilty	William Redman	1594–1602
1601	Joan Robertson	pleaded not guilty		
1602	Rose Debnall			
	Joan Debnall	guilty		
1603	Helen Hodges	not guilty	John Jegon	1603–1618
1605, 1604	Rachel Webb	not guilty		
1618	Diana Taylor	not guilty		
No trials held			John Overall	1618–1619
1622	Anna Puce	guilty		
No trials held			Samuel Harsnet	1619–1628
1624	Thomas and Agnes Pye	not guilty	Francis White	1628–1631
No trials held			Richard Corbet	1632–1635
No trials held			Mathew Wren	1635–1638
No trials held			Richard Montagu	1638–1641
1640 Fall and later trial of Archbishop Laud and loss of power by bishops				
	Katherine Dameron	not guilty		
1645	Margery Sutton	not guilty		
	Rose Parker	not guilty		
	Alice Daye	not guilty		
	James and Mary Emerson	acquitted on major charges, found guilty on lesser charge; imprisoned and pilloried		
	Alice Denham	guilty		
	Mary Lakeland (Lackland)	guilty; burnt		

This pattern shows a commencement and a peak of activity at the end of the reign of Queen Elizabeth I, just a sprinkling of Jacobean cases, and nothing at all under the rule of Charles I or Archbishop Laud. It was only after the Laudian bishops of Norwich had been removed from power that the next and final wave of legal persecutions began in earnest.

In Ipswich at least twice as many were acquitted as convicted. The leaders of a community could go through the expense, disruption and bitterness of a trial only to fail to get a conviction. Magistrates really needed more certainty that, having brought a case, they would actually get a result.

Hopkins and Stearne had devised a series of methods to exert extreme pressure on individuals to force them to confess. This amounted to a reliable confession-generating machine that could bring to a head, and then resolve by means of a judicial execution, feuds and problems which had been bedevilling small communities for decades. All they needed was a list of suspects and local backing. Tendring was intended to be the place for the demonstration of their methods.

The power of Hopkins and Stearne lay in their ability to offer rural JPs and clergy a solution. They were the experts. Above all, they allowed the authorities firstly to be seen doing the right thing in protecting the community by calling them in, and secondly the responsibility for sending members of the local community to their death became that of the witchfinders. Seventeenth-century authority was no different from contemporary authority in being keen to see the responsibility for difficult decisions fall on to someone else's shoulders, and in being prepared to pay a commission for the service.

Hopkins and Stearne were in fact the most modern of figures: the outside professional expert hired to find what the local authorities wanted them to find, and quite well aware that their next contract depended on not displeasing or challenging the prejudices of their backers. Of course, the authorities had made the decision to invite the witchfinders, knowing pretty clearly what their views and methods were and, of course, they supplied the witchfinders with the lists of suspects. Hopkins did not simply appear in rural villages a long way from his home, unannounced, and select potential witches randomly. Apart from his book, the sole surviving document written by Hopkins is a letter, discussed in more detail later, in which he asks a local man whether or not he will be welcome and supported in a village, and stating that if not he will go elsewhere where his services are appreciated.

But who was backing Hopkins and Stearne? And who was finally to bring them down? The two actors behind the scenes were Sir Harbottle Grimston and Sir Robert Rich, Earl of Warwick.

Robert Rich is a highly complex and interesting figure. His great house, Leeze Priory in Essex, has been described as the intellectual centre of the Commonwealth movement. His father had owned over 100 Essex manors, and Rich still held around sixty. Rich was the son of Penelope Devereux, and thus linked to the noble family of the Earl of Essex. Throughout his career he pushed the old Essex policy of war with Spain in the Caribbean, based on pirates and colonies, of promoting naval interests and the cause of Protestant freedom against Catholicism and tyranny (as he saw matters). Rich spent his life promoting the colonies and trying to make them pay by whatever means came to hand. These were, of course, commercial ventures based on the investment of private shareholders. They were all highly speculative and they were promoted as sure ways to get rich fast, but often seemed a surer way to lose money. They were highly controversial and led to all sorts of bitter financial quarrels.

Rich was the political figure most bound up with English maritime interests, whether military or civilian, which at this time were inextricably linked in any case. This meant that the Orwell ports of Ipswich and Harwich were places with which he had many varied links. There was a very high proportion of Suffolk and Harwich men amongst the first colonists of Jamestown in Virginia. The Borough of Ipswich had held shares in Virginia which it had passed to its lecturer, Samuel Ward. Ward was the principal organiser of emigration to New England in East Anglia. Samuel Ward's brother, Nathaniel, was to write the first law code of Massachusetts. Rich was desperate to find settlers and labourers, voluntary or otherwise, for his projects, and must have been well aware of and interested in Samuel Ward's activities.

In 1619, Robert Rich had covertly supported and backed a privateer called Daniel Elfrith. He had managed to get Elfrith papers issued by the Duke of Savoy licensing him to attack Spanish shipping in the Caribbean. Elfrith was basically a near pirate. On his cruise he captured a Spanish ship full of African slaves from the kingdom of Kongo. He took the ship and its cargo to Jamestown, Virginia, where the colony was starting to finally to prosper as the tobacco boom took off. Labour was in high demand, and the enslaved Africans found ready purchasers (technically, because slavery had not yet been legalised, they were sold as indentured apprentices for life, a distinction without a difference). This was the first landing of the enslaved in the English parts of the Americas. The next year Captain John Dameron of Ipswich landed his cargo of 200 indentured English poor children for the Virginia Company at Jamestown. Twenty years later, a close relative of his, Katherine Dameron, was to be accused and acquitted of witchcraft in Ipswich.

In 1624, divisions within the Virginia Company were one of the major concerns of Parliament; 10 per cent of the MPs were involved as Virginia Company shareholders. The company had attracted large amounts of investment but was faced with serious financial problems. Rich and his supporters had always been interested in using Virginia as a base for privateering raids against the Spanish, and he was also interested in making Virginia pay through building up the only commercially viable crop, tobacco, which needed large amounts of unfree labour in its cultivation.

King James wished Virginia to proceed as a colony with a balanced economy, and had encouraged the setting up of glassworks and other skilled trades. He actually sent out some Bohemian glassworkers to set up a workshop. The king was opposed to the sale of tobacco on principle and he had published a famous book against it in 1604. He had also built his foreign policy around securing some sort of peace with Spain.

Supporters of Rich were publishing details on just what a bad condition the colony was in, and just how far many projects had failed or been illusions in the first place. Robert Rich's interests in Parliament were represented

THE RIGHT HONO.ble ROBERT EARLE OF WARWICK BARON
of Leeze etc Lord high ADMIRAL of England, one of his Mai:ties most hono:rble
privie Councell, & his Mai:ties Lievtenant of Norfolck & Essex etc.
ſould by Peter Stent

Sir Robert Rich by Wenceslas Hollar. (National Portrait Gallery)

Sir Harbottle
Grimston. (Suffolk
Record Office)

S.ᵗHAREBOTTLE GRIMSTON.
*from an Original Picture by S.ᵗ P. Lely in the Collection of.
Lord Verulam.*

Pub.ᵈ 1 May 1796. by S & R. Harding Pall Mall.

by his kinsman, Nathaniel Rich, who became MP for Harwich for the first time in 1624. It was Nathaniel Rich who presented the case against Sandys, the Virginia Company's governor, which led the king to withdraw the charter and make Virginia into a royal colony with governors appointed by the Crown.

The charter of the Virginia Company allowed all shareholders only a single vote, no matter how many shares they had. Therefore, shareholder's meetings were noisy and acrimonious public debates. At one stage things became so bad that the Sandys faction had to be confined to their houses, and Sir Robert Rich openly accused a member of that faction, called Cavendish (possibly a member of the Cavendish family of Grimston Hall in Trimley), of lying. A duel was feared, and official action had to be taken to prevent it. Warwick wrote to the Secretary of State Conway about various problems and requesting that letters should be sent to the lord lieutenant of Suffolk and the town of Ipswich to send 1,000 men from the Suffolk trained bands. He asks that the recusants should be

disarmed and enclosed information of a meeting held by night at the house of
Mr Benfield, a recusant at Redingfield in Suffolk. Conway wrote back to say
that 'orders shall be sent touching recusants', but in fact nothing seems to have
been done.

By now, Rich was already involved in the Somer Island Company which
ran Barbados (there is a Warwick tribe, as parishes are called on Barbados,
named after Robert Rich, Earl of Warwick). Robert Rich then moved on
to involvement in the settlement of New England, the Massachusetts Bay
Company and the Saybrook plantation in Connecticut. He was also soon to be
involved in the creation of Rhode Island.

The Grimston family had originally been associated with Suffolk. Sir Edward
Grimston had been the last English governor of Calais, and had been imprisoned
in the Bastille in Paris. At the same time he had been charged with treachery
in England for his part in the fall of Calais, in an attempt to shift the blame
from Queen Mary. He escaped from the Bastille and faced down his accusers
in England. In the reign of Elizabeth I he was MP for Ipswich 1562–1563 and
was very active in tracking down Catholic sympathisers in the 1590s. His son,
another Edward, who became MP for Eye, married into a family (the Risbys)
that had inherited Harbottle property and so Edward Grimston II's son became
the first Harbottle Grimston.

The family had a large house in Ipswich – Grimston Hall in Northgate
Street. Sir Edward became a freeman of Ipswich and therefore by the laws of
the town his sons, Harbottle and a younger son, became freemen of Ipswich
as well (duly recorded in Bacon's *Annalls of Ipswche*). The borough records
of Ipswich show junior members of the family in legal work about the
town afterwards, work which would have linked them to the witch trials in
due course.

Harbottle Grimston the Elder had Tendring estates around his mansion at
Bradfield, and was an MP for Essex 1569–1648 (apart from the period when
Charles I ruled without Parliament). He became High Sheriff of Essex in 1614
and was MP for Harwich that year.

Meanwhile, as a condition of his marriage to Sir George Croke's daughter,
Sir Harbottle the Younger (II) was building himself a career in the law. Harbottle
Grimston II owed his advancement to his father-in-law, Croke. Croke was a
leading judge. He had made a record of his cases and the reasons behind his
decisions in Norman French, unbelievably still the official language of the law
in England at the time. Harbottle was to write an enormous compilation of
these cases, translating them from Norman French into English for the benefit
of young lawyers.

As well as seeking to immortalise his father-in-law, Harbottle Grimston was
mentioned in sixty-one of the cases. Of these, a number involved witchcraft,
but principally in an unusual fashion. All the witchcraft references in the Croke

trials were cases of slander, in which someone had brought a case against another person who had called them a witch, for example:

35 year of Queen Elizabeth.
Action for these words: 'Thou art a witch, an enchanter, a necromancer, and a sorcerer, and therby wast the cause of death of my husband.' Additionally the widow had said, 'He is a witch and bewitched my husband to death; for he made his picture in wax, and roasted it every day by the fire, until he roasted my husband to death.'

The widow was guilty because she had accused someone of a definite crime for which the punishment was death.

4 year of King James.
'Thou art a witch' and 'I will prove thee a witch'.

The speaker was not guilty, because there was no allegation of a specific crime and the term was just a general insult. However, there was some concern that the Act of King James, which made all witchcraft a felony even if there was no proven attack on a person, might have changed this.

14 Year of King James, Loyd against Cook.
'Thou art a witch and that I will prove. I have seen thy imps or spirits in the night and thus didst unbewitch my child.'

The accuser above was not convicted because, once again, the charge was general and the second charge 'I have seen thy imps' was 'but a matter of fancy'.

17 year of James I, Oliver and his wife against Stephens.
'Thou art a witch.'

This is too general a charge but, because of the Act of James I making all witchcraft a crime, the court was uncertain.

17 year of James I.
'Thou art a witch and by thy means I have lost my mare.'

Again, this is too general.

18 year of James I, Martin and his wife against Stradling.
'Thou art a witch and hath bewitched my wife's milk.'

Landguard Fort. (Ipswich Museum)

Here, the court was undecided, because the first part was too general and, as far as the second part went, it was argued that if the charge was that the alleged witch had bewitched the milk of the wife's cow then the case failed because the wife could have had no cow to bewitch since any cow of hers belonged, of course, to her husband. But then it was counter-argued that it could have meant the milk in the wife's breast. However, the court decided that in cases of uncertainty they should give the benefit to the person accused of the libel or slander.

20 year of James I, Hunn and his wife against Parker.
'Christian Hunn is a witch and hath bewitched two of the servants of JS to death.'

4 year Charles I
'Thou art a witch and didst bewitch my mother's drink.'

8 year Charles I, John George and his wife against Harvey of Bury.
'She is a witch and a strong witch.'

Harbottle Grimston had spoken as a lawyer in this case.

> 9 year of Charles I, Thomas Broxon and his wife against Dager and his wife. 'Thou art a witch: I will make thee come and say "God save my mare". I was forced to get my mare charmed for thee.'

In this case, the fault lay with person making the accusation because they had admitted taking their horse to be charmed.

Some important general points emerge from all this: that mutual accusations of witchcraft often took place between people sufficiently wealthy and at ease with the legal system to go to court; that people were often accused of libel and slander for calling others with good lawyers, witches; but that Sir George Croke and other judges were very keen to interpret the law in such a way as to protect the people who had made the accusation of witchcraft from the charge of slander, sometimes with a logic which seems very forced. In all these cases it was accepted that the accused had called the plaintiff a witch, but that this in itself was not enough to secure a conviction: the accused must also have accused the plaintiff of a specific crime punishable by law.

As a sign of his success in the law, Harbottle Grimston had become the recorder of both Colchester and Harwich. Grimston then followed his father into politics. Initially this would have required them to defer to Sir Robert Rich, Earl of Warwick and the greatest power in Essex. However, as they grew in power they would have escaped his influence and become his rivals.

In 1626, Sir Robert Rich became even more involved in Harwich and more especially with the rebuilding of Landguard Fort, on the other side of the Orwell in Suffolk. This was a troublesome undertaking surrounded by all kinds of disputes; perhaps this first caused Sir Harbottle as the chief legal authority of Harwich to clash with Rich who was based in Harwich to oversee the project.

In addition, he had to help with organising the troops already there – 3,000 foot and a 100 horse. A total of 1,000 local militia men (trained bands) had been called up to protect the Orwell estuary. Warwick wrote to Secretary of State Conway about various problems, and requested that letters should be sent to the Lord Lieutenant of Suffolk and the town of Ipswich to send 1,000 men from the Suffolk-trained bands. He asked that the recusants should be disarmed, and enclosed information of a meeting held by night at the house of Mr Benfield, a recusant at Redingfield in Suffolk. Conway wrote back to say that 'orders shall be sent touching recusants', but in fact none seem ever to have been.

The Lord Lieutenant of Suffolk and the town of Ipswich did all that they could to avoid sending any support to Warwick. Squabbles between the Earls of Sussex and Warwick, the two Lord Lieutenants of Essex over precedence, and between the Essex lords and the Earl of Suffolk, meant that things were disorganised. In all, 150 men, including twenty-five from Ipswich, were assembled, but were not fully enlisted for months. The mismanagement and corruption were such that it nearly caused a mutiny amongst the troops stationed in Ipswich. By 1628, matters had got even worse. No money could be raised in the county to pay for the various groups of soldiers, so the deputy lieutenants had to borrow money themselves to support the men. The sums were: to pay the soldiers at Ipswich £68 10s and £24 4s; for those at Woodbridge £68 10s and £14 13s; and for those at Beccles £74 14s 8d.

In 1628, the governor of Landguard Fort was Robert Gosnold. He was a member of the family at nearby Otley, a nephew of the Bartholmew Gosnold who went to Jamestown, and as such he was a long-time Rich supporter. He was a professional soldier with a chequered career, who was associated with the Essex interest and had been imprisoned for his part in the Essex revolt. The only other thing known about him is a second round of political trouble that he experienced right at the beginning of the reign of James I in 1604–1606. It took place while he was staying with a relative of Robert Rich, (who had become the leader of the former party of the Earl of Essex), another soldier called Barnaby Rich, at a friend's house at Shanklin on the Isle of Wight. Robert Gosnold had had a falling out with Barnaby Rich's wife Katherine, who did not like some of the dangerous remarks Gosnold was making about the new king. She had kissed Gosnold on first meeting him but refused to do so when he left. It is difficult to pick up all the nuances of the story but it does link Gosnold with the Riches in some fashion, and also includes the themes of witchcraft and the fear of undercover Papists. It is possible that his claim that James I killed bucks but was good to does is a reference to the king's homosexual tastes. It underlines the dangerous rivalries that ran beneath the surface of all social life:

Ryche, his wife, and Captain Christopher Levens, being in company with Captain Gosnole, Mr Bowyer Worsely, and others at Mr Denyse's, the new book of statutes of the last Parliament was called for, and Gosnole made trifles of many of them, namely of that against conjurors, and against the marriage of two wives. Gosnole also used the following speeches to Ryche's wife: 'he never before had heard any woman speak so well of the King as she had done'; 'the King is a good hunter and he kills bucks, but he is good to does, and he grows weak in the back, his date is almost out'; and 'his back is weak and he is going on his last half year.' Mr Denyse thought Gosnole to be a counterfeit Papist, and ill affected to the King.

(Calendar of Cecil Papers in Hatfield House, 29 September 1604, in British History Online.)

The matter was quickly smoothed over, and Gosnold released to carry on his career. By 1628 he had become Governor of Landguard, probably through Robert Rich's influence.

The problems over finding the money for soldiers' pay led to a protest or mutiny in 1628 at Landguard. Captain Robert Gosnold of Landguard New Forte compelled the six 'chiefest auters' to draw lots for 'one of them to dye'. The unlucky winner who happened to be 'the veriest villayn of them all' was handed over to the Walton constable for transmission from constable to constable to Melton Gaol, but the constable at the next parish, Trimley St Mary, most contemptously sent back the warrant to Captain Gosnold and himself dismissed the prisoner (*Suffolk Invasion*, Frank Hussey, 1983). That is, the lowly parish constable was so shocked and so sure of popular backing by the local authorities that he was quite prepared to release a man described as a dangerous mutineer by the army commander at Landguard.

A few years later, the fort's commander actually opened fire on Ipswich ships which had not correctly saluted the flag on the fort.

In the 1626 Parliament, Harbottle the Elder was one of the two county MPs for Essex, and Nathaniel Rich represented Harwich. In this Parliament, Warwick had tried to get the lords to impeach Buckingham, the king's favourite. He had also attempted to silence the principal spokesperson for the Laudian movement, through the York House conference. This backfired and intensified the split between the Laudians and the Puritans. Far too important to be directly seriously punished himself, he and his clients lost influence in their power base of Essex. Warwick lost the lord lieutenancy which had only been granted the year before, and all his deputy lieutenants, including Harbottle Grimston, lost their positions too.

Sir Harbottle's tactics during the 1628 election were reported to Secretary of State Nicholas by Edward Nuttall, and are contained in the Calendar of State Papers Domestic, for March 1628:

> Knights of the Shire for Essex were that day chosen. The free holders were called upon by the Constables to give their voices for the side supported by most of the justices of the peace; and there was also a very irregular creation of freeholders in order to secure the return of Sir Francis Barrington and Sir Harbottle Grimston.

> (p.6)

In 1631, Harbottle Grimston and Sir Robert Rich co-operated in making William Bridge Lecturer of Colchester against the wishes of Bishop Laud of London. Bridge held this post until 1637 when he moved to Norwich. There, he inevitably fell out with Matthew Wren. Bridge fled to Rotterdam, returning after 1640 to become one of the five leaders of the Independents in the Westminster Assembly.

The same Daniel Elfrith who had first brought slaves to Jamestown in Virginia, had also discovered a little island off the Miskito coast of modern Nicaragua, which had been named Providence Island in 1629. Elfrith had contacted Nathaniel Rich, who had contacted Robert Rich, who then started the Providence Bay Company in 1630. Other members of the company were all Parliamentarians, and several were relatives: his brother Henry (Earl of Holland); their half-brother Mountjoy (Earl of Newport); their cousin Robert Devereux (Earl of Essex) and his brother-in-law William Seymour (the Earl of Hertford); Lords Saye and Brook who had already been in partnership with Robert Rich in New England over the Sayebrook plantation; John Gurdon, MP for Ipswich and Edmund Moundeford, the MP for first Thetford and then Norfolk.

Their aim was to create an ideal colony (from a Puritan perspective) which included plantations and a little pirating. In 1638, it was to become the scene of the first slave revolt in British America and, at one point, the notorious pirate island of Tortuga was added. As well as their membership in the Providence Company and their complex inter-relationships, they were all opposed to Ship Money, and included the two famous Parliamentary leaders, Pym and Hampden. In fact, they were all members of the Parliamentary opposition to the king.

Rich was closely connected with the Devereux family of the Earl of Essex, and by the 1640s Earl Robert Devereux was the commander of the Commonwealth Army. Once Rich had become admiral and delivered the navy to the side of the Commonwealth, he and his associates were a mighty force in the land. Locally, in Ipswich, Leicester Devereux, the nephew of the Earl of Essex, had fought off a number of legal challenges and become Lord of Christchurch Mansion which gave him a dominant position in Ipswich as well as being an officer in the army of Parliament.

The Short Parliament of 1640 saw Harbottle the Elder as one of the two county MPS, and the Younger as MP for Harwich, with no members of the Rich family. When the Long Parliament first sat in 1640, Sir Robert Rich was one of the two county members, and the younger Harbottle sat for Colchester and the older for Harwich.

Grimston led the attack in Parliament against Archbishop Laud in speeches filled with violent abuse and later published: Laud was 'the roote and branche of all our miseries and calamities – the sty of all the pestilential filth that hath infested the state and the government of this commonwealth – a viper which should no longer be permitted to distil his poison into the sacred ears of the king'.

Such a speech would have been in line with the known position of Sir Robert Rich, but it also included remarks which would have certainly given Rich thought. Grimston attacked Laud because, amongst other things, 'He had condescended so low as to deal in tobacco by which thousands of poor people had been turned out of their trades.' Grimston also described, 'The whole nation overrun with swarmes of projecting canker-worms and caterpillars, the worst of all the plagues of Egypt.'

'Projectors' were those who had got up projects – schemes designed to get people to invest, such as in trading companies. Robert Rich had been on the board of every company that had sought to build up colonies in the New World, including the Virginia Company which had finally proved successful through the sale of tobacco, a strategy Rich had promoted. Robert and Nathaniel Rich were the leading examples of projectors in the kingdom. Grimston, who had forced Nathaniel Rich out as MP for the Harwich seat, was definitely attacking them.

In March 1642, the Militia Ordinance was passed by Parliament, but without royal assent. Harbottle Grimston helped get it through the house. The ordinance allowed Parliament, through those lord lieutenants who supported the Parliamentary cause, to raise the local militia as soldiers. It was designed as a counter measure to the king, who was already assembling his own forces. In Essex, Robert Rich was made lord lieutenant and Harbottle was made one of his deputy lieutenants.

Harbottle Grimston accepted the commission, but only on condition that he was not to be made to fight the king. To Rich, this kind of legal fudging would have seemed both ridiculous – after all why was the militia being raised if not to fight the Royalists – and cowardly. Rich himself had just also been made lord admiral by Parliament, against the express veto of the king and had swung the (formerly Royal) navy behind Parliament. He was also actively raising troops in Norfolk and Essex while his relative, the Earl of Essex, was the commander of the Parliamentary forces actually in the field. Rich knew that in defeat he could well have faced a charge of treason, and he also knew that Grimston was giving himself an escape clause in the event of a Royalist victory.

On 22 August 1642, Sir John Lucas was prevented by a Colchester mob from taking horses and arms to strengthen the king's forces. Lucas was an ultra-Royalist, who had been at odds with the people of Colchester for years and the previous focus of popular violence. At one point, he was in danger of his life, but was rescued by Harbottle Grimston who got him away to London under guard. His brother, Charles, was to be one of the Royalist commanders executed after the siege of Colchester Castle in 1648.

The attack on Lucas was the signal for an attack throughout the area, on the houses of noble Catholics like Countess Rivers. The Countess Rivers' house at Long Melford was destroyed by a mob estimated at 1,000 strong, and Sir Francis Manocke's house at Stoke by Nayland was destroyed too, along with his writings and his dogs. A little later, Sir Harbottle Grimston was to become the executor of Lady Rivers' estates. These mob attacks on gentry families along the Stour, occurring before the Civil War itself, would have been terrifying to the gentry families of the area, no matter their politics or their religion. This perhaps helps to explain the obviously tense situation further down the Stour estuary in the Tendring Hundred, and the fears of Harbottle Grimston.

In 1643 the Solemn League and Covenant was drawn up. Grimston was reported by Burnet (in *Burnet's History of My Own Time*) never to have signed it. This was an odd position for a Presbyterian, because the Solemn League and Covenant was an agreement between Parliament and the Scots to remove the bishops and impose a Presbyterian system of church government and religion on England. It also committed the signatories to supporting the king, working together with Parliament. Signature of the covenant became the litmus test of loyalty to Parliament. King Charles Stuart himself was to sign the covenant later when he formed an alliance with the Scots to support the Royalist cause. In other words, the Solemn League would appear to have been exactly what Harbottle Grimston would have wanted. Yet, for many Royalists, and for the king in his heart, the Solemn League and Covenant was unacceptable because it made loyalty to the king conditional on the king's own loyalty to the oath, and not an absolute duty. If this was Grimston's reason he was clearly a more hardline Royalist than is usually supposed.

Harbottle Grimston also stood out against the Solemn League and Covenant in an extremely unusual and difficult position. The Solemn League and Covenant was a major symbolic act, carried out by all officials and by all parishioners in churchyards across the land. An equivalent formal rejection of the Solemn League and Covenant was required of all officials on the Restoration. It actually gave the name of 'covenanter' to the opposition to the restoration of bishops in Scotland.

But, what is interesting for us is that the signing of a covenant had also become a kind of symbol to Stearne and Hopkins. One of the things that they demanded the witches confessed to was the signing of a league and covenant, but this time with Satan. Stearne, in his *Confirmation and Discoverie*, uses the phrase over and over again:

ELIZABETH DEEKES of Rattlesden in Suffolk, she did make a League and Covenant with the Devil.

JOANE WALLIS of Keyston in Huntingdonshire, she had consented to the other of his demands, and confirmed the Covenant.

ELIZABETH FINCH of Wattisham in Suffolk, let him have blood to seal or confirm the Covenant or agreement.

NICHOLAS HEMPSTEAD of Creeting in Suffolk, he had made a League and Covenant with the Devil.

Of a boy of Rattlesden in Suffolk, confessed likewise his renewing of the League and Covenant with the Devil.

One MOORES wife of Sutton, in the Isle of Ely, she had confessed the League and Covenant made.

ANNE RANDALL of Lavenham in Suffolk, after she had confessed the Covenant, for still you must remember, that this is first done, before the Devil, or their Familiars, or Imps, act, or do anything.

PARSON LOWES the Devil took advantage of him, and he covenanted with the Devil, and sealed it with his blood.

That there is some kind of mental connection between the Solemn League and Covenant to defend Parliament and the witches' league and covenant with the Devil is obvious. Whether it means that Stearne saw the world dividing into two great camps, those that had covenanted with the godly cause and those that had covenanted with the ungodly cause, or whether he wished to suggest that the Solemn League and Covenant was itself ungodly, cannot be known. However, if Stearne was backed by Harbottle Grimston and if Grimston refused to sign the covenant it is at least possible that they did see the Solemn League and Covenant in this light.

Around this time the Mayor of Colchester, Richard Buxton, invited Sir Harbottle Grimston, Sir Thomas Bowes and the 'Rest of the gentlemen' to Colchester. This certainly was an invitation to the patrons of the witchfinders, and it may have included Hopkins and Stearne under the heading of the rest of the gentlemen.

The new rigour of their methods had led to thirty women being held in Colchester Castle, in conditions so bad that four died 'of visitation by God'.

In addition to the women from Tendring, a Colchester woman, Widow Alice Stansby of St Giles was also accused. Her genitals were duly searched by two female searchers from Wivenhoe. Although it is not known whether these searchers had worked for Hopkins and Stearne earlier in the Tendring case, it is more than likely that they were working for the pair now. After several months in gaol, Stansby was eventually freed, and she was possibly the woman protected by unnamed powerful people according to Stearne. The total costs of the case, borne by the town council, amounted to £1 13s 4d, a rough modern equivalent to £1,000. Already there is some evidence of unease surrounding such large numbers and there is no evidence that Colchester Borough ever paid Hopkins or Stearne

So, from the very start of the campaign, Stearne, Hopkins and the whole project had its enemies. This humiliation at Colchester must have overlapped with the main trial of those already arrested, who were being tried at Chelmsford.

In 1645, the witches accused at Tendring were brought to Chelmsford for trial. The appearance of the witches, who had spent long months imprisoned in the dungeons of Colchester Castle, and the whole nature of the trial, was to give one of the observers a profound shock. He wrote about what he saw in his autobiography, written some years afterwards, and it is worth quoting at some length:

> There is nothing upon the stage of the world, acted by publique justice, comes so crosse to my temper, as putting so many witches to death. Nor is it a new thing. The Scripture not onlie making mention of them, but condemning them. And it hath bene, in a long series of time, the practize of all states and kingdoms, not to suffer those they call witches to live.
>
> About this time in Essex, there being a great manie arraigned, I was at Chensford at the trial and execution of eighteen women. But could see nothing in the evidence which did perswade me to thinke them other than poore, mellenchollie, envious, mischevous, ill-disposed, ill-dieted, atrabilus constitutions; whose fancies working by grosse fumes and vapors, might make the imagination readie to take any impression; whereby their anger and envie might vent it selfe into such expressions, as the hearers of their confessions (who gave evidence) might find cause to beleeve, they were such people as they blazon'd themselves to bee.
>
> And they themselves, by the strength of fancie, may thinke they bring such things to passe, which, many times, unhapelie they wish for, and rejoyce in, when done, out of the malevolent humor which is in them: which passes with them as if they had reallie acted it.
>
> And, if there be an opinion in the people that such a bodie is a witch, their owne feares (coming where they are) resulting from such dreadfull apprehensions, do make everie shaddow, an apparition; and everie ratt or catt, an imp or spirit. Which make so many tales and stories in the world, which have no shadow of truth. This will bee better asserted in another place; and those texts of scripture genuinelie interpreted: which will bee too large for this place.

In fact, his concerns were such as to cause him to have some kind of crisis of faith, about which, as a man of his time, he wrote at length:

> But one day, not long after this execution, my meditations fixing upon that subject, I had a great conflicting in my spirit, how to discover this blind path, which the world for so many ages hat trod in, to be a mistaken way. And again some hoerse, in my secret thoughts, admiring the justice and mercies of God; mercies restrayning Satan, and keeping him in chaines; justice, in letting him loose, for the execution of his owne decrees. At last I fixt upon this assertion; That it did not consist with the infinite goodnes of the almighty God, to let Satan loose, in so ravenous a way, upon poore, mellanchollie, dark-minded, discontented creatures; and lett him be bound up from acting

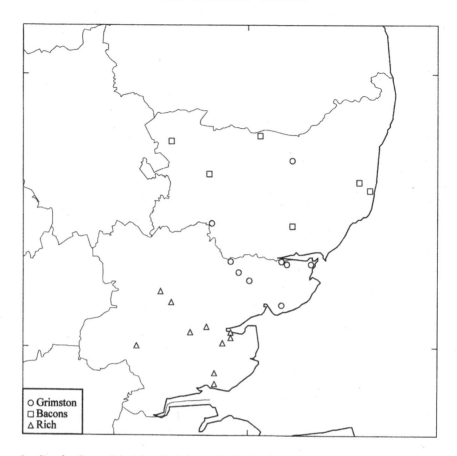

Leading families and their local influence. (Author's collection)

this, his most sordid part, with such whose constitutions were readie to kick at heaven, by all kinds of atheisme, prophanes, and wickednes. Though I did conceive, that God, in his wisdome, had his severall dispensations; and could proportion punishments to everie man's sin: which was not fit for mee to prie into, but humblie to submit! to the almightie Power, with, O the depth, &c. yet could I not be satisfied. But (with struglings and wrastlings with God, with teares and prayers) I humblie besought him, either to take this opinion from mee (which is, that Satan doth not worke these effects by witches, which themselves confesse) or to confirme it to mee, some way or other, that hee doth: that I might not live in an error. And this was presented to God with all humilitie of soule; submitting my will to his; and that hee would not impute this to mee as a presumption. Laying my desires at his feet, and being wing'd with such a spirit, as, I thought at that time, was able to overcome Satan arm'd with his mallice. I came to this conclusion. That if it be true, that Satan doth worke theise effects (in a particular way) I might see something to

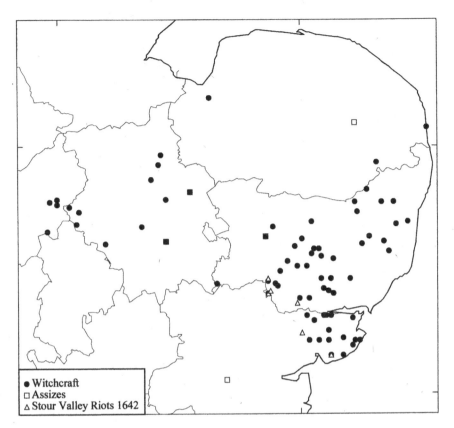

Places involved in the 1645 witch prosecutions. Comparison with the map of influence shows how the trials took place in Bacon/Grimston areas and not in Rich areas. (Author's collection)

assure it to mee. If not, that I might see nothing. The writer trembled at his presumption in asking a sign from God, but none came – But I have never had cause since to alter this opinion; nor do I find it anyway derogatory of God or inconsistent with His justice and mercie, that I do not believe the vaine chimeras, without any superstructure of reason which the people build upon this foundation.

This advocate of reason was Arthur Wilson, the steward of the Earl of Warwick. A cultured man, but also a duellist and a soldier as well as a playwright and a convinced Puritan, Arthur Wilson is an interesting character and unusual for the time in that he wrote a readable autobiography, not taken up entirely with his moral concerns. Wilson, for all his opposition to Archbishop Laud, was no fanatic and was perfectly happy to ride at the head of a body of men in an attempt to rescue the Catholic Countess Rivers from the hands of the mob at Long Melford.

If the trial had troubled Wilson so deeply, it is very likely that his master, the Earl of Warwick, would have known of his concerns as well. For, although Wilson doesn't say so, seated at the centre of the bench of magistrates that heard the case was none other than the Earl of Warwick himself. As Lord Lieutenant of Essex he was also the *custos rotulorum*, or senior magistrate, of the county. Wilson's concerns go right to the heart of the matter – he simply cannot credit the confessions the witches are making.

We don't know how Warwick reacted to his steward's concerns that he and his fellow magistrates had convicted innocent women. But we do know that, after the trial, Warwick was approached by six concerned magistrates and a clergyman to beg reprieves for the witches. Despite being convicted at the trial, nine were actually reprieved afterwards, fifteen were hanged at Chelmsford and four were hanged at Manningtree. Of the accused witches, all of those from the Tendring Hundred whose trials had been brought about by Hopkins and Stearne, working for Sir Harbottle and Sir Thomas Bowes, were executed.

So far, opposition and disquiet were relatively muted and it was possible for Hopkins and Stearne, and their backers, to rush into print with two triumphal pamphlets, circulating the most lurid details of witchcraft, insisting on the veracity of the confessions and suggesting that more was to come. The first, with a typically lengthy title, was:

A true and exact
RELATION
Of the severall Informations,
Examinations, and Confessions of the late Witches,
arraigned and executed in the County of Essex.
Who were arraigned and condemned at the late Sessions,
holden at Chelmesford
before the Right Honorable ROBERT, Earle of Warwicke,
and severall of his Majesties Justices of Peace,
the 29 of July, 1645.
Wherein the severall murthers, and devilish
Witchcrafts, committed on the bodies of men,
women, and children, and divers cattell,
are fully discovered.
Published by Authoritie.
LONDON,
Printed by M.S. for Henry Overton, and Benj. Allen,
and are to be sold at their Shops in Popes-head Alley.
1645.

The second was rather more populist in its approach. It was called, equally long windedly:

A True
RELATION
Of the
ARAIGNMENT
Of Thirty
WITCHES
At Chensford in Essex, before Iudge Coniers, fourteene
whereof were hanged on Friday last, Iuly 25. 1645.
there being at this time a hundred more
in severall prisons in Suffolke
and Essex.
Setting forth the Confessions of the
principall of them.
Also shewing how the Divell had carnall copulation
with Rebecca West, a young maid, daughter to
Anne West.
And how they bewitched Men, Women, Children, and
Cattell to death: with many other strange things,
the like was never heard of before.

Both of these pamphlets are very clearly a justification of the Hopkins-Stearne machine, and imply that the search for witches should be greatly extended. It is obvious why the first pamphlet refers to Robert Rich's part in the trial, and in the second pamphlet he is not mentioned, while Judge Conyers is – Rich had distanced himself from it.

Hopkins and Stearne had clearly run into some difficulties in Essex, but they still had very powerful backers and they now had been invited to work in Suffolk. Working very quickly, around thirty witches had by now been arrested and were being held in Ipswich, and soon many more were being held in Bury St Edmunds ready for trial. Perhaps as many as 300 were involved in some fashion. The speed at which such large numbers of accused witches from all over Suffolk were identified and investigated by Hopkins and Stearne cannot be due to their own unsupported efforts. They must have had heavyweight backing somewhere in the background and must have been working to prepared lists of suspects. The kind of deep local knowledge that is revealed in the depositions of the witches could not have been collected by two minor figures from Manningtree, about events far outside their own locality in North or West Suffolk, let alone in Norfolk and Huntingdon.

It is obvious that the trial of Mother Lackland and her fellow accused at Ipswich was linked in some way to the accusations made in the same county and tried at Bury at the same time. The Ipswich authorities both supported Hopkins and his backers, but also were keen to uphold their own independent authority.

On 24 July 1645 an assize commission was drawn up for Suffolk. Amongst the twenty-seven commissioners were Nathaniel Bacon, the recorder of Ipswich, a father-and-son team both named Brampton Gurdon, and Sir Thomas Barnardiston. All these men had worked together on the committee set up in 1643 to raise money for Parliament in Suffolk, which included in full:

> For the County of Suff. Sir Edmond Bacon, Sir William Playters, Knights and Baronets; Sir Butts Bacon, Sir William Springe, Baronets; Sir Roger North, Sir William Soame, Sir Nathaniel Barnardiston, Sir Philip Parker, Sir John Wentworth, Sir Robert Brook, Sir Thomas Barnardiston, Knights; William Heveningham, Maurice Barrowe, Thomas Baker, Henry North, Sen. Brampton Gurdon, Henry North, Jun. Nicholas Bacon, Nathaniel Bacon of Freston, John Clench of Creating, Thomas Terrell, Robert Reynolds, Francis Bacon, William Cage, John Gurdon, Robert Brewster, Isack Appleton, Nathaniel Bacon of Ipswich, William Bloyse, Thomas Cole, Richard Pepis, William Ryvet of Bilson, John Clynch of Cullpho, Theophilus Vaughan, Edmond Harvy, Esquires; Francis Brewster, and John Base Gent.

This represents a list of the moderate Parliamentarian faction in Suffolk.

Nathaniel Bacon, Sir Thomas Barnardiston and two other Gurdons had also sat on the Committee for the Ejection of Scandalous Ministers. Nathaniel Bacon was recorder for Ipswich. Brampton Gurdon Senior, whose home was in Assington, had been MP for Sudbury and High Sherriff of Suffolk. He was on the Council of State and had benefited from the sale of bishops' lands, having gained Taunton Castle and all its estates from the Bishop of Winchester. His son was now MP for Ipswich, and later was to sit for Sudbury. He had commanded the Suffolk Cavalry to victory at Naseby, and was to take part in the siege of Colchester. Nathaniel Barnardiston, brother of Sir Thomas, was the MP for Suffolk. These were quite clearly men at the centre of power and the Parliamentary cause in the county, and men who were experienced and well informed in the exercise of power.

However, soon after the list of commissioners was drawn up, Parliament had received from an unknown source a report from Suffolk expressing considerable concern at the number of witches accused in Suffolk, and strongly suggesting that something was not quite right about what was going on. 'As if some busie men had made use of some ill Arts, to extort such confessions from them' is how the report expressed itself, pointing the finger directly at Hopkins and Stearne without naming them. This report must have come with some serious backing, because Parliament decided to act on it quickly and used its powers to set up a special commission of oyer and terminer to investigate the situation. This was a procedure normally reserved for the most important cases, especially high treason. It had been used against Anne Boleyn, and was to be used in 1660 against the regicides. It was nearly always a handpicked commission of senior lawyers, not connected with the locality and hence impartial.

In this case, John Godbold was a Suffolk man, and his two colleagues were leading Presbyterian ministers with powerful local connections and influence – Samuel Fairclough and Edmund Calamy. Therefore, this commission was irregular in that the members were local and two were clergy not lawyers. This was an exceptional way of dealing with the situation, and evidence that someone with great influence was working behind the scenes.

Fairclough had been born in 1594. His father, Laurence, had been the vicar of Haverhill and his mother was the daughter of John Cole, the most influential man in the town. His initial religious crisis was brought on by stealing pears and then listening to a sermon by Samuel Ward, not yet at that time lecturer at Ipswich, but still at Haverhill. At Cambridge, which he attended before he was 14, he showed his principles and determination by refusing to take a woman's role as an actor in a comic play entitled *Ignoramus* that was to be performed by Queens College for James I. Ward remained

Samuel Fairclough.
(Suffolk Record Office)

qui obiit 14 Decemb 1677 *Ætatis* 84.
P.H. van. Hove. sculp:

Fairclough's spiritual mentor during most of Ward's remaining life. Inevitably, Fairclough fell foul of Bishop Samuel Harsnett during his time as a lecturer at King's Lynn, and again after a sermon which he preached at Oldbury. At Kennington his sermons were extremely popular. Kennington church, Samuel Clarke tells us, was:

> … so thronged, that (though, for a village, very large and capacious, yet) there was no getting in, unless by some hours' attending before his exercise began; and then the outward walls were generally lined with shoals and multitudes of people, which came (many) from far, (some above twenty miles), so that you could see the Church yard (which was likewise very spacious) barricaded with horses, tied to the outward rails, while their owners were greedily waiting to hear the word of life from his mouth.

He had, apparently, two levels of teaching, one for the learned and one for the people. As a pastor he catechised, examined before monthly communion, visited and counselled his parishioners, acted as a peacemaker, and engaged in practical charity, from regular almsgiving to distribution of large-print Bibles for the elderly. He had a number of run-ins with the archdeacon at Bury over such things as altar rails and the *Book of Sports*. In 1641 he preached a sermon calling for the punishment of the Earl of Stafford.

We also know that he married twice, both times happily. So much so, that his sorrow on his first wife's death drew adverse criticism from some people as showing insufficient resignation to the will of the Lord.

The second of the two ministers was Edmund Calamy. Edmund Calamy was the Puritan of Puritans. He had been the town lecturer at Bury St Edmunds for ten years, overlapping with Samuel Ward's tenure at Ipswich. He had been forced out of the lectureship at Bury by the bishop, but had become a leading, clerical protégé of none other than the Earl of Warwick, who had found him a living at Rochford from 1636–1639. So close was Calamy to Warwick that he often prayed alone with him, and in due course in 1658 it was Calamy who preached Warwick's funeral sermon.

After Rochford, his patron secured him the perpetual curacy of St Mary Aldermanbury, London. In 1641 he had been one of the men who had written an attack on the bishops, whose various initials were joined into the jaw-breaking acronym 'Smectymnuus'. His initials were the third and fourth letters of the mysterious name. He had given sermons to the Houses of Parliament which had so pleased them that he had been awarded a huge silver plate as a reward for his sermon entitled 'England's Looking Glass.' He was elected to the Westminster Assembly of Divines, and accused by Charles I of high treason in 1643.

Warwick had sent down to Suffolk, not just anybody, but his best man amongst the clergy, one of the most experienced and able brains in the country,

Edmund Calamy, Rich's spiritual
counsellor. (Suffolk Record Office)

and the guardian of his own conscience. Calamy and Fairclough had arrived to
find hundreds of women and some men on trial, most of whom had apparently
confessed. The two men cannot have known what to think. Both were
convinced that witches did indeed exist, but they also clearly believed that some
of these women had been falsely accused. Their patron and Parliament had sent
them because they were concerned at what was happening; but obviously a lot
of the respectable gentry, and a powerful group of local lawyers drawn from
that section of the population who seemed to support their politics and beliefs,
believed in the trials.

The situation was chaotic. Prisons were so full that barns had to be used to
hold the accused and the condemned. The trials were rushed through at great
speed, but nevertheless had to be interrupted for fear of a raid by Royalists.
What had been started could not be stopped by the arrival of the ministers
from London. Things had gone too far to simply halt.

Fairclough knew exactly how Stearne operated, for he had been involved in
one of his witchcraft investigations in Haverhill. Stearne described the occasion
in his book, written after the trial in 1648, entitled *A Confirmation and Discoverie
of Witchcraft*:

Also some witness of God himself happening upon the execrable curses of Witches upon themselves, praying God to show some token, if they are guilty: who by bitter curses upon themselves, think thereby to clear themselves: as one BINKES of Haverhill in Suffolk, who confessed to me that she was guilty, and amongst other things told me, that the Fly which was seen to fly about the chamber, was one of her Imps; but desired to speak with one MASTER FAIRECLOTH, who lived not above two miles, or thereabouts, from the Town, being an able Orthodox Divine; who was immediately sent for, and came. This woman, notwithstanding her confessing to me, denied all to him, wishing and desiring withal, that if she were such a manner of person, that the Lord would show an example upon her; and that if she had any Imps, they would come whilst he was there: presently after, she cries out, A just judgement of God, they are come indeed, said she. This Imp, in the same shape it was seen formerly flying in the room, was seen fastened upon another place of her body, not far from the other marks, but not upon them, and so remained above half a quarter of an hour, till some women came near a quarter of a mile, who saw it fastened on her body, she only crying out to have it pulled off, which at first they were fearful to do; but at length they wiped it off, as they say, with a cloth; and what became of it after, they knew not; but it had drawn a new mark, like the other.

Was this woman fit to live, this evidence, with others, being against her, by credible witnesses? I am sure she was living not long since, and acquitted upon her trial: for she never confessed any more, but denied what she had formerly confessed--

They come likewise invisible; as one BINKES of Haverhill had an Imp sucking of her whilst she was talking with others, and presently confessed it.

It is interesting that the woman, Binkes, knew exactly which local minister to call upon. Stearne was obviously beside himself over this case. It must have been especially frustrating that Samuel Fairclough was so well connected that Stearne, once he had mentioned him, had to describe him as an able and orthodox minister. Fairclough never wavered in his own opinion of Binkes' innocence, for she was acquitted once put on trial.

Fairclough was not the only person to protect the accused. Francis Hutchinson, Vicar of Hoxne in the Restoration, recounted a case in his own parish in which a gentlewoman had told him of her own experience. A woman had been accused, and it was said that she confessed to having an imp called Nan, after long fasting and without sleep: 'This good gentlewoman told me [that is, Francis Hutchinson] that her husband (a very learned ingenious gentleman) having indignation at the thing, he and she went to the house, and put the people out of doors, and gave the poor woman some meat, and let her go to bed.' When she woke up she remembered nothing of her confessions and, on being asked about the diabolic Nan, said it was the name of one of her chickens.

Fairclough and the 'gentleman' of Hoxne were both taking something of a risk. It could be quite dangerous to speak up for an accused witch, as one case shows. Perhaps the most famous victim of Hopkins was the nearly 80-year-old vicar of Brandeston, John Lowes. Lowes was certainly the highest placed of all those convicted of witchcraft.

Lowes had been locked, for more than thirty years, in a feud with the biggest farmers of Brandeston, originally over tithes. The main rival of the vicar was a Jonas Cooke who, back in 1615, had failed to win a case against Lowes as a 'barrator' (a man who seeks to intimidate others by bringing false legal charges against them). Following this case, Cooke had accused Anne Annson of being a most wild and wicked witch. Lowes had intervened to protect her, and had sheltered her in his house while a mob had gathered outside shouting threats. A constable came to arrest her but Lowes denied that she was there. Later men broke into the house and had her committed for trial. Lowes' brother, Nicholas, bailed her out. However, at the trial she was convicted and hanged.

During all the shouting and pushing, Lowes, clearly a man of personal courage and principles, had said that Anne Annson was no more a witch than he was. To the ears of a man like Jonas Cooke that was tantamount to a confession, Anne Annson was a witch and so therefore John Lowes was a witch.

Sure enough, livestock began dying. At some time, Lowes was said to have tried to cure a son of Jonas Cooke, using a gold chain. The boy only partially recovered and another healer said that the boy had been bewitched by Lowes. Cooke had also had nightmares in which he saw Lowes and imps in his bedroom.

However, Lowes was no impoverished widow and he was able to sue Cooke successfully for slander, leaving him with a bill of more than £28 and an even greater hatred of the vicar. So, by 1645 this had being going on for years. The parson's opponents seized their moment and had Lowes denounced to Hopkins. To break an 80 year old using Hopkins' methods was hardly a challenge, especially when he was swum in the moat of Framlingham Castle. His confession proved fatal and Lowes was amongst those hanged at Bury.

Fairclough would have been very aware of this case, both as a fellow minister who must have seen Lowes at Bury, and as the protector of Binkes. Perhaps it was this case that persuaded Godbold to rule that 'swimming' was illegal. Both Stearne and Hopkins were very defensive about the use of swimming in the earlier cases and very keen to underline that once Godbold had spoken the practice finished.

Things had not gone as they would have wished for Stearne and Hopkins at Bury St Edmunds: their powers had been undermined, just as they had been at Colchester and Chelmsford. It was time for Stearne and Hopkins to move on.

Their next centre of activities was to be around St Neots and Huntingdon. They forced their usual confessions with their usual methods, and the usual crop of victims were due to be delivered to the local assizes. Once again a minister who had had contact with one of the witches (Francis Moore) and believed her innocent, spoke out. Once again, this minister, John Gaule, had connections with important people. In this case, it was not just the Earl of Warwick, but a man fast coming to be the major figure in English politics, whose strongest supporter was the Earl of Warwick, Oliver Cromwell himself. John Gaule had the living of Great Staughton. The lord of the manor of Great Staughton was Valentine Walton, who had married Cromwell's sister and who had been a commander at Edgehill.

By this time, and most probably much earlier, Hopkins knew that there were forces definitely moving against him. One of the very few personal records concerning Hopkins is a letter which he addressed to a contact called M.N. in the village of Great Staughton:

> My service to your worship presented, I have this day received a Letter &,- to come to a Towne called Great Staughton to search for evill disposed persons called Withches (though I heare your Minister is fare against us through ignorance) I intend to come (God willing) the sooner to heare his singular Judgement on behalf of such parties; I have known a Minister in Suffolk preach as much against their discovery in a Pulpit, and forc'd to recant it (by the Committee) in the same place. I much marvaile such evill Members should have any (much more any of the clergy who should daily preach terrour to convince such offenders) stand up to take their parts against such as are Complainants for the King and sufferers themselves with their families and estates.

It is not surprising, perhaps, that Hopkins appears to be telling an outright lie in this passage, for there is no evidence that either Fairclough or Calamy were censured and then humiliated in their own church in such a manner. But the last sentence is remarkable, and has not been commented upon previously. Read it carefully.

Some of the clergy and other people are standing up for such 'evill Members' (witches) against the witchfinders and their supporters. Who are the supporters of witchfinders? Complainants for the king who themselves have suffered with their families and estates, meaning suffered for their support of the king? Royalists and malignants are behind Hopkins.

This is completely opposed to the normal depiction of Hopkins, and completely in line with the facts. This will become clearer, and it will be shown that Hopkins is referring to the deep splits emerging within the Parliamentarian movement.

Hopkins goes on to say that he will probably come to this area, but goes on to ask 'whether your Town afords many Sticklers for such Cattell, or willing to give and afford us good welcome and entertainement'. If he was supported he would come, otherwise he would take himself elsewhere 'and betake me to such places where I doe and may persist without controle, but with thankes and recompence'.

Such places were becoming hard to find. In April 1646 in Yarmouth, five people were accused of witchcraft, all were acquitted (contrasting the December 1645 trial in which all six accused were found guilty, and five actually were hanged). In May 1646, Hopkins had visited King's Lynn at the invitation of the mayor. He had arrived in some style, being welcomed by a mounted trooper and a drummer for an agreed fee of £15. He had the nine witches (eight women and one man) that had already been accused searched for marks, and then left to investigate cases elsewhere. He then returned to King's Lynn for the trial in September. There he met the same mayor, the recorder Miles Corbett, who was also recorder of Yarmouth and had worked with Hopkins in sentencing Yarmouth witches in 1645. All would have looked set for a successful trial, followed by nine hanging bodies.

Except that is not what happened. The jury acquitted six of the accused, released one as insane and not able to stand trial, and hanged two. Two days later, three witches were tried in front of none other than John Godbold, the sergeant of law who had proscribed the swimming of witches. All three were acquitted.

This is clearly far more than just freak decisions by individual juries. The political tide was turning against Hopkins and his backers in an organised and co-ordinated fashion. In April 1647, after a gap of a year caused by unrest, the Norwich assizes were opened with their usual civic pageantry, and visiting judges from London. If Hopkins was present, as Gaskill suggests, he had ridden into a legal ambush. Unfortunately, we only know about this from Hopkins himself. 'Some gentlemen of the county' had drawn up a careful list of questions which they wanted the judges to put to Hopkins. According to Hopkins these questions were:

- Did Hopkins' special knowledge of witches mean that he had acquired special, diabolical, information about them?
- As he was not known for his learning [he had not attended university, and was not a clergyman] where then did his knowledge of witches come from?
- Why does the devil, a bodiless spirit need to suck blood?
- How could one trust the evidence of the mark when so many people were 'troubled with natural wretts on severall parts of their bodies, and other naturall excrescencies'?
- Were they forced to confess by unlawful torture?

- Were they deprived of sleep?
- Were they forced to walk continually?
- Were they subject to the water ordeal?
- Did Hopkins browbeat them and put words into their mouths?
- Was it not all a scheme to make money?

These questions were carefully chosen to be lethal to Hopkins in several ways. They forced the argument to engage specifically on his own worldly methods.

Hopkins and Stearne had the right of it theologically. The Bible makes several references to witches and witchcraft and Exodus makes it clear that the punishment was to be death. The medical debate over whether or not witches were, in fact, sufferers from delusions who confessed out of depression to things they couldn't do, was too complex and involved. After all, some doctors thought that it was this depression which allowed patients to be actually led astray by real, external devils, and that whether or not they actually could harm people they were at least guilty of really bitterly wishing to harm people, and were therefore in some sense guilty as charged. Such arguments could go round and round for ever.

This group of gentlemen carefully side-stepped the theological and medical arguments. Witches are possible, they were saying, but in any case you, Matthew Hopkins, are suspected of torturing the helpless into making false confessions for your own profit. There was to be no long list of accused witches at Norwich that year. The tone of the questions is quite clear; these leading gentlemen of Norfolk were not setting out to understand or debate witchcraft, they were intending to destroy Hopkins, at the least as a person of credibility, but in all probability personally too.

A suggestion that Hopkins' special knowledge came from the Devil, was clearly an ironic joke, but made in a legal setting in that time and place it was also a personal threat. Immediately after his death, strong and persistent rumours spread that Hopkins had himself been put on trial for witchcraft and had been swum for a witch. If anything like that really did happen then this would have been the moment for it. Hopkins was forced to retire to Manningtree, where he still had the support of the Grimstons, to write up a defence of his methods and activities as fast as he possibly could, in an attempt to get public opinion on his side.

The pamphlet rapidly appeared under the tile of *The Discovery of Witches*, published both in London and Norwich. In full, it is called *The Discovery of Witches: in Answer to severall Queries LATELY delivered to the Judges of Assize for the County of NORFOLK*. By the time the pamphlet was published in May 1647, Hopkins was a very sick man, dying of consumption. He breathed his last in August 1647, in his bed at home.

John Stearne was still busy finishing up a series of cases in the Isle of Ely, which led to several acquittals and one hanging. Concerned at what had happened to Hopkins, and the attack on both their careers, he returned to his home at Lawshall, dividing his time between there and his property in Manningtree. He too was to go into print with a much longer but less well-known book, *A Confirmation and Discoverie of Witchcraft – also some objections answered.*

Stearne, in a key section of *The Confirmation and Discoverie of Witchcraft*, reveals his frustration at the opposition they had encountered. He is very guarded and and is careful to mention no names, although he does give very strong hints to a contemporary audience. Because it is so crucial, I give it in full and then unpack it bit by bit:

> And in truth, was there no alteration in England at the beginning and continuance of the suppression of this sin, and in some Counties more than others? And who are they that have been against the prosecution of, or been partakers with such, but only such as (without offence I may speak it) are enemies to the Church of God? I dare not instance, not only for fear of offence but also for suits of Law?
>
> For was there not above forty in Essex, (as I take it) all in Tendring-hundred, there where some were discovered, illegally outlawed, contrary to the law of this realm, upon a Writ of Conspiracy (as I have been credibly informed) I being one of the number, as I was likewise informed by some which were my neighbours when I lived there, by the means of one who is reported to have been one of the greatest agents in Colchester-business, within the Town; when as there was never any notice given to any upon the Proclamations, as ought, I am sure? This man, with another who is likewise reported to have been fellow-agent with him in that business, and the two chiefest in it, was the cause that some were not questioned in that town: but for his part, I saw him labour and endeavour all he could to keep this woman, whom he so much held withal from her legal Trial, and likewise heard him threaten both me and all that had given evidence against her, or informed what manner of woman she had been in her life and conversation, to their knowledge, or as they had heard: Yea, as I since have heard, she was condemned at that Assize, and by his procurement reprieved. Since which time, on her behalf, this has been done.
>
> Was not this an animation to all such people in those parts, when so many Gentlemen and Yeomen thereabouts should be thus questioned for testifying their knowledge? And was it not a fit object for the Devil, to work upon others? Let the world judge.

Stearne is asking his readers to remember and agree several things. First of all that there had indeed been a mighty 'alteration in England', a change in power, between the 'beginning of the suppression of this sin', that is, at the beginning of their campaign in 1645 and the 'continuance of the suppression of this sin', that is, their attempts to keep it going in 1648. He is asking them to remember that this political change and the change in attitude towards witchcraft had been biggest in the East Anglia, the area of the Eastern Association, and in some counties more than others.

He explains that his greatest enemies, who are also 'enemies to the church of God' (which in his language could simply mean non-Presbyterians) are too powerful for him to risk offending, and that they could charge him with slander: 'who are they that have been against the prosecution – I dare not instance, not only for fear of offence but also for suits of Law?' He reminds his readers, too, that this enemy was so strong that he, and forty like-minded people all connected with Tendring, had been technically outlawed for their part in the trials 'upon a Writ of Conspiracy' which Stearne claimed had not followed due legal process.

He points out that the most powerful man in Colchester and his agents had blocked the prosecution of a number of witches and had protected one woman in particular (he had, in fact, threatened anyone who sought to give evidence against her). He had even got her acquitted at Chelmsford assizes, and Stearne cannot name him:

> This man, with another who is likewise reported to have been fellow-agent
> with him in that business, and the two chiefest in it, was the cause that some
> were not questioned in that town: but for his part, I saw him labour and
> endeavour all he could to keep this woman, whom he so much held withal
> from her legal Trial and had been able to have her reprieved after she had
> been convicted at [Chelmsford] Assize Yea, as I since have heard, she was
> condemned at that Assize, and by his procurement reprieved.

At Chelmsford, nineteen women were hanged, nine died of gaol fever, six were still in prison in 1648, one was acquitted and one gave evidence for the prosecution. If the records are complete, then the woman that Stearne is referring to can only have been Mary Coppine of Kirby, in Essex, acquitted on the request of an identified minister called Grey, or Rebecca West, the prosecution's witness.

So who was the immensely powerful man who had acted in this way, bringing writs of conspiracy against forty people, blocking the prosecution of witches, protecting a single guilty woman and getting her reprieved after conviction, and all this despite Harbottle Grimston and other friends in high places of Stearne and Hopkins? He is very powerful indeed in both Colchester and Chelmsford, he is more powerful in 1648 than in 1645 – he is not a Royalist, therefore, and he is connected with the people in power at the time and an enemy to the Church of God.

There is only one individual to which Stearne can be referring, and that is Robert Rich, Earl of Warwick. In looking at the career of Matthew Hopkins, it has been shown how his difficulties began from the first moment of his campaign at the prison in Colchester, and then at the trial in Chelmsford. The key role of Rich's steward, Arthur Wilson, in raising concerns over the Chelmsford trials has already been described. It is Robert Rich's personal spiritual guide who is sent down to investigate events at Bury.

So, we have Harbottle Grimston promoting the witch trials and Robert Rich opposing them. This rivalry between the two men continued after the end of the witch trials. Sir Robert Rich was one of Cromwell's closest supporters, while Sir Harbottle Grimston ended up helping Charles II to return, and became Master of the Rolls in the Restoration.

Clarendon, the leading contemporary historian of the Civil Wars from a Royalist perspective, describes Harbottle Grimston as not being of the Parliament party but as someone who 'continued with them'. He was forbidden to sit in Parliament after Pride's Purge and, although he was allowed back in due course, he remained tolerated in part precisely because he was a bridge to the Presbyterian Royalists.

Meanwhile, Grimston was about to become even more wealthy through marriage, linking his family with the powerful legal dynasty of the Bacons. Members of the Bacon clan were extremely powerful in Suffolk. Edmund Bacon was Baronet of Redgrave, and Edward Bacon Baronet of Mildenall. Nathaniel Bacon was recorder of Ipswich and Bury, and his brother Francis was recorder of Aldeburgh. Another Nathaniel Bacon, of Friston, was on the panel of the committee that heard charges against the 'Scandalous Ministers'.

The great Lord Chancellor Francis Bacon had left his own estates in a mess, as a result of which his private secretary, Sir Thomas Meutys, took over the Bacon property and the great house of Gorhambury in 1626. Meautys married a niece of Francis Bacon called Anne Bacon, who was also a daughter of his cousin. When Meautys died in 1649, it was Harbottle Grimston that married Widow Anne and became head of the family and owner of the magnificent Gorhambury estate. The Bacons and Grimstons were not only a powerfully interconnected body of major landowners in East Anglia, they were also immensely powerful within the legal profession, nationally and regionally.

In 1648, in the Second Civil War, the rivalry between Rich and the Grimstons became more open and violent. In 1648 the members of the party in Essex who sought to come to an arrangement with Charles, in combination with fellow thinkers across the country, began to co-ordinate their attempts. It began with a request, deviously straightforward, that the earl, as lord lieutenant, should order a general muster of the county militia, all units turning up to be issued with weapons from the various arsenals at the same time on the same day and under the control of the deputy lieutenants. Many of the deputy lieutenants, men such as Harbottle, were closet Royalists, and this would have created large bodies of armed men under Royalist commanders able to counterbalance the Independents' control of Cromwell's New Model Army.

Warwick ordered that, instead of a general muster, the militia should be called out and inspected at different times and in different places, obviously so that it could be supervised and controlled better. The deputy lieutenants, still pretending to be good Parliamentarians, then complained that when different militia units were inspected separately they were, in fact, swopping and exchanging weapons to give the impression that they were fully equipped, whereas the reality was that the stores had been plundered by corrupt quartermasters, and the equipment sold on.

Warwick's steward, Arthur Wilson, was sent down to Essex to investigate the situation. He found that 'Sir William Hixe one of the deputie Lieutenants and Farr and Smith, Lieutenantt Colonel and Maior to my Lord's regiment now without order, sent out their warrants [for calling the militia trained bands to arms] and brought the train'd bands to Chensford; pretending the service of the countrie.'

The situation immediately became even more volatile, for the Royalist commander Lord Goring now crossed into Essex from Kent to meet up with the Essex trained bands and incorporate them into the king's army:

> That day the lord Goring crost the water, with a partie of four or five hundred of them; crossing the Thames in boates, came to Chensford; where they found spirits of as malignant temper as themselves.

Wilson's task now was to try as best he could to keep the deputy lieutenants and the trained bands of Essex loyal to the Parliamentary cause, and to secure Rich's mansion at Leaze, as it contained an important arsenal, as well as part of Rich's wealth:

> That day that Goring crost the water, My Lord sent me to Leeze with a great part of his familie, to secure his house. I mett Mr [Henry] Rich [a Royalist member of the family] Sir Harbottle Grimston and Sir Martin Lumley in the way who had bene at Chensford, to offer these tumultous indempnitie from the Parliament, if they would retire to their owne homes. But they slighted their [Parliament's] offer [in other words Grimston threw his lot in with the Royalist side]. And the Parliament men, with some difficultie, got from them; they having committed Sir Henrie Rowe and others of the countie, intending they should run the same hazard they did.

It is quite difficult to follow Arthur Wilson's description of the tense and difficult situation. What had happened was this: as part of a co-ordinated plot the Royalist deputy lieutenants of Essex had called out the county militia without authorisation, to get them to gather at Chelmsford. Once all the militia of the county were gathered together, it was hoped that the arrival of a successful Royalist army from Kent would be able to overawe the Essex militia and get them to join the Royalist cause. Harbottle Grimston, Lumley and Rich had gone to Chelmsford with the aim of bringing the militia over to the king. Mr Rich was Sir Robert's younger brother, the Earl of Holland, and the Rich family, like so many others, was divided by the war. Robert Rich's brother was a Royalist commander who was later to be captured at St Neots and beheaded in 1649, despite Robert Rich's pleas.

Wilson had ridden to meet them under a flag of truce, to tell them that Parliament would pardon them if they returned to their own homes. They, however, were expecting news of Royalist victories. Wilson told them of the failure of Goring's Royalist plans; that the Kentish rebels had been defeated at Maidstone; that there had been no Royalist rising in the City of London, and that they were on their own. Nevertheless, Grimston and the others knew that Goring and the Royalists were close by and refused Parliament's offer. In the arguing and confusion, Wilson still managed 'with some difficulty' to get the loyal Parliamentarians to join him and leave the Royalist forces.

Leaving Harbottle Grimston and the others to decide which side they should back, Wilson hurried on to Leeze, where he organised the house and hid the Parliament arsenal, while having to surrender to Lord Goring's larger army and its cannon. Wilson vividly describes the chaos that he faced in trying to organise the house, hide the weapons, and pretend to Goring's officers that he knew nothing about any arsenal while Goring's regulars tried to prevent the militia from pushing into the house and looting it.

As Parliament forces rushed into Essex, the Royalists withdrew to Colchester and found themselves caught in the famous siege. Later Daniel Defoe, in his guide to England, was to publish a diary of the siege. One entry reads:

23rd. The besiegers [the Parliamentarians] began to fire with their cannon from Essex Fort, and from Barkstead's Fort, which was built upon the Malden road; and finding that the besieged [The Royalists] had a party in Sir Harbottle Grimston's house, called, 'The Fryery,' they fired at it with their cannon, and battered it almost down, and then the soldiers set it on fire.

This made it clear which side Grimston supported. Later on, Sir Robert Rich's men plundered Grimston's house and forced out Grimston's wife, Anne.

Of course, what was eventually to happen is that the execution of Charles I removed the prime obstacle (i.e. Charles himself) from Harbottle and like-minded people, and enabled them to make the deal that they had always wanted to.

His son, Charles II, in exile was quite happy, gave them precisely what they wanted and signed the Declaration of Breda. He was equally happy to tear it up once in power. Harbottle Grimston's support of the Restoration gained him the position of Speaker of the House and Master of the Rolls. He was also part of the commission that tried the regicides.

Rich went on from the personal tragedy of his brother's execution to carry the sword of state at Cromwell's inauguration as Lord Protector, and to see his grandson marry the Lord Protector's daughter, Frances Cromwell. He died in 1658.

I have been trying to draw a picture of the way that witch trials reflected all kinds of local rivalries behind the scenes, and to underline the intensity of the campaigns to combat the trials. This picture is supported by events in Newcastle in the 1650s, as depicted in a pamphlet published in 1655 which

The search for a balanced world and a balanced community. The frontispiece to John Gauden's *Hierapistes*, with the king as the lion, and the bishop as the lamb in an ordered and peaceable world. Gauden came from an East Anglian family and was educated at Bury St Edmunds. He became Sir Robert Rich's chaplain after 1625 but broke with him later on. He became a convinced Royalist, and Bishop of Exeter. Compare this with Ward's image on page 49. (Suffolk Record Office)

shows a parallel situation where the opposition to witch persecution is directly linked to other struggles.

Ipswich was the centre of the coal fleet which brought coal from Newcastle to London. The Newcastle end of the operation was under the control of the hostmen of Newcastle who had a protected monopoly over the trade. On Newcastle council, the monopoly had been challenged by the Brandling family; especially by John Brandling, who had made himself extremely unpopular as a result. This monopoly was particularly hated by the Ipswich traders, as Charles I had allowed the hostmen to raise their dues threefold in return for their support. Newcastle had been blockaded by the Parliamentary navy, under the Earl of Warwick, and as a result London had experienced a severe coal shortage.

In 1641, John Brandling became Bailiff of Ipswich, to which he had recently moved. The pamphlet claimed that the hostmen of Newcastle had so mismanaged the town that their monopoly over the coal trade should be broken. It is called *England's Grievance Discovered, in Relation to the Coal Trade* and was written by a man called Ralph Gardiner, a gentleman of North Shields, a town completely opposed to Newcastle's attempt to control the trade. He ran a brewery for the use of the collier fleets; a brewery which Newcastle claimed was illegal under their monopoly. This was something for which he had been imprisoned. Gardiner's case against Newcastle is based on the cruelty of the magistrates and the manifest illegality and injustice of their rule as demonstrated by three types of case: the treatment of witches, the treatment of women scolds and the treatment of drunks.

Thus, improbably perhaps, a trade dispute over local protectionism in the coal trade is equally an attack on the use of witchfinders, by a man profoundly shocked by what he saw and who included the evidence of Ipswich men in his case. His tone, from which one can see that he could hardly credit the reality of what was going on, matches that of Arthur Wilson in Chelmsford. It is probably the most dramatic account of what searching for witchcraft could really be like at its worst, and it is very interestingly linked to punishments for scolding. This account makes the sexual abuse of searching absolutely clear. It also reveals how, if an external authority was in a position to intervene, the case could be overturned (in this case by a senior officer in Cromwell's army). It is worth quoting at length:

Thirty women were brought into the town hall and stripped, and then openly had pins thrust into their body – when the said person [the witchfinder] was searching of a personable and good-like woman, the said Colonel [Lieutenant Colonel Hobson] said 'Surely this woman is none and need not be tried', but the Scotch man said she was, for the town said she was, and therfoe he would try her; and presently in the sight of all the people laid her body naked to the waist, with her clothes over her head [she was naked to the waist in the sense that her genitals were exposed, not her breasts], by which right and shame all her blood contracted into one part of her body, and then he ran a pin into her thigh, and then suddenly let her coats fall, – then he put her hand up her coats and pulled out the pin and set her aside as a guilty person.

Because she had not bled, Gardiner, following Hobson's account, put this down to the shock of the exposure having cause the blood flow to the thigh to have stopped. Hobson had the test repeated after a period, when the woman then bled normally and she was released.

The MP John Ogle had the Scots witchfinder arrested. However, he fled to Scotland where he was again imprisoned and confessed to having been responsible for the deaths of 220 women, for which he was hanged. Part of Gardiner's case was that a Scots witchfinder should not have been used in an English town, as further evidence of Newcastle misrule.

The case of the scold's bridle (or 'branks' as it is called) is described as follows:

John Willis of Ipswich, upon his oath said, that he, this deponent, was in Newcastle six months ago, and there he saw one Anne Biulestone, drove through the streets by an officer of the same corporation, holding a rope in his hand, the other end fastened to an engine called the branks, which is like a crown, being of iron, which was muzzled over the head and face with a great gap or tongue of iron forced into her mouth which forced the blood out. And that is the punishment that the magistrates doth inflict on chiding or scolding women, and he has often seen the like done to others.

Willis also accused the Newcastle authorities of making drunks parade about enclosed within a specially made wooden barrel, out of which their heads projected and which also had holes for their legs. The effect of this would have been like the notorious Chinese cangue. The weight of the barrel falls on the shoulders, the prisoner cannot feed himself or reach his face with hands trapped inside the barrel, and it would be extremely difficult to walk.

6

EVIDENCE OF SIN

As She Confessed

The fullest records relating to any case are found in documents called 'depositions'. They contain the actual evidence taken down against the individual charged with witchcraft. Depositions have survived from a number of witch prosecutions and most of them, including those connected with Matthew Hopkins, were collected and published by C. L'Estrange Ewen. They are not a full record of everything that went on in 1645, for Stearne mentions other cases and, frustratingly, the Ipswich cases are not mentioned, though those in several villages bordering Ipswich, like Bramford and Copdock, are described. And they only record the accusations brought to the trial, they are not verbatim records of the trial. Actual records of what really went on in any such trial, any statements made by the accused, any questioning of witnesses and any statements by the judges are missing.

Nevertheless, they take us directly to the heart of the matter, to what actually went on in the rooms where the accused were held in the villages, and through them we can get a glimpse of the reality of the interrogations. They give the most valuable and direct evidence of what an accusation of witchcraft in Suffolk under the influence of Hopkins and Stearne was like. Though they have been used regularly by writers since their publication, they are of the greatest interest and what can be learnt from them is far from exhausted.

The depositions are arranged in groups of cases relating to different groups of villages, and there are different recording styles which suggest that they were compiled from records made by different individuals. For example, while most only record successful confessions, one unusually honest recorder at Glemham noted that Anne Driver, Alice Glemfield, Margerie Blake, Ellen Bishop, Rosa Charlfield and Thomas Clarke all refused to confess.

Many of the depositions show some women confessed to becoming witches many years, even decades, earlier and that some of their crimes were equally as old. This suggests that Hopkins and Stearne were, in some sense, clearing a backlog of cases that had been impossible to progress under the authority of Laud and Wren.

Alongside the depositions must be read the accounts of various Suffolk cases given by John Stearne in his *A Confirmation and Discoverie of Witchcraft*. He gives fewer cases, and those he records sometimes overlap with those in the depositions. They are clearly written with an eye to justifying the whole process, and with that aim differ in subtle ways from the accounts of the same cases found in the depositions.

The Reverend John Gaule (*Select Cases of Conscience*, 1646) has left particulars of the method in which the watching was carried out by Hopkins and his colleagues:

> Having taken the suspected witch, she is placed in the middle of a room upon a stool or table, cross-legged, or in some other uneasy posture, to which if she submits not, she is then bound with cords; there is she watched and kept without meat or sleep for the space of 24 hours for (they say) within that time they shall see her imp come and suck. A little hole is likewise made in the door for the imp to come in at; and lest it might come in some less discernible shape, they that watch are taught to be ever and anon sweeping the room, and if they see any spiders or flies, to kill them. And if they cannot kill them, then they may be sure they are her imps.

There is another description of their procedure in a single case – that of John Lowes, the Vicar of Brandeston, recorded around twenty or more years later by John Revett, the lord of the manor:

> I have heard it from them that watched with him, that they kept him awake several Nights together & ran him backwards, and forwards about ye Room, until he was out of Breath. Then they rested him a litle, & then ran him again; & thus they did for several Days & Nights together, till his as weary of his life, & was scarce sensible of what he said or did.

That is, Hopkins and Stearne had already perfected modern interrogation techniques, and the individual was assaulted and shamed by having their private parts searched for anything out of the ordinary, during which they were humiliated and mocked. They were accused of sexual deviance and other horrible things. They were kept in a stress position, balanced on a stool in an awkward pose, and sometimes tied. Gaule says that they were kept like this for twenty-four hours but the depositions seem to suggest that many were subjected to the process for days on end. Perhaps they were given a short break between sessions.

Although they were standing or squatting on a stool, nevertheless they would tend to drop momentarily asleep and come to with a start as they nearly fell off. It is highly unlikely, and completely against the logic of the process, that the person being watched would have been allowed privacy for their natural functions, and this would have been a further part of the process of humiliation and shame. Where the person had been swum for a witch they had, in effect, been subjected to waterboarding, but with a perverse psychological twist: the longer they were under, the better.

The depositions give the details of the duration of the process in a number of cases (around half), but the details are given slightly differently in the individual cases so that it is sometimes a little difficult to know exactly how long is meant. Two to three days and nights seem be quite common. A couple of witches confessed before they had been accused; twelve confessed as soon as they were formally accused; five after a day; four after two days; nine after three days; one after four days and two after six days. A couple are said to have confessed, and then withdrawn their confessions only to be watched again. This must be the reason why Payne of Bramford is entered as having confessed on both the third and the eighth night of his interrogation. It is surprising that any of them held out as long as they did, for they were not committed, trained and fit young militia men but often elderly, half-starved and sometimes unstable.

This form of interrogation meant that, as well as dramatic moments, there would have been hours of watching in which nothing much happened. The discomfort of the awkward position slowly but surely would have turned into a deep aching muscle pain, and the accused would have become absorbed by an obsessive desire to just move, to be allowed to ease their position ever so slightly. If only he or she could make even a tiny change in position.

Time would have changed for them and become elastic, seeming to stretch out and then moving quite fast. The light in the room would have seemed to take years to move around from wall to wall and for the shadows to change, and then it would be dark apparently all of a sudden. Fear and disorientation would have been strong. What to do, what to say, which of the people present might prove sympathetic and listen – desperately trying to work out some kind of strategy will have alternated with seconds of passing into blackness, only to jerk awake as one began to sway and fall on the stool. They may have experienced memories so vividly that they seemed like another physical world one could reach out and step into; almost but not quite. Then one would be back in the room, obsessed once again by a pain like cramp and pins and needles, all mixed up. All this, going round and round in a circle that seemed to have become endless.

For the watchers themselves the experience would have been similar in some ways. Their thoughts would wander off too and then come back with a snap. This was all very important, and they would have been chosen for this key task to protect their families and villages against evil. It is quite probably the most exciting thing in which they would ever have taken part. At the back of their minds they would wonder if they could be at risk – Anne Marsh, of Tattingstone, apparently told her watchers that they would be better at home looking after their children and, inevitably, one of the watchers' children did indeed fall in the fire. They might be worried that the imps could come and they could have missed seeing them. Which one of them would prove the most vigilant? Did anyone else see me yawn? How are the others doing? They would also be wondering when their shift would end, when they could go and eat, or get a drink.

The atmosphere within the room would have become powerfully charged, as people were keyed up and expecting to see something exceptional – they were, after all, really expecting to see an imp, and quite possibly see a woman suckle a demon creature, not necessarily from her breasts but from secret nipples hidden in her private parts. One could watch so intensely that they forgot to blink, so that the object on which they focused seemed to jump and move around, in and out of focus. The imp could be any shape, maybe the bird that just flew up to the window, maybe a mouse that had run into the room, stopped and scuttled out again, maybe even that loudly buzzing fly. Add to this the whole village watching outside, and the threat of mob violence. Everyone would want to get close to the witchfinders, to ask their opinions, to carry out errands, to groom their horses – anything really to be a part of the action.

In certain cases the watchers were rewarded for these long periods of tension and boredom with some particularly exciting event. Susanna Smith, of Rushmere, apparently tried to commit suicide. The deposition records: 'The Devil told her to kill herself with an old rusty knife while being watched.'

Margaret Mixter of Shotley went into fits:

After the third night she seemed to be very sick and have strange fits, in the time of her watching she cried out and said Satan was within her and prayed them that watched with her to hold her body and to work and had wrought Satan down Satan which they – and she after thanked them and said they had done her great good out of her.

Stearne, in his *Confirmation*, actually records cases in which he says that the imps were invisible and that he could detect that they were there in the room and invisibly feeding while the woman was watched:

> Another whilst I was in the room with her, at Huntingdon, I perceived by her carriage that she was feeding her Imps, Spirits or Familiars so called; I laid it to her charge, but she denied it: Yet presently after she confessed it was truth, when she was asked by the Justice of Peace.

He records a particularly nasty example at Coddenham. This is how he describes it:

> And so at Coddenham in Suffolk, being told how a woman there carried her self, I caused her to be searched again, and there was alteration of the marks, and the woman presently confessed it, and made a large confession; and so it has been common in all our proceedings, and a great cause for keeping them; for the blood has sometimes been found on the end of the mark, or to be stroked out when they are taken on a sudden.

He is saying that he saw a woman that he already knew had some abnormal growth somewhere on her body, and was holding herself awkwardly (perhaps in pain), and he had this growth squeezed (stroked out) until it bled and called this bleeding evidence.

In Stearne's mind, even the absence of evidence was evidence of diabolic cunning, never of innocence:

> But there is one, a very remarkable thing concerning this, that was done at St Neots in Huntingdonshire, of a woman that had been searched two or three times, and not found, for they can hide their marks sometimes, as you shall herein, yet was still in great suspicion of many of the Townsmen to be guilty (the brand is difficult to find if she had notice) and the rather, for that she fled or went away after she was searched twice, for some are not found at first, yet are in the end.

Not infrequently, this stage of the process had begun before the arrival of either Hopkins or Stearne, and in some cases it is obvious that the local minister had begun himself by copying their methods. John Curtise seems to have done this at Bramford, Mr Willan at Wickham and Mr Browne, minister at Dunwich. Sometimes, as in the case of Katherine Tooly of Westleton, this gave the minister an opportunity for a little self-promotion of his own:

Upon a difference with Mr Driver minister she sent Jackly to meet him as he was to go to preach from Kelsale to Westleton and strike him and his horse dead and the imp required blood of her to do it but he returned to her and told her he could not do it he had no power over him and the reason was he served God. witness Mr Driver.

In the case of Eliza Southerne, it was the kindly piety of the minister which was stressed: 'The minister used no other argument to make her confess. Only by saying you do wrong yourself but clear your conscience.'

Stearne also sometimes directly reports some of the dialogue between the accused and himself and Hopkins. He reveals himself again as having so little insight that he fails to see what the woman is saying. Elizabeth Clarke's case is the best recorded. She seems to have been one of the more courageous and to have threatened her persecutors, for she is alleged to have said when accused of having imps: 'but said, one was still to come, which was to tear me [Stearne] to pieces, then I asked her why, she said, because I would have swum her, and told me that now she would be even with me.'

It is, however, Stearne's perverse literal-mindedness which most reveals the persecuting mentality, the drive to prove the impossible true by corrupt means:

Then he replied and said, tell the truth, if it is the truth, say so, but if not the truth, then say so, Has not the Devil had the use of your body? She said, why should you ask such a question? he answered, I desire to know the truth and no otherwise, then she fetched a sigh, and said, it is true, then said Mr Hopkin, in what manner and likeness came he to you? She said, like a tall proper black haired gentleman, a proper man like yourself, and being asked which she had rather lie with, she said the Devil, and so particulized everything, and how he came in, and his habit, and how he lay with her, and spoke to her, as she then affirmed to be the truth.

It is not surprising that Elizabeth Clarke should have said she would rather have sex with the Devil than with Matthew Hopkins even though the Devil looked just like him, nor that she gave him a thrill by describing the event. It is also not surprising that, given their perverse mentality, the witchfinders should have taken the statement 'I would rather sleep with the Devil than Matthew Hopkins' and turned it into 'I confess to sleeping with the Devil'.

This perversion of an everyday statement into something sinister can be seen in other cases. Ellen Driver of Framlingham confessed to the sorrow of her life which had begun sixty years ago when the Devil courted her to marry her:

The Devil appeared to her like a man and that she was married to him in one — parishes and that he lived with her 3 years and that she had 2 childeren

A panel from a closet painted for, or possibly by, Lady Anne Drury at Hawstead near Bury St Edmunds, sometime between 1600 and 1615. A black man with the caption 'we are all equal now'. Joseph Hall, Lady Drury's spiritual guide, published a sermon upon first meeting a black person, in which he speaks of a common spiritual value beneath outward experience. (Ipswich Museum)

Sir Nicholas Crispe, Cavalier, and organiser of the West African slave trade. In the background of the engraving can be seen the slave castle he built in Courmantine, Ghana, and a chain of slaves. He had connections with the Glemham family, and his daughter and heir married Sir Thomas Cullum of Thorndon, who owned Hardwick Hall next to Hawstead. The Hawstead panels were later moved there. Crispe had large estates in Hammersmith, while Cullum was Sheriff of London. (Suffolk Record Office)

by him in that time that were changelings after she were married he had the carnal use of her but was cold, she said that she did not know that any of his neighbours did ever see him, she further said that being in bed with him she felt of his feet and they were cloven and he lived with her two years and then died as she thought.

She was surely not the only woman who would describe a man who deserted her after three years, leaving her with two sickly children, as a devil. Margaret Benet of Bacton confessed to a forceful seduction, possibly a rape:

The devil met her as she came from Newton with a long cloak, and she knew him by his feet, the devil in the shape of a man at the first ... carried her body over a close into a thicket and there lay with her. She was promised she should be revenged on all that angered her.

The way that the depositions regularly interpret encounters very obviously of this world through a distorting supernatural lens is revealed by another tiny story which is interesting for another reason. Eliza Southerne of Dunwich:

She met the devil midsummer last like a black boy ten years old by a white thorne as she went to Westleton and there he promised her 2s 6d and he had not then but she should have it the next time she came that way but he failed of his promise, he met her indeed, but complained of the hardness of the times the boy was hairy though young.

So in the heat of the summer under the thorn tree in blossom on the scented heathland between Westleton and Dunwich, she had had a liaison with a young black boy who let her down but did come back with a feeble excuse. It is not at all far-fetched to think of black people living in rural Suffolk at this period. The first named black man known to have lived in Suffolk is recorded in the burial register of Little Wenham on 7 June 1618:

John a Moore by birth brought out of his contrie by Captayne Cauendish liued the latter part of his dayes at Wenham Hall hee dyed the sixt day of June and was buried the seauenth, his body lyeth in the churchyard of Little Wenham, and his soule wee hope resteth with God.

(As transcribed by Charles Partridge, *East Anglian Miscellany* 1934, No 9,293.)

Around this time the very successful merchant John Eldred, who had made a fortune from the sale of tobacco, built himself a grand mansion, Nutmeg

Hall in Great Saxham. He is known to have had a black servant. At Hawstead, Lady Dury had employed a chaplain called Joseph Hall, who had published a book of Sermons entitled *Occasionall Meditations* (London: 1631) towards the end of his life in 1638. The thirty-eighth of these Puritan meditations is called 'Upon the sight of a Blackemore'. Black people, one of them smoking tobacco, appear on the strange, almost surreal, painting that she had prepared for her own closet, now preserved in Christchurch Mansion (*see* p. 130). Thomas Warner of Parham was trying to settle St Kitts and Nevis just at this time.

So, when Elizabeth Hobart of Wetherden was tempted by a small black boy, or Margery Spara of Mendham met the Devil in the woods in the likeness of a black man, or when Katherine Tooly of Westleton, like her neighbour Elizabeth Southerne, met a black boy, that is quite possibly exactly what did happen. Another sign that New World influences were spreading fast through the county is when Maria Bush of Bacton destroyed the livestock of a Mr Pritiman; they included twenty turkeys.

Amongst those targeted as witches, the saddest group were a number of people clearly depressive and wracked with guilt for some failure to be a good mother or wife. A number confessed to having gone over to the Devil shortly after their husbands had died, and in terms which make it clear that this was a folk description for surrendering to despair: Payne of Bramford had been tempted to hang himself; Ellen Greenlif of Bacton was often tempted to kill herself; for Mary Scrutton of Bacton, the Devil 'tempted her in a hollow voice to kill her child'; Susanna Smith of Rushmere was tempted to kill her children but refused. Prosilla Collit of Dunwich was:

> … in a sickness about 12 years since the devil tempted her to make away with her children or else so should always continue poor, she carried one of her children and laid it close to the fire to burn it and went to bed again and the fire burnt the hair and the head lining and she heard it cry but could not have power to help it but one other of her children pulled it away.

Mary Bacon of Chattisham 'sent her imp Thomas to kill her daughter and he did kill her and she wished her son's child cold in the mouth and it died likewise'. Meanwhile, for Susanna Stegold of Hintlesham:

> After her husband being a bad husband she wished he might depart from her meaning as she said that he should die and presently after he died mad, and when this informant went from her there followed a dor [jackdaw] after him which this accusant saith was an imp which she sent after him but it could do him no harm and being in the – art she cried out Oh! My dear husband but

being asked whether she bewitched him to dead or no and said she wished him ill wishes to him.

For Anne Moats: 'The devil did appear first to her when she was alone in her house and after she had had been cursing of her husband and children.'

The witchfinders did not control the courts, but they did control this horrible little world which they exploited to build a successful career for themselves, for a time.

7

Women, Witches and Quakers

The said Mother Lakeland hath been a Professor of Religion, a constant hearer of the Word for these many years.

Most of the accused were women (though there were some men). As previously discussed, their power was said to lie in suckling imps through extra nipples hidden in their private parts and many allegedly had had sex with the Devil. In other words, they represented a perversion of the most powerful elements of women's sexuality, and if anything this was even more transgressive when the accused was a man. While there is no evidence that witches were, in any sense, priestesses of an old religion (as we have seen, the agents of a protean ancient tradition were, in fact, the cunning men), or village midwives, these popular ideas are indeed true in one respect. There is an element of gender politics in witchcraft, and there is to some degree a fear of the feminine. This is what Stearne had to say:

> Women therefore without question exceed men, especially of the hurting Witches; but for the other, I have known more men, and have heard such as have gone to them say, almost generally they be men.
>
> Now, why it should be that women exceed men in this kind, I will not say, that Satan's setting upon these rather than man is, or like to be, because of his unhappy onset and prevailing with Eve; or their more credulous nature, and apt to be misled, for that they are commonly impatient, and being displeased more malicious, and so more apt to revenge according to their power and thereby more fit instruments for the Devil; or that, because they are more ready to be teachers of Witchcraft to others, and to leave it to Children, servants or to some others (but that you shall find to be a great inducement thereto by their confessions) or that, because, where they can command they are more fierce in their rule, and revengeful in setting such on work whom they can command, wherefore the Devil labours most to make them Witches: for Satan is subtle and seeks whom he may devour …

But as St Paul says, Witchcraft being amongst the fruits of the flesh, one may fall into this sin as well as into any other (if God prevent it not) and therefore whether men or women.

(Stearne, *Confirmation and Discoverie*.)

Any study of popular seventeenth-century writing on morality, from whatever religious point of view, clearly does reveal a strong critical current directed against women. The works of Nathaniel Ward, the brother of Samuel Ward the Ipswich town lecturer, are a vivid example, in part because he obviously had such fun in writing them down: 'It is a most unworthy thing for men who have bones in them, to spend their lives making fidle-cases for futulous womens phantasies, which are the very pettitoes of Infirmity, the giblets of perquisquilian toyes.'

In the same book, he denounces fashionable women as 'bullymong drossocks' (*The Simple Cobler of Aggawam*).

However, these attacks are not principally to do with witchcraft. What infuriated Puritans like Nathaniel Ward, or the better known Philip Stubbes in his *Anatomy of Abuses*, was the vanity of fashion and, above all, the ruff. Prints showing women led astray by Devils who sold them ruffs were sold across Europe to accompany stories of how ruffs had led women to hell. Stubbes included the 'Fearful example of the ruff-wearing woman of Antwerp whose neck the Devil broke'. In some ways, as the fashions were so very expensive, these charges were as much class as gender-based and male fashions were also bitterly ridiculed. Pleated and stiffened ruffs bedecked the carved and painted figures of vanity personified across Europe, along with the mirror and the serpent appearing on carved overmantles in Ipswich.

This rhetoric was not anti-women as such, after all it was combined with a glorification of the sober, careful and modest housewife, but it certainly was directed against the 'bad woman', and there is a suggestion at least of the woman who uses her sexual power to extract wealth from men. The desperate, embittered, unattractive and poor witch is the opposite of the 'scarlet woman' in every respect, save being both evil.

Fear of women can be seen in the punishment of women as 'scolds'. In Ipswich, women who were found guilty of being common scolds could be paraded through the town and then sat in a special chair in which they were ducked in the river. Confusingly, its correct title is a 'cucking stool', from the Norman French word *coquiner* (to scold), not from the English word 'duck'.

The laws of Ipswich were quite precise. Their offence was not to scold their family or their husbands, but to quarrel loudly with their neighbours. It is women who were married and all of whose property belonged to their husband, and who therefore had no money of their own with which to pay a fine, who were to be ducked.

Detail of an overmantle carving showing the vice of vanity, based on a Dutch engraving of a woman strangled by a devil for her fancy ruff. (Ipswich Museum)

Although on the face of it the cucking stool is a form of corporal punishment for a simple, straightforward, and un-supernatural offence, it does have a kind of connection with witchcraft. Most cases of witchcraft started as quarrels between neighbours, the same offence for which the cucking stool was the punishment, and more particularly between neighbours who were women. Grimston's list of legal cases concerning claims of libel against people for calling someone else a witch are usually between women, and obviously arise from quarrels between neighbours.

A dispute can lead to a quarrel, a quarrel to an outburst of scolding and name calling, and this in turn can very easily turn into cursing and ill-wishing, and now the parties are on the slippery slope towards witchcraft. We do not like to be cursed, but in modernity we usually do not think a curse will have an effect. However, in the seventeenth century, when a slip of words by a drunkard could lead to his death and damnation (according to Ward in *Woe to Drunkards*), a hard word in a quarrel could indeed be deadly – God, or something else, might listen.

Moreover, the very nature of the punishment, strapped into a chair attached to an arm allowing the victim to be ducked under water, was highly reminiscent of the folk practice of tying someone up and throwing them into a body of water to see if they were a witch. So much so, that there is hardly a book on witchcraft which does not include the same woodcut of a woman being ducked as a scold to illustrate swimming a person for a witch.

Women were ducked at the quayside in Ipswich for being common scolds in the years immediately leading up to the witch trials, and the cases were recorded in the Sessions Book: 'Sessions 29 April 1645 – The King v Mary Paine upon the indictment and for a scold, Plea not guilty, found guilty and to be dupped three times.'

There is an important group of cases in which gender politics of a very modern kind, relating to the proper role of women in the Church, is crucial. It concerns the role of women in various groups of the small separatist and independent movements. The evidence, I think, is overwhelming in some key cases and circumstantial in others. However, at the moment it is an obvious element only in a minority of cases.

One aspect of the cases of heresy that had earlier led to the burning of men and women by the Catholic Church in Ipswich in the reign of Mary Tudor, and recorded in detail by Foxe in his famous *Book of Martyrs*, is the number of women victims, such as: Agnes Potten, 1556; Joan Trunchfield, 1556; Alice Driver, 1558; Anne Bolton and Agnes Wardal. Somehow, the religious disputes of the day had drawn women clearly into them and had, in some way, empowered women in quite ordinary positions to have the confidence to openly debate theological ideas at the risk of their life, with the great, the powerful and the educated, in terms of Catholic bishops. No longer called heretics, but reclassified as witches, women of strong religious views found themselves persecuted once again.

It is a complicated story, and it takes us first to New England. The emigration to New England was a movement of people refusing to be compelled to follow the teachings of Archbishop Laud. Almost immediately, its leadership became embroiled in problems over what they themselves could tolerate. The 'simple cobler of Aggavam', as Nathaniel Ward called himself in his pamphlet, was quite clear that religious toleration was another name for chaos:

> That if the state of England shall either willingly tolerate, or weakly connive at, such courses the Church of that kingdom will sooner become the Devil's dancing-school, than God's temple, the civil State a bear-garden, than an exchange, the whole realm a Pays-Basse [Netherlands] than an England.
>
> (*The Simple Cobler of Aggavam*, p.9.)

> If there be room in England for familiars, Libertines, Erastians, Antitrinitarians, Anabaptists, Anti-Scripturists, Armininians, Manifesterians, Millenaries, Antinomians, Socinians, Arians, perfectists, Brownists, Mortalians, seekers, Enthusiasts etc, religious men but pernicious heretics–in a word for hell above ground.
>
> (*The Simple Cobler of Aggavam*, p.11.)

Massachusetts, under the laws drawn up by Nathaniel Ward, like Ipswich under the influence of his brother, Samuel, saw itself as an embattled corporation of Mansoul, and it had decided to allow no room for such divisive voices. Yet the Puritans of New England had brought with them their deeply ingrained habits of deep theological study, independent thinking and their profound determination to stand up for what they believed to be correct, no matter what any external authority might say or think. Dissent was their nature, and conflict inevitably broke out. This is known as the 'antinomian debate' and it deeply divided the society of New England in the mid 1630s.

Antinomianism is the doctrine that because Christians are saved by faith and the free gift of God's grace they are no longer subject to moral laws, at least in the conventional sense. For its believers, this has usually been understood to mean that the love of God and love for God is more important than the previous moral codes superseded by the sacrifice of Jesus, and of man-made morality in general. To its opponents, it can easily seem to be a rejection of all rules to be replaced by a complete anarchy in which anything goes. While the former governor, John Winthrop, and most ministers held to an orthodox Presbyterian approach, the new governor, Sir Henry Vane, and Sir Robert Rich supported the antinomians.

Overmantle from a house in Carr Street, carved with three graces and one vice. The house was known as 'The Old House Carr Street' and was the home, in the 1850s, of the industrialist James Allen Ransome. More work is needed to establish who commissioned such fine carvings in the seventeenth century, but this house was clearly very close to the site of Harbottle House which had belonged to Sir Harbottle Grimston Snr, and it is quite possible that the 'Old House' and 'Harbottle House' are different names for the same house. (Ipswich Museum)

Robert Rich, as described previously, had become deeply involved in the English settlement of the New World, firstly in Virginia, then in Massachusetts and what was to become the Saybrook Colony in modern Connecticut. In 1638, he sold the Saybrook Colony to a group of people who were all associated with Oliver Cromwell, the Parliamentarian movement, and the nascent Independents in religion. Cromwell, Pym, Hampden Haselrig, Lord Saye and Lord Brook were all involved, and it was rumoured that they had plans to fortify the colony and hold it as a refuge in case England became too dangerous for them. Their success in the Civil War rendered this pointless and in 1644 the Saybrook Colony was sold back to Connecticut.

Sandwiched between Connecticut and Massachusetts is Rhode Island. Rhode Island was to become Massachusetts' own 'new England', the place where the dissidents and freethinkers gathered. First to arrive in 1636, was an outstanding preacher-scholar called Roger Williams, and his followers, who named their settlement Providence Island, and organised it on the basis of majority rule in civil matters and freedom of conscience in religious matters. In the next year, 1637, the remarkable Anne Hutchinson, her husband and followers set up their own settlement on Rhode Island at Portsmouth, and two others, Coddington and Clarke, set up another at Newport.

Anne Hutchinson had been in trouble almost since her arrival in Massachusetts. She was a devout follower of the Reverend John Cotton, a member of an important Suffolk family who had also emigrated. However, she went considerably further than her more cautious mentor. A record survives of her confrontation with the Massachusetts authorities, and it is important when it is compared with Stearne's accounts of his own interrogation of alleged witches.

This was not a formal trial as such. One of the principal accusations against Anne Hutchinson was that groups of women had been meeting privately in her house for prayers and Bible study. Linked to this is the charge that, during these meetings, Anne was putting forward her own theological ideas and also saying that only the Reverend John Cotton was preaching true doctrine, and the other New England ministers were preaching a false doctrine based on law not love. The interrogation is recounted in what seems to have been a transcript which makes clear the frustration of the governor, who is clearly completely opposed to the idea of private female Bible study groups, but can't really find a law or a theological reason against it. The further accusation is then made that some Bible study groups led by her were mixed, and this is seen as more serious. Anne becomes more heated and more open about her ideas. As she does so, she begins to speak of various voices which give her the spiritual insight and confidence she needs, and begins to speak of the voice of the Spirit. She ends by getting close to saying that God will curse the governor if he persecutes her. It is worth quoting in full:

Mrs H: I bless the Lord, he hath let me see which was the clear ministry and which the wrong. Since that time I confess I have been more choice and he hath let me to distinguish between the voice of my beloved and the voice of Moses, the voice of John Baptist and the voice of Antichrist, for all those voices are spoken of in scripture. Now if you do condemn me for speaking what in my conscience I know to be truth I must commit myself unto the Lord.

Mr Nowell: How do you know that that was the spirit?

Mrs H: How did Abraham know that it was God that bid him offer his son, being a breach of the sixth commandment?

Dep. Gov: By an immediate voice.

Mrs H: So to me by an immediate revelation.

Dep. Gov: How! an immediate revelation.

Mrs H: By the voice of his own spirit to my soul. I will give you another scripture, Jer. 46. 27, 28 – out of which the Lord shewed me what he would do for me and the rest of his servants. -- But after he was pleased to reveal himself to me ... Ever since that time I have been confident of what he hath revealed unto me ... Therefore I desire you to look to it, for you see this scripture fulfilled this day and therefore I desire you that as you tender the Lord and the church and commonwealth to consider and look what you do. You have power over my body but the Lord Jesus hath power over my body and soul, and assure yourselves thus much, you do as much as in you lies to put the Lord Jesus Christ from you, and if you go on in this course you begin you will bring a curse upon you and your posterity, and the mouth of the Lord hath spoken it ...

Gov: The court hath already declared themselves satisfied concerning the things you hear, and concerning the troublesomeness of her spirit.

In 1642 they were joined by another settlement, led by Samuel Gorton, on the mainland near the island at a place then called Shawomet. Originally each of these settlements were more or less independent of each other and had their own internal squabbles. By 1643 they had joined in a loose alliance, and were trying to get recognition as a separate colony in response to various police actions against them by Massachusetts.

Roger Williams, the first of the settlers, sailed back home to London in 1643/44 to get recognition of their independence from Massachusetts and support for these loosely linked communities. In 1644, he published his remarkable pamphlet *The Bloudy Tenet of Persecution for Cause of Conscience, Discussed, in a Conference Betweene Truth and Peace. Who in all Tender Affection Present to the High Court of Parliament* ... This book was probably the first reasoned plea for religious toleration in the English language. It begins: 'First, That the blood of so many hundred thousand soules of Protestants and Papists, spilt in the Wars of present and former Ages, for their respective Consciences, is not required nor accepted by Jesus Christ the Prince of Peace.' Building to a rousing (and quite amazing, for the period) statement:

Sixtly, It is the will and command of God, that (since the comming of his Sonne the Lord Jesus) a permission of the most Paganish, Jewish, Turkish, or Antichristian consciences and worships, bee granted to all men in all Nations and Countries: and they are onely to bee fought against with that Sword which is only (in Soule matters) able to conquer, to wit, the Sword of Gods Spirit, the Word of God.

(This is available on Google Books, digitisation of the Narranganset Club reprint of the original.)

Robert Rich was their patron and their supporter with the London Government. Robert Rich successfully helped establish Anne Hutchinson, Roger Williams and Samuel Gorton's settlements as the separate colony of Rhode Island and Warwick town and river are both named after him. He was helped in this by Sir Henry Vane, who had returned to London after a clash with Winthrop. In 1644, the Long Parliament granted the dissidents of Rhode Island a charter, but in it appointed a governor, something the colonists rejected in favour of a president and council, both elected.

Massachusetts claimed that the new colony was in fact part of their state, and used force to try impose their authority. Gorton, still in Rhode Island, became embroiled in all kinds of legal problems with the Massachusetts Bay General Court. He too travelled to London to appeal directly to Warwick to use his influence to sort matters out. Rich, as we have already seen, was committed to making the new colonies successful, and for this to happen it was essential that he should be able to attract settlers and a work force to them. Supporting religious freedom in New England was an acceptable price to pay to get settlers, especially as he was moving away from Presbyterianism towards the Independent position anyway.

In 1648 Gorton returned with the necessary letter from Rich, ordering Massachusetts to leave Rhode Island alone. During the following years, Rhode Island became a centre for some very progressive ideas, including banning witchcraft trials, imprisonment for debt, restricting capital punishment and, on 8 March 1652, banning chattel slavery, whether of whites or blacks.

In one sense, these settlements of a few hundred people could be described loosely as obscure hippy communes on the far side of the Atlantic, but from another perspective they were also social experiments backed by two of the most powerful men in England at the time. The Earl of Warwick must have known of Samuel Gorton or indeed Anne Hutchinson's ideas, and he cannot have been totally opposed to them. Political events in New England and old England were completely intertwined. The inhabitants of New England were still largely first-generation emigrants with living brothers and other family in England. Ships were passing to and fro, and some preachers who had gone to New England were to return to England with the fall of Laud. The same religious and political debates absorbed both communities.

Events in New England would have sent alarm bells ringing throughout the Presbyterian movement. Sir Henry Vane apparently came to believe that, while the Roman Catholic Church represented 'the first beast of Revelations', the Presbyterians and all state-backed religion represented 'the second beast of Revelations'. The struggle between Independents and Presbyterians was a bitter division within the Parliamentary forces.

The date of Gorton's visit to London to try and sort matters out is quite possibly significant for another reason. Contained within letter 2624 of the

Clarendon Manuscripts in the Bodleian Library is the earliest known reference to the term 'Quaker' for a religious sect. It suggests that they came from New England and were women. It runs as follows:

> I heare of a Sect of woemen-- come from beyond the Sea, called Quakers and these swell, shiver and shake, and when they came to themselves (for in all this fitt Mahomet's holy ghost hath bin conversing with them) they begin to preache what hath bin delivered to them by the spirit.

If female believers were in fact going into dramatic prophetic trances, then they would have looked very threatening, not to say demonically possessed to the conventional Presbyterians of the period. Later, in the 1690s, Richard Baxter in his book *The Certainty of the World of Spirits* was to describe the Quakers as follows:

> When the Quakers first rose here, their societies began like witches, with quaking, and vomiting, and infecting others with breathing upon them, and tying ribbons on their hands. And their actions, as well as their doctrines showed their master [Satan]. When some as prophesying walked through the streets of the cities naked; and some vainly undertook to raise the dead [as Susan Pierson at Worcester]. And usually they disturbed and publickly reviled the most godly ministers worse than the most debauched of the rabble did.
>
> (*The Certainty of the World of Spirits*, p.65)

Baxter's remarks allude to things which are not very clear. What associated Quakers with vomiting? Was it something to do with the long fasts some undertook? Does it have a connection with the Lowestoft and later trials, and the vivid descriptions of the vomiting of strange objects that was described in some Restoration Suffolk witch cases? What about tying ribbons on hands? However, one thing is pretty clear; to their Presbyterian opponents, Quakers were close to witches.

If, then, events in Rhode Island are connected to Warwick, and if Warwick is connected with the opposition to witch trials in Suffolk and Essex, then it is at least possible that events in Rhode Island have a direct bearing on what was going on in East Anglia – that part of England most intimately involved with the New World.

What I am going to suggest is that the same religious conflict which was expressed openly in New England appeared in a disguised or even deliberately distorted form in East Anglia during the witch persecutions of 1645. In November 1644 the committee of Suffolk at Bury (consisting of Edward Bacon, Francis Bacon, Henry North, Samuel Moody, M. Barrowe, Sheriff of

Suffolk William Spring, William Laurence and Gibson Lucas) wrote formally to the committee for both kingdoms as follows:

> The Ordinance of the posture of Defence is now Happyly executed within this Country so that they will be able to defend themselves, but the Antinomians & Anabaptists Doe soe exceedingly increase amongst us, that if there be not speedily proved a posture of Defence for the Church as well as for Comon Wealth wee evidently foresee our ruyne approaching …
>
> (Item 4552, in the University of Chicago Library, Sir Nicholas Bacon Collection of English Court and Manorial Documents.)

Stearne, in his attempts to answer all his critics, was to write:

> Then some will say, How shall they be known one from another, or how shall they be found out, if these difficulties be? **For it cannot be denied but that many of them have made great shows of Religion.**
>
> I answer, It is truth: as the Devil can transform himself into an Angel of light, so have many of these Witches made outward shows, as if they had been Saints on earth, and so were taken by some; as one of Catworth in Huntingdonshire, who made as large a Confession, in a manner, as ever any did, & confessed at the gallows before her death, in my hearing. Likewise one LENDALL of Cambridge, who suffered also, carried herself as if she had been no less: and so did the mother of the said REBECCA WEST, and many others, which by their carriage seemed to be very religious people, and would constantly repair to all Sermons near them: yet notwithstanding all their shows of religion, there appeared some of these probabilities, whereby they were suspected, and so searched, and so by that means discovered and made known.

To Stearne's own list of cases can, of course, be added that of Mary Lackland herself: 'The said Mother Lakeland hath been a Professor of Religion, a constant hearer of the Word for these many years, and yet a Witch (as she confessed) for the space of near twenty years.'

The pamphlet on the trial of Rebecca West lists amongst those executed at Chelmsford, 'Mrs Wayt, a minister's wife.' Stearne also mentions: 'RICHMOND, a woman which lived in Bramford, confessed the Devil appeared to her in the likeness of a man, called DANIEL THE PROPHET.'

Joanne Balls of Wickham Market was described by her parish minister as follows: 'This woman professed ANABAPTISM and runner after new sects, teste Mr Willan clerk.'

The depositions record how Mary Skipper of Copdock received satanic instruction in deception: 'The Devil bade her go to Church and make a great show but if she attended diligently he would nip her she felt of a week after.' The depositions also record how Susan Marchant was singing psalms and milking when she was tempted.

Stearne himself describes how eighteen of the alleged witches convicted at Bury, who had been imprisoned separately in a barn, made a pact to reject their confessions and say nothing on the scaffold. To fortify themselves they sang psalms. So, a body of accused women organised themselves as a group and sang psalms together as they waited for their deaths …

The first of Hopkins and Stearne's cases, the one that they worked on most closely with Harbottle Grimston and which served as the pattern for their future career, was the one at Manningtree involving the group of women allegedly led by Anne West. The confession of the daughter was central to this case, and it is retold in the two pamphlets about the trials and in Stearne's *Confirmation*, differing in detail each time.

It is possible to take the confession of Anne West as a straightforward and accurate account of events by removing from it all the pejorative words and replacing them by neutral ones, as well as removing Stearne's glosses and manifest impossibilities regarding imps. If this is done, the confession can be presented as follows:

The said Rebecca confessed at the Barre, that about Shrovetide last her mother bad her make haste of her worke, for she must gee along with her before Sunne downe: and as they were going over the fields, her mother gave her a great charge never to speake of what shee should heare or see, and she faithfully promised to keep counsel. When she came to the house of meeting there were five women more; the two chiefs were Mother Benefield and Mother Goodwin: this Mother Goodwin pulled out a Booke, they prayed out of it, and presently six Kittens about a weeke old in Mother Benefield's lap, and after she had kissed them, she said unto Rebecca that those were all her children which she had by as handsome a man as any was in England – then Mother Benefield called to mother West, and asked if she were sure that her daughter Rebecca would keepe counsel, or else she might seeke all their blood. She answered, Rebecca had promised. They all then replyed, if shee ever did speake of it that shee should suffer more tortures and paines on earth. Presently mother Benefield said, for more certainty let her take our Covenant and Oath as we have already done. Then they taught her what to say, to beleeve as they did, and to serve and obey as they did. Shortly after, when she was going to bed, appeared unto her a handsome young man, saying that he came to marry her. The manner was thus: he took her by the hand, and leading her about the roome, said, I take thee Rebecca to be my wife, and doe promise to be thy loving husband till death, defending, thee from all harmes; then he told her what shee must say, whereupon she

took him by the hand and said, I Rebecca take thee to be my husband, and
doe promise to be an obedient wife till death, faithfully to performe and
observe all thy commands; And being asked by the Judge whether she ever
had carnall copulation with the handsome young man, she confessed that
she had. She further affirmed, that when she was going to the Grand Inquest
with one mother Miller she told mother Miller that shee would confesse
nothing, if they pulled her to pieces with pincers: she said she found her selfe
in such extremity of torture and amazement, that she would not endure it
againe for the world: and when she looked upon the ground shee saw her
selfe encompassed in flames of fire: and presently the Grand Inquest called
for her, where they admit but one at a time, and so soone as she was thus
separated from this mother Miller, the tortures and the flames beganne to
cease: whereupon she then confessed all shee ever knew, and said that so
soone as her confession was fully ended, she found her conscience so satisfied
and disburdened of all her tortures, that she thought her selfe the happiest
creature in the world: (The Confession of Rebecca West, daughter to Anne
West of Colchester in Essex.)

This sounds very much like the clandestine meeting of dissident women
Christians, and what was this book out of which Mother Goodwin read if not
the Bible? Having taken a sacred vow of secrecy it is not surprising that she was
wracked with guilt and fear of divine punishment for informing on her mother
and her co-believers. It was only when separated from them that she confessed
and then, according to the official version, felt at ease.

There is another version of her confession in which the kittens and the
young man all vanish, but far more detail was given of the witches' evil plans. If,
however, the imps and devilish plots are removed we are left with:

The Confession of Rebecca West,
Taken before the said Justices at Mannyntree, the 21 of March, 1645.
This Examinant saith, that about a moneth since, the aforesaid Anne Leech,
Elizabeth Gooding, Hellen Clark, Anne West, and this Examinant, met all
together at the house of the aforesaid Elizabeth Clark in Mannyntree, where
they together spent some time in praying----, and every one in order went
to prayers; afterwards some of them read in a book, the book being Elizabeth
Clarks; And lastly this Examinant saith, that having thus done, this Examinant,
and the other five, did appoint the next meeting to be at the said Elizabeth
Goodings house, and so departed all to their owne houses.

More or less contemporaneously with this case across the Atlantic in New
England, Anne Hutchinson was being interrogated by the Governor of
Massachusetts. Anne Hutchinson's group, which was linked to the Reverend

John Cotton (from a Suffolk family), was specifically accused of antinomianism, or in other words rejecting moral laws.

If Governor Winthrop had been as good at distortion and persecution as Stearne, his description of the interview might have read something like this:

> Mrs Hutchinson, as she confessed, said that four voices came to her called My Beloved, Moses, John Baptist and as she confessed the Antichrist. It was these voices or spirits that did lead her on so to miscall those godly Ministers as she confessed. She claimed that these spirits spoke to her soul. She then began to call down curses upon the governor and his children, as she confessed. The governor spoke of the troublesomeness of the spirits that she had within her.

Anne Hutchinson spoke with Moses, and the woman Richmond in Bramford spoke with the prophet Daniel. Stearne makes a further reference to Anne West, Rebecca West's mother:

> But one thing observe, that the Devil imitates God in all things as he can, much after the Book of Common Prayer. Then in his outward Worship. She likewise confessed that her mother prayed constantly (and, as the world thought, very seriously) but she said it was to the Devil, using these words, Oh my God, my God, meaning him, and not the LORD.

Thus, depending on how the case of Anne Hutchinson and the case of Anne West is recorded, we can see how Winthrop the governor of Massachusetts, an intolerant but basically decent and straightforward man, would have recorded Anne West as a religious dissident and how Stearne, who gives the impression of being neither of these things, would have recorded Anne Hutchinson as a witch.

There is strong reason, therefore, for suspecting that these Manningtree women and a scattering of the other victims of the witchfinders were in fact groups of women Puritans, related to the groups becoming known as Quakers. There were of course all kinds of small dissident groups – Ranters, Waiters, Searchers, and Fifth Monarchy Men – and Fox had not yet organised the Quakers into a coherent group. It is impossible to be certain, and it hardly matters to what particular strand of religious dissent they belonged.

To the Presbyterian establishment, male ministers who deviated from standard Presbyterian theology or suggested that each congregation be free to choose its own minister were bad enough and not to be tolerated, but that groups of poor village women should be doing the same thing was intolerable. In that sense, a feminist or gender-based explanation for some aspects of the witch trials is one major factor in what was going on.

The Ranters Ranting:

W ITH

The apprehending, examinations, and confession of *Iohn Collins,* *I. Shakefpear, Tho. Wiberton,* and five more which are to anfwer the next Seffions. And feverall fongs or catches, which werefung at their meetings. Alfo their feveral kinds of mirth, and dancing. Their blafphemous opinions, Their belief concerning heaven and hell. And the reafon why one of the fame opinion cut off the heads of his own mother and brother. Set forth for the further difcovery of this ungodly crew.

LONDON
Printed by *B. Alfop, 1650*

The Ranters Ranting. This attack on the alleged behaviour of English religious radicals includes several themes taken from earlier illustrations of the meetings of witches and the kiss by which they honoured Satan. (British Library)

The persecution of Quakers continued after the witch trials, under circum-stances which make it clear that it was their beliefs that were the real cause. Once again, however, it was not Quaker beliefs as such that were the formal reason for their punishment. For example, a travelling preacher would be whipped, not as a Quaker, but as a vagabond; attendants at a Quaker meeting would be charged with keeping a disorderly house. Any history of the Quakers will underline the emotional intensity of their beliefs, leading to visionary experiences and behaviour similar to possession; the importance of women, especially women preachers, in the early movement; and the degree of virulent persecution that they suffered throughout the Interregnum and Restoration, which not infrequently charged them with sexual immorality and denounced them as secret, hypocritical agents of the Devil. The title alone of Ellis Bradshaw's attack on James Naylor, *The Quakers whitest divell unvailed or their sheeps cloathing pulled off that their woolvish inside may be easily discerned*, shows how Quakers were seen as the Devil's agents. Naylor replied by writing *The Railer Rebuked*, in which Naylor charged that Bradshaw had only discovered (revealed) a dark Devil in himself. Both men meant this literally.

The persecution of female Quaker preachers in New England clearly reveals the connection with witchcraft; I have only selected a few cases. In 1656, two women preachers, Mary Fisher and Ann Austin, arrived in Boston after a visit to Barbados in which they spoke against slavery. In Boston they fell foul of the governor by calling him 'thou'. They were imprisoned and, very significantly for my argument, stripped and searched as witches, held under harsh terms of complete isolation and then sent back to England. The main Quaker source for the persecutions in New England, Edward Burrough, describes the event as follows: 'Two honest and innocent women stripped stark naked and searched after such an inhumane manner as modesty will not permit particularly to mention.'

The degree to which intense religious belief could empower ordinary women is also very clearly demonstrated. Mary Fisher was originally a housemaid. After her experiences in New England she then went to the Ottoman Empire and gained an audience before Sultan Mehmet IV, who heard her preach and received her writings (which he might well have found similar to Sufism if he ever examined them).

In Ipswich, the situation was more complicated for, perhaps uniquely, two members of the town oligarchy, Samuel and Robert Duncon, were themselves Quakers. Robert Duncon, a tanner, was to be bailiff three times in the Commonwealth. He, along with Edward Plumstead, were both MPs in the nominated Parliament of 1653, the 'Barebones Parliament.'

In 1656 George Whitehead, one of the most significant early Quaker leaders, was imprisoned in Bury St Edmunds. He was sentenced to be 'beaten till his back be bloody' as a vagrant, but really this was for his preaching in Bures. That year, the diarist John Evelyn recounts visiting Quakers in prison in Ipswich.

A QVAKER

Weake as you say we are, yett wee commands
all flesh to fall, that doth againct us, stand.
The light within us, of such force tis found,
showld satan come, twill lay him on the ground.

The Light they talke of keepes a heavy rout,
ile search all corners, but ile find it out.
By yea and nay, she is a dareing Gurle,
ile try a fall, or els I am a Churle.

With face of brass, this woman that you see
most Impudently doth afirm, that shee,
The mind of God, in all poynts, more doth know,
then from the Sacred Scriptures, ere could flaw.
Presumptious wretch: it were more fitt that shee,
at home showld keepe, and mind hir howsewifery,
And if noe meanes to live on, woorke for bread,
then idlye gossop with hir maget head.
Their light within doth so prevayle,
it makes them hot about the tayle.
Exsept afreind that poynt doth cleare,
they could them selves in pecces teare.

An engraving of a Quaker woman preacher inspired by the Devil. The original inspiration for this engraving was a painting of a Quaker meeting with a woman preacher, by the Dutch artist Egbert van Heemskerk who worked in London during the reign of Charles II. (© The Trustees of the British Museum)

In Colchester, according to John Gough, James Parnell was imprisoned in the castle in a special cell called 'the Oven', high up in the castle wall. Parnell, who was not out of his teens, had to reach his cell by climbing a ladder and then a rope. This he had to do every day to get his food. One day he fell to his death, although the gaolers claimed he had starved himself.

That year Quakers were also being whipped and imprisoned in Ipswich, Massachusetts. In 1658 John Causton was imprisoned in Ipswich and kept in an unheated cell throughout the winter, dying of exposure. A little later, the Mayor of Colchester was encouraging mobs to set about Quaker women using clubs with nails in them.

After George Whitehead had been released from imprisonment in Bury he continued his career, and seems to have provoked an argument with the minister at Hoxne who had him sent to prison in Ipswich for about sixteen weeks in 1658. Whitehead recalled that he was better treated in the Ipswich prison and:

> ... my dear friend Robert Duncon of Ipswich making application to his uncle Duncon of Ipswich (as I remember) and to Justice Edgar I was set at liberty from that imprisonment.
>
> After I was released from my imprisonment at Ipswich, as before related, I had very good and comfortable service – in several places in the country, particularly at Trembly [Trimley, near Felixstowe] and Walton Side [part of modern Felixstowe, near Landguard Fort] in Suffolk and at Harwich, Manningtree, Colchester and other places in Essex.
>
> A meeting of our friends with me, being desired in the town of Ipswich, some weeks after my release out of prison and our honest Friend Timothy Grimble (Ship Master) and Mary his wife – but our adversaries in that town, still possessed with prejudice and envy against us.
>
> (George Whitehead, *The Christian Progress of George Whitehead*
> *that Ancient Servant & Minister of Jesus Christ*.)

Timothy Grimble and the others at the meeting were indicted for keeping a disorderly house, and amongst those present was Robert Duncon. The charge seems eventually to have been dropped. The Duncons also appear in a pamphlet called *Quakerism A Grand Imposture* (1715), one of a series of anti-Quaker pamphlets issued by Francis Bugg of Mildenhall in Suffolk, whose aunt, Anne Docwra, was a Quaker preacher. Bugg himself had been a Quaker, and later an informant against Quakers. Here Bugg is pursuing the common charge that Quakers were sexually immoral:

> Stephen Crisp, going to Norwich by Mendelsham, and tho' cautioned by Robert Duncon to carry wifely with his cousin, Samuel Duncon's wife, yet

THE QVAKERS DREAM:

O R,
The Devil's Pilgrimage in England :
BEING

An infallible Relation of their several Meetings,

Shreekings, Shakings, Quakings, Roarings, Yellings, Howlings, Tremblings in the Bodies, and Risings in the Bellies : With a Narrative of their several Arguments, Tenets, Principles, and strange Dœtrine : The strange and wonderful Satanical Apparitions, and the appearing of the Devil unto them in the likeness of a black Boar, a Dog with flaming eyes, and a black man without a head, causing the Dogs to bark, the Swine to cry, and the Cattel to run, to the great admiration of all that shall read the same.

Free-vvill.

walk answerable to the light within you.

be thou merry.

Above Ordinances

London, Printed for G. Horton, and are to be sold at the Royal Exchange in Cornhil, 1655.

The Quakers Dream. This uses much of the same imagery as the *Ranters Ranting* and shows very clearly how religious radicalism was linked to devil worship in the minds of the established church. (British Library)

A Neſt of Serpents 12

Diſcovered.

OR,

A knot of old Heretiques revived,

Called the

ADAMITES.

Wherein their originall, increaſe, and ſeverall ridiculous tenets are plainly layd open.

Downe
luſt

Printed in the yeare 1641.

A Nest of Serpents. An attack on members of the Adamite sect in London. Little is known
for certain about the English Adamites, but they were believed to hold their meetings in the
nude, just as Adam had lived in Eden before the fall. (British Library)

having set up his horse in Norwich, went to Sam. Duncon's house, takes his wife up into the Chamber and there kept her to 10 a clock at Night. Nay his son in law told me that looking through a crevice of the door he saw Stephen upon the bed with Hester Milksopp of Ipswich, another female Preacher, very sweet together, not fit to be spoken, and this I know, that when I was a Quaker with them we looked upon him little better than a Ranter.

(Francis Bugg, *Quakerism A Grand Imposture, Or, the Picture of Quakerism Continued.*)

He is also seeking to undermine the testimony that the Quakers had given in support of James Parnell, the teenage preacher who died in Colchester castle: Stephen Crisp had given him a character reference.

In 1660 Robert Duncon was released from his imprisonment for refusing to swear an oath of allegiance to Charles II (as Quakers refused to swear oaths), as part of a general pardon to Quakers.

In 1666, according to Clarke's *History of Ipswich*, Robert Duncon wrote to the bailiffs of Ipswich asking that five Quakers held in gaol should be liberated.

In 1677 when George Fox went into exile in Holland, Robert Duncon was amongst those who saw him off at Harwich.

8

WITCHES AND THE POOR

Telling her that if she would serve him she should want Nothing.

It is rather too simplistic to explain witchcraft trials as a way of policing the poor. It is far too complex to be reduced to any single cause. However, it is very obvious that poverty was deeply connected with witchcraft. What the trial cases of witches show in an overwhelming and obvious fashion is that witches, including the smaller group of male witches, were three things: they were very poor, they were powerless, and they had no powerful friends or backers. Most seem to have been illiterate.

Witchfinders themselves, while convinced that witches were agents of Satan, nevertheless saw them as essentially pathetic rather than powerful. Stearne wrote that, while in many instances one could see sinners benefitting temporarily in worldly terms from their sinning, he had never known of a case where a witch – in his terms a 'hurting' witch – was materially better off. This is how he puts it:

> … but as for that I think it is seldom or never known, that any get estates or thrive, that thus give themselves over to Satan, bur rather consume their estates, if they have any: yet the word of God says, The wicked man thrives as well as the godly in this world: But for Witches, I never knew any.

Stearne's stories and the depositions often make reference to people hoping to get money; whether it be the rusty coins in a lord's strong box, some money hidden under bushes, or a man's despair at losing his money. Indeed, the number of cases in which the accused confesses how she had dreamt of a figure saying that he would be a good husband to her and provide for her, points the same way.

The depositions or witness statements for the Bury trial sometimes describe the incident that caused the alleged witch to attack their victim. These incidents are all connected to neighbourly disputes, and usually to the denial of minor requests for charity:

The Ipswich cucking stool.
(Ipswich Museum)

A falling out with oaths (Ann Ellis Mettingham).

Victim denied her husband a load of hay (Ellen Crispe Sweslinge).

Victim denied her woodchips from a tree he was felling (Thomasine Ratliff).

Because the victim took her collection from her.

Because he would not give her relief (Maria Bush of Bacton).

Because the victim denied her a pint of butter (Margaret Benet of Bacton).

Because she was denied a pot of beer (Anne Palmer of Framlingham).

The victim gave her some milk but not as much as she wished (Mary Edwards).

The victim had taken away a hat which Mary Edwards had just taken from a relative of the victim.

Victim had asked for 12 shillings which she owed him (Mary Lackland).

Victim refused to lend a needle and asked her to return a shilling previously lent her (Mary Lackland).

Witchcraft in seventeenth-century England is definitely linked to poverty and misery. This is not inevitable – there is a typical African pattern in which it is the man who gets rich and powerful, while his extended family stays poor, who is most likely to be accused. Deaths amongst his relatives may be signs that he has sacrificed them to gain his success. Witchcraft becomes an idiom for explaining how some individuals gain undeserved wealth and success at the expense of the community,

In many parts of the world certain people have a link to spirits in animal shape – familiars. In most parts of the world this familiar ('bush soul' in Nigerian English, 'nagu al' in Mexico) is a powerful, and dangerous wild animal, a leopard, crocodile or jaguar. But in England it could be an insect, vermin, even shellfish, at best a dog or maybe a cat.

Inescapably then, we must look at the position of the poor. The pre-Reformation Church had dealt with poverty through the concept of religious charity, especially of funeral gifts to the poor, an act which would help the soul of the dead in Purgatory. The concept was captured vividly in the famous 'Lyke Wake Dirge', first recorded by John Aubrey in 1686, but which he said was at least as old as 1616:

> If ever thou gavest meat or drink,
> The fire sall never make thee shrink;
> If meat or drink thou ne'er gav'st nane,
> The fire will burn thee to the bare bane;

However, the whole concept of Purgatory had been eradicated root and branch from the Church of England. By now, society leaders wanted more than unconditional handouts. They wanted targeted schemes to reward and care for the deserving poor and schemes to get the work-shy set to work.

There were several factors creating a crisis amongst the rural poor. Both their number and the depth of their poverty seems to have been growing, Explanations include a series of poor harvests, a period of very severe winters in which the Thames regularly froze, and hyperinflation caused by import of Spanish silver from the New World. Gaskill has pointed out that the price of grain had risen by 15 per cent and of livestock by 12 per cent. They governed the price of food. However, wages and the amounts disbursed as parish charity had stayed the same.

Early Tudor law controlling the poor had been ferocious. The village memory of the poor would have been imprinted vividly, with memories of legislation imposing branding, ear-boring, flogging, enslavement or even hanging for the able-bodied poor deemed work-shy, especially the vagrant.

In 1554, it was made a hanging offence simply to be a gypsy (Romani), or to join the gypsies or pretend to be a gypsy. It is interesting that the authorities' anger was also directed at anyone joining the gypsies or pretending to be gypsies – a feature of Romani society is that settled people have always been able to enter Romani life if they adhere to Romani purity rules. This has enabled some families and some individuals to pass to and fro from settled life to traveller. The wording of this Elizabethan law strongly suggests that some of the English rural poor were leaving house life for the travelling life.

The Act, legitimising a sort of genocide, was in force until 1783, ready on the books if the local magistrates felt they needed it. The law was not, however, just a sleeping tiger. It was used, and the main period of actual persecution seems to have been in the 1640s. In 1641, William Hawkes of Bury was paid 10s a quarter for an apprentice gypsy child. In 1646, William Hawkins of Bury was paid £5 a year 'to keep a poor child who is an innocent and a child of one who was formerly executed as an Egipitian'. Quite possibly this was the same man who had a convenient deal with the council, in which his friends paid him out of the public purse to take care of children legally separated from their parents, and profit from their labour. In 1649, John Holmes the gaoler was paid to take Egyptians to Bury assizes. At this Bury assize, eleven gypsies were hanged.

In 1645, the famous Act for the Relief of the Poor was only forty-four years old, having been passed right at the end of Elizabeth's reign in 1601. This law made the poor the responsibility of every parish within the kingdom, and co-opted very large numbers of the rural gentry into operating it. The local well-to-do were charged with setting themselves a rate from which to support the local poor. The poor were divided into two classes: 'the impotent poor', those who for whatever reason could not work, being disabled, sick or elderly, and those deemed work-shy. Reyce (*Breviary of Suffolk*) gives a general snapshot of the Suffolk poor from the perspective of the rich, criticising their complaints about the burden that the poor represented:

… the corrupt and froward judgement of many in these dayes, who esteeme the multitude of our poore heere to bee matter of heavy burden, and a sore discommoditie, thinking that no greife is greater than their own, so no incommoditie to bee greater than that which is where they dwell. Butt if such did remember that as well the poore as the rich cannott stand withoutt the poore, of if they did see how far the nomber of the poore in other shires do exceed ours, they would nott esteeme of oure poore as a burden, butt as a looking glasse wherein the rich may see his owne estate, if once the Lord should bereave him of his benefitts which he doth dayly abuse. Indeed I must say as it hath pleased the Lord to voutsafe us some poore, so what with powerfull effort of the prevayling word, and the due regard of the commanding law. Much charitable reliefe is heere used, so that few there bee that goe unrelieved, whither they bee poore by impotence or by casualty. As for the thriftles poore, whither hee bee riotous, idle person, or vagabond, the list of the late godly lawes, if it may still by execution bee increased, will so reform the quality of them, or diminish the number of them that here will bee much spared to add to the reliefe of the other.

Which can be modernised as:

… complain too much of the heavy burden and painful inconvenience of the large numbers of the poor here, because they believe that no one bears a heavier burden of grief than them and no inconveniences are greater than those where they live. But if they would only remember that the rich would not survive without the poor, or if they saw how much greater the number of the poor is in other counties than Suffolk they would not see our poor as a burden, but as a looking glass in which the rich can see what their own position would be if the Lord should strip them of the advantages which they misuse everyday. Indeed I have to say that just as it has pleased the Lord to entrust us with some poor, so because of the powerful effect of the successful Preaching of the Gospel, and the necessary care of the commands of the law much charitable support is common here, so that there are few that are left unsupported, whether they are poor due to lack of ability or due to an accident.

As for the irresponsible poor, whether they are antisocial and idle or a wanderer, the number of the recent Godly laws if they are really put into operation, will either improve their nature or reduce their number, that there will be substantial savings to help the other poor.

This is a classic statement of the basic English categorisation of the poor into the genuinely unfortunate, those without the ability to work, the impotent poor, and those who were 'thriftless vagabonds'.

Charity and the administration of the poor in Ipswich was a large and quite complex feature of corporate life. It was organised through Christ's Hospital, which had been set up in the former Blackfriars Priory, which also housed the grammar school, Christ's Hospital School and the bridewell. A term as a guide, treasurer or warden at Christ's Hospital, helping the administration of the place, was an essential step on the upward career of any seventeenth-century Ipswich oligarch. Christ's Hospital in Ipswich was a large and, for its day, efficient organisation, something no rural parish could expect to run.

Considerable power was delegated to the four wardens of Christ Church who were almost always ex-bailiffs. They had been delegated by the council with the authority to:

> … enquire and examine diligently – all and all manner of suspicious houses, taverns, inns, gaming houses, ludos saltarios and other suspicious places – or idle ruffians, slothful vagrants, vagabonds and sturdy beggars and other suspected persons whatsoever and men and women of bad name and reputation – That masterless idle persons, hedge breakers, harlots drunkards & shall be sent to the Hospital and whipp'd and forced to work. At their entrance the Guide shall have two pence for every such person and shall take the benefit of their work for their maintenance.

> Four beadles to be appointed to have the care and oversight of the House of Correction and to restrain all poor people from begging and to set them on to work and to punish all rogues and vagabonds: four were elected to be paid £5 yearly to be levied by the church wardens.
>
> (Sessions, 12 May 1627.)

There are several accounts demonstrating how the town had set up a preaching place in Christ's Hospital, so that the incarcerated poor would not be denied instruction. The corporation awarded the hospital the monopoly of candle-making within Ipswich so that its inmates laboured unpaid at a lucrative trade with which to fund its activities.

In 1597, a survey of the poor was carried out in Ipswich and from it we learn that the writer was suggesting that the council should purchased forty spinning wheels to replace the use of the distaff, and instruct the poor in their use, and also that a rope maker had been encouraged to move from Barnstaple in Devon and set up business in Ipswich in the Rope Walk.

There were educational charities funding the Grammar School, Christ's Hospital School, a town library for the lecturer and to provide scholarships for local boys at Cambridge. There were business charities: nineteen separate charities were rolled into one unit called the Lending Cash Fund. This fund lent money to enterprising men just starting on their careers. They got the money interest free for different periods of years, and then were supposed to repay the original sum. In some cases they were expected to give a proportion of their profits to the Lending Cash Fund to increase the amount it had available for more loans. White's gift, for example, financed a sum of £104 which had been lent to four poor freemen for four years interest free, with any profits to be made over to the fund.

Trading in Ipswich was restricted to freemen of the borough. Foreigners, that is those English people not freemen of Ipswich, were subject to all kinds of extra charges and payments if allowed to trade at all. One charity was set up to undermine this system of local protectionism by having as its aim the payment of all such charges on the behalf of incomers to Ipswich.

Provision for the poor was the most significant though. The principle provisions for the poor were Tooley's (1550) and Smart's (1598) almshouses. Smart's charities really were all-encompassing; they included repairing St Mary Tower church; £20 to the poor; twelve gowns annually for the poor; support to twenty poor and virtuous maids; scouring and cleaning the port; providing wood, seacoal, butter and cheese to the poorest drapers and taylors in the town; providing poor scholars in the Grammar School with books, ink, paper and convenient apparel; money as a gift to the master and usher of the school and supporting his almshouses; to support and repair the two hospitals (St Lazarus and St Edmund Pulteney); to help the poor prisoners in the Common Gaol and provision to buy grain for the poor.

Reference is made to a fund called 'The Poor's Corn', while Scrivener's charity provided £7 a year to be spent on gowns, shirts and smocks. Hunwick's charity was administered by Colchester, which sent the Ipswich poor £10 a year. Hunt's 1635 charity provided £100 annually to be lent to five poor tradesmen and the interest used to buy shirts and shifts for the poor. A more modest gift was that of Leonard Carston, who left money to buy bread to feed thirty poor.

Then there were single payments too; Mr Baxter gave the hospital £20 and Thomas Goodings also gave £20 to the hospital. In exceptionally bad years, even Sir Edmund Withipole (usually at total loggerheads with the town authorities) had given money to purchase Baltic rye for the poor. All the smaller charities tended to be organised through Christ's Hospital. These were charities for the whole town, and there was another layer of charities set up to benefit the poor of each of the parishes. The records do show genuine leadership, care and compassion for the unfortunate.

That is one side of the story ...

However, it is also clear that substantial sums of land, rents and ready money were floating around the system, structured in complex ways. It is pretty obvious that there were all kinds of opportunities for the less than perfectly scrupulous amongst a tightly organised bunch of self-selected businessmen, monopolising posts in the corporation. When the town council applied the reserves in Christ's Hospital to paying for the war, they were not working for personal benefit as such, but they were still clearly breaching the terms of the charities.

We don't have any evidence for corruption at this date, but in 1747 a book entitled *An Enquiry into the Gifts and Legacies of the Town of Ipswich* was published. It was the report of a damning internal enquiry into how various sums of money had been administered:

> … and then the poor men whose property the overplus [on the charities] is might be satisfied that they are not defrauded of it; at present it is certain they are.
>
> (Canning, *An Enquiry into the Gifts and Legacies of the Town of Ipswich*, p.101.)

> … that care should be taken to prevent persons who are employ'd in furnishing the Bread and Cloaths from imposing upon the poor, and in the modern phrase, which every man in the Corporation knows the meaning of, from making a jobb of it. The bread, the linen and the woollen are brought for the poor, not with the town's money, but with their own.
>
> (Canning, *An Enquiry into the Gifts and Legacies of the Town of Ipswich*, p.154.)

In other words, those with the contracts for supplying the hospital were providing sub-standard goods at greatly inflated prices. The same book claimed that not a penny of the lending money fund was being used correctly.

Poor children could also have been taken in to a parish house so that they could be looked after, educated and then bound as an apprentice, to work unpaid for a master who was paid by the parish for feeding and clothing and training them. If a boy or girl was being educated in a skill for life that would enable them to take up a reasonable place in the community, this was a kind and generous act. However, if a master got a subsidy from the parish as well as a child to provide him with unpaid hard manual labour for seven years with no skill at the end of it, it was something else again.

East Anglia was a major source of emigrants for the New World, and Ipswich was at the centre of the migration. In 1640, Samuel Ward accused Matthew Wren, Bishop of Norwich, of driving 3,000 people from East Anglia into exile in New England. Wren's defence was that it was poverty and poor wages that drove them. Both charges were true.

There is some indication that Ipswich may have been involved, not only in voluntary emigration to the New World, but in compulsory emigration of pauper children as bonded apprentices. This was to become quite common practice in many port towns under the Restoration, lasting until the American War of Independence, and is the subject of a full-length study by Peter Wilson Coldham in *Emigrants in Chains*.

Hawstead panels. It shows a black man smoking, with the caption 'as outside so within'.
The association between enslaved Africans and the Virginia plantations is already made.
(Ipswich Museum)

The indications of such a trade to and from Suffolk are as follows:

1   1618 recorded the first burial of a black slave in Suffolk.

2   Captain John Dameron of Ipswich appears in different sources as the captain of the ship *Deuty* that arrived in Virginia in 1619, carrying about fifty poor children to be apprenticed as servants. In 1620, he shipped another 150 or so on the *Diana*. After delivering the child apprentices, the *Diana* was sent northwards to trade and fish in Canada. A letter from John Pory to the Virginia Company, dated 17 June 1620, indicates that John Dameron had made a number of other such voyages, because he was arguing over the best course over the sea:

> JOHN DAMYRON not withstandige he made a kinde of a
> vowe upon our untoward northerly passage in ye *Dyana* that
> he would never stand ye like course for Virginia againe
> preferred now obedyence before sacrafice, and followed ye
> companyes directions by ye way of ye north, and by
> longe contynuance at sea (besides other inconveyence)
> lost to ye colony ye benefytt of those silkworms which
> his majesty had so gratiously bestowed upon us.

The Dameron family had built up lands in Nacton, and the extended family in Ipswich are often mentioned both as successful traders and people in trouble with the council. A Bailiff of Ipswich, Tobias Blosse, acquired most of their Nacton land. Katherine Dameron was tried for a witch in Ipswich in 1640 but acquitted. The Damerons were near neighbours to Mary Lackland.

3   Although the king was trying to set up a silk industry in Virginia, the colony was finally becoming profitable based on the sale of tobacco and there was a growing need for cheap labour. This trade was of direct interest to Robert Rich, whose political and financial interest in Virginia has already been mentioned. Rich, through his captain Daniel Elfrith, first brought slaves to Virginia in 1619.

In 1643 Edmund Calamy, Rich's conscience and leading minister had been appointed by Parliament as collector of donations to transport children from Ireland and England to New England. This was to turn into a voyage organised by the corporation for the 'propagation of the Gospel' in New England, in which 200 children were transported and settled there. Finding them the passage money to make a new start in the colonies sounds quite laudable. Benevolence could mask crude exploitation, however. In reality, the system was soon to become abused co-existing as it did with the growth of plantation slavery. Soon laws were passed that equated a days absence from labour with an additional year of servitude, and apprentices were forced into debt for food and clothes, and not a few masters realised that an apprentice who did not survive their apprenticeship was an apprentice who did not need the final cash payment and land grant they were supposed to receive. They became, in effect if not law, white slaves working alongside enslaved Africans.

On 9 May 1645, Parliament passed an ordinance against the stealing of children with permission to search vessels and ships: 'All such lewd persons as shall steal, sell buy inveigle purloin convey or receive any little children' were to be imprisoned without bail and meanwhile a proper punishment was to be decided for such people. This law was to be publicised as widely as possible. In connection with this legislation, the Borough of Bristol began recording the details of all apprentices shipped to English colonies from 1654 to prove this had been done legally and that they were not stolen children.

4   In 1645 some witches confessed to sexual relationships with black men in circumstances that strongly suggest they are talking about real people, presumably slaves.

A few decades later Evelyn, in his travel diaries, was to note that there were absolutely no beggars in Ipswich owing to the actions of the magistrates, but he had no idea how they managed it. Was he perhaps being ironic? Port towns have always had a bad reputation when it comes to finding men to crew ships. It would have been very surprising if the waterfront taverns of Ipswich did not have their share of crimps. A hundred or so years later Aberdeen Council was convicted of having organised child theft to supply plantations in the American colonies. The people involved in the trade in stealing children were called spirits and the children were said to be spirited away.

A less prosperous town or a rural parish could not support either the elaborate charitable provisions or the possibilities of corruption that were open to rich port towns like Ipswich. In the seventeenth century an active adult, temporarily ill or injured, could be expected to either return to work or to die. A poor child would fairly soon be able to labour. So neither was likely to be a charge on the local Poor Law for long. But the older poor, especially the women, had little value as unskilled labourers anymore. A poor widow in good repute amongst her neighbours and with the local vicar, had a chance of a secure place in an almshouse.

Most could not expect to be so lucky. If they were sickly and unable to work fully or make a go of life as a cottager, they inevitably became a long-term burden on the poor rate, and indeed a burden on the whole community in all sorts of minor ways. Good neighbours in a village would look after each other; they offered help in a myriad of tiny but vital ways. But the point is that everybody did it for everybody else, they each took turns in helping. These were people who would not ever be able to return the favour or balance the books. They needed all the help they could get, and more each year as they got older just to barely get by themselves, so that they never had the power to repay. Bitterness and depression were their constant temptation. They could become the sort of people that we would currently say 'were always on the earhole', complaining, whining and generally making a nuisance of themselves.

The specific details of the depositions, and the more general remarks of Stearne and others show that it was precisely these people who were often accused of being witches. In so very many of the witchcraft accusations one can see the breakdown of what were obviously at one stage, neighbourly and affectionate relationships, of misunderstood acts of kindness towards children (for example, offering them apples), even in the later Lowestoft cases of breastfeeding them. In other words, of community relations finally rupturing under the stresses of life.

Before the Reformation charity was a religious duty and the uncharitable could expect punishment not only in Purgatory but in this life too. The Puritans taught that misfortunes were punishments sent by God to turn sinners towards him. A farmer or successful cottager experiencing a run of bad luck had the alternatives of either believing that it was God's punishment for his lack of charity to the poor, or that God was punishing him for his secret sins, or that he was an innocent victim, unjustly being attacked by a wicked witch.

A series of witchcraft accusations, a trial and an execution could actually release the tensions of decades and resolve them in acts of cathartic vengeance and violence. The witch was the human sacrifice that allowed the village community to continue to exist. The community could carry on believing in its goodhearted neighbourly ways, rather than face its own failure of compassion.

Potential Royalists amongst villagers were another group of malcontents. Malcolm Gaskill, and others, have suggested that some witches were connected in some way with the Royalists, and there is certainly conclusive evidence that Parliamentary propaganda in general accused the Royalists of witchcraft. This charge was all the easier to make because of Buckingham's hated 'wizard', Dr Lambe, and the charge that Buckingham's mother had bewitched the king. Prince Rupert was the principal target of such accusations, including the famous assertion that his dog 'Boy' was a familiar. Two or three depositions do, in fact, make specific connections between witchcraft and at least a lack of enthusiasm for the Parliamentary cause, but I would say that the evidence points more to this being an individual feature of some cases rather than a major element. The Everards at Halesworth were said to have sent imps to help Prince Rupert, and Anne Smith's son at Great Glemham had apparently ridden off to join the Royalists with one of his mother's imps for company. Glemham saw large numbers of accused. The lord of the manor, Sir Henry Glemham, was a leading Royalist, fighting with the king.

Some of those accused of witchcraft were those amongst the poor who did not accept the system, and who broke the law. It is pretty obvious that Thomas Everard of Halesworth was some kind of poacher; he had had weird experiences when out with his dogs and he had sent his imps to kill deer and a sheep. If Everard was a poacher, then Anne Randall at Lavenham may have been something of a militant. Amongst her crimes was the use of her imps to remove bushes which the lord of the manor, Henry Copinger, had laid out ready for planting. At first sight this might seem a rather pointless crime but,

A Dutch image of two beggars.
(© The Trustees of the British Museum)

as Gaskill has pointed out, these bushes were probably to be used as a part of a hedge to enclose lands for private use by the lord. Certainly this particular case was not a simple squabble between villagers, but between a very poor woman and her lord in which she was to end up accused of causing the death of his daughter.

A stray case, at an earlier date than the main witch-hunt, also seems to link witchcraft and poaching. It relates to Christchurch Mansion in Ipswich. Christchurch had a fine deer park and this attracted poachers, including one case which frustratingly hides what may have been a far more interesting story:

> Nicholas Sanders indicted for killing and carrying away a deer out of the park of Sir William Withipole and formerly pleaded not guilty: now *relict venific* he pleads guilty-Judgement that he remains in prison for a day.
>
> (Sessions of the Peace, 1 Jan 1637.)

What makes this so intriguing is that the phrase *relict venefic* appears to mean the 'widower of a witch'. To be precise, *veneficia* was a form of natural magic which depended not on demons but on the natural powers of potions, poisons and drugs to achieve its results. Why did this cause Nicholas to change his plea? And why did he then get such a light punishment? As we have seen, religious dissidents among the poor were a major target.

Malcolm Gaskill may well be right in suggesting that one of the factors that brought the witch-hunt to a conclusion was the not-inconsiderable costs born by a community in accusing, arresting and holding in prison, trying and then executing very poor people, with no goods of their own from which the costs could be recovered. If an external expert – a witchfinder – was called in, then the cost increased a great deal. He writes:

> Silver was cherished and its expenditure – even, in due course, on witchfinding – was resented.

> The crowd that enjoyed the executions of John Lowes and the others soon found themselves paying for the privilege, and forced to reconsider the wisdom of witch-hunting in that light.

> Like the inhabitants of Ipswich, Aldeburgh was now to learn the true price of witch finding, and to realise that--- it was not a sustainable campaign.

However, what we see in Ipswich, Bury, Aldeburgh and elsewhere is that the response to costs was to make the charge a burden on the whole community, so that those in control at the time were clearly gearing up for further costs, not running away from them. The conflict was not so much as to whether to pay or not, but more about *who* was to pay. After all, for the obsessed believer this was a matter of life and death, for individuals and communities.

If Gaskill is right, and the treasurers of towns and parishes were shaking their heads over witch trials because they had cost too much, it is equally possible that the same careful guardians of the communities' finances would have thought of the saving to the parish if various troublemakers were no longer alive to be a burden on the rates. Had every witch accused by Hopkins and Stearne been executed, as was their intent, then Suffolk parishes would not have faced the costs of continuing to support a minimum of 300 people for years on end. Bluntly, yes, there was a cost to killing a poor woman accused of witchcraft, but there was also a cost in continuing to keep a poor woman alive on public charity indefinitely.

It is difficult to know, because of course no one is ever going to confess such motives in writing. Witchcraft trials, for all their expense, offered the local lord of the manor and JP, as well as the local vicar, an opportunity of ridding themselves of local troublemakers and burdens on the rates. It is the case that riots had broken out along the upper Stour, in which resentment at enclosure was just one element, only a few years before Harbottle Grimston, who had been affected directly himself by the riots, launched his anti-witchcraft campaign along the Stour estuary.

9

Re-examining the Trial of Mary Lackland

The justices of the peace may not always expect direct evidence, seeing all their works are workes of darknesse, and no witnesses present with them to accuse them.

So far we have been trying to establish what kind of wider society would feel driven to burn to death an elderly woman, especially when part of the community must have had serious doubts about her guilt. By now, we know that we cannot take accounts of witchcraft at face value, that there are deep currents going on under the surface of our narrative. It is clear that this is true in the case of Mary Lackland. Somewhere, in that nexus of interests and rivalries which criss-crossed her world like a series of live electrical cables, lay the causes which destroyed her. But there are no new accounts, no new facts to reveal what actually happened, to close our case and to put the question of who killed her, and why, to rest once and for all.

However, once the facts can go no further, our imagination can take a leap. We can guess what people said to themselves in privacy, we can use all our skill to imagine the things never committed to any document. This is how I read what happened, how do you read it? Part of the fascination of the subject is due precisely to the fact that it is possible to reach different conclusions.

Starting at the top, one can imagine Robert Rich in his private cabinet in Leaze Hall thinking something like this (these are the words we don't know that he ever spoke; these are the thoughts he would never have recorded):

I am the head of the Essex party. The way forward for England lies in the New World Colonies. There is just so much wealth there lying ready to be picked up. Send our younger sons, send all our discontented, send out all our poor to serve them. Planters need labour, the poor need work. This is the solution. Incidentally, it will make me very wealthy indeed.

England should not be ruled by royal favourites but by us, the peers of the realm in the House of Lords, we *are* England. And who are these Stuarts anyway? Perhaps the Poles have the right idea, the nobles there elect their king. A strong navy, defending our shores for the first time and weakening the power of Catholic Spain.

In any case, I have gone too far ever to retreat now, and I know quite well what happened to the first Robert Devereaux, Earl of Essex, executed for treason – it is family history after all, my grandfather married his sister.

The city merchants did not rise at his call and the lawyers, the Cokes, the Bacons and their like, they brought him down. The same lawyers and the merchants want to use me and my cousin, another Robert, Earl of Essex, to frighten the king so badly that he will do what they want. They will have the king they want, and me and my cousin will face the axe. Harbottle Grimston is one of that crew. It was my influence that gave the Grimstons their start in politics, and now they challenge my family in Harwich? I think not. Essex and Suffolk are my territory and are going to stay that way.

I don't believe a word of all this witchcraft nonsense. My divines tell me it is bad theology. My steward says that the charges are all the result of bullying. I am not going to let Grimston impose his personal rule of terror throughout East Anglia through his two nobodies, the witchfinders Stearne and Hopkins.

Equally, Grimston may have believed or at least told himself that the king was bewitched by his favourites:

The whole court is rotten with wizards. To defeat the king in battle is to free him from enchantment and to go back to the rule of law. There is no way that I, as a lawyer, will sign a Solemn League and Covenant. Merchants want peace, they don't want exciting adventures. If Warwick annoys Spain, where will the Dunkirk raiders hit first? Harwich, Landguard and the Orwell. Warwick will go too far one day with all his projects and schemes, and when he falls I just need to be ready.

I have seen what social unrest will bring, the mobs that caused my neighbours to flee while their mansions were burnt are not far away, and I am not having villagers turn up with torches at my mansion one night. Such unrest amongst the lower orders can only logically be the work of Satan. The only possible explanation for women preaching is the Devil at work and I am going to be vigilant in my own estates. These two, Stearne and Hopkins, get things done, they get the evidence and the results that we want. We can clear the villages of troublemakers, dissidents, the complaining ungrateful poor. I have my ear to the ground in Ipswich through my family members and interests. Women seem to be preaching there too.

Now it is necessary to narrow the focus down to Ipswich. In Ipswich, maritime trade is the source of the town's wealth, and it has always been a risky business. It has been the cause of many a loss, but it has also been the cause of quite a few fortunes. Tobacco, turkeys and the odd black slave are to be seen, while new mansions have already been built on the back of the Virginia trade. Not just sailors, but captains and merchants want to know the future, they want to prevent disasters and they want success. Superstitions of all sorts have always surrounded the sea, and cunning men are to be found in St Clement's, ready and willing to explain why some ships float and others sink, and to do something about it with their 'powers'.

The town council believes firmly in their divine duty to act as godly magistrates, constructing a holy city of Ipswich, but this project is at risk from within and without. Secret sinners can bring down God's wrath on the whole community – plague carriers, whose bodies need to be examined to see if they are carrying the secret marks of infection, and whose very disease is a direct consequence of God's displeasure. Conspiracies of Catholics inspired by Satan, joining with Dunkirk privateers. Master bailiffs are answerable to God for all this, charged with leading their community. The idle, able-bodied poor of all sorts, including Romanis and English who have joined the Romanis, must be whipped into work. The town walls, which have been left to slowly fall down for the last 200 years, have to be put in readiness. Groups of town militia must be organised into watch and ward.

Some councillors have been enjoying the usual profits of the system for years. Properly handled, the Christ's Hospital and the other charities represent a gold mine in terms of supply and building contracts, the labour of the inmates and the outdwellers, issued with their spinning wheels. Planters and settlers in the New World need child apprentices. Despite all the uncertainty and fear, the town is growing – new buildings are going up, and there are many ways such developments can enrich a member of the town's oligarchy.

Now, focus still more, on Mary herself. There are at least three alternative ways in which the story of Mary Lackland can be told. The first 'traditional' explanation is that Mother Lackland had done something that could be understood as witchcraft by the people of the time. We can, if we choose, imagine a deeply embittered woman living in the poorest part of the town on the fringes of the underworld.

For years she has been the terror of the neighbourhood. Her neighbours take trouble to avoid her, but once they realise that she has focused on them, they slap a grin on their face and do their best to ingratiate themselves with her. She has become adept at hinting at her terrible powers, and suggesting in roundabout ways the awful fates of those who have crossed her. If she hears of some disaster, perhaps the sinking of a ship, she may even hint that it was her work, not openly of course, but by suggestion. Thereby, she is able to extort favour after favour. Just try and get her to pay back a debt or turn down a loan she has set her heart on, and see how she reacts.

How she gloated when she heard what had happened to her daughter's former young man. Desperate girls go to see her from time to time, and some of them die in great pain afterwards. There are dark whispers that she knows things that can be added to the food of elderly relatives who live inconveniently long, and can free wives of husbands that they hate. It has long been strongly rumoured that she has done just this herself by removing her husband before his time.

In an attempt to ingratiate herself with the clergy, to make sure she gets any handouts going and as a kind of spiritual insurance policy, she has made a huge show of going to hear sermons, which teach her nothing but how to despise others. Always one to invent and hold on to any possible grievance for a long time, she has been embittered over her dealings with Christ's Hospital. It is the vigilance of the officials of the hospital and of the godly ministers of Ipswich that have brought to light her reign of fear and who, secure in the protection afforded them by their holiness and faith, have dared to challenge her. In this, they have been supported by the campaign carried out by Hopkins and Stearne, and endorsed by such prominent people as the recorders of Ipswich, Harwich, Colchester, Bury St Edmunds and Aldeburgh.

Unless we are prepared to accept the literal reality of her crimes of witchcraft, then this kind of scenario, give or take a few details, seems the only way that one can see the case against Mary Lackland as having been brought in good faith, and a way in which she was indeed guilty of some kind of extortion and active malice.

Another version is that the dominant belief system of the time was a sexually repressed gloomy fanaticism. Its leaders were obsessed with destroying ancient buildings and art. They had no respect for any traditional power, save for their own. They hated beauty in worship, they hated pleasure in life and they especially hated and feared women. They were also totally hypocritical. They used fear of witchcraft as a way of whipping up mobs in order to attack the Crown and imposing an insane rule of fear over the country. Hopkins and Stearne were mad preachers, working more or less on their own. Mary Lackland and the other witches were kindly village healers and midwives – guardians of traditional wisdom, vulnerable women unfortunate enough to be swept up at random. It was just her bad luck that we are discussing her and not her neighbour, Widow 'Anybody'.

There is a third opton – Widow Lackland was selected to be punished for a specific reason, but that reason was *not* witchcraft.

The trial gives her name and that she is a widow. A search through the records of the Borough of Ipswich allows us to learn a little more about her and the small world within Ipswich in which she lived. Around 1595, Mary Lackland was living in St Stephen's parish with her husband, John, who was a barber. A relative, Theophilus Lakeland (Lackland) lived first in St Mary Elms, and then St Peters. However, by the 1620s John and Mary appear to have moved to St Clement's parish, and a few years later John Lackland was old and sick; unable to look after himself or his wife. He was, in fact, being helped by his son George:

> George Lakeland a parishioner of St Clement's rated at 1*d* a week is discharged thereof from henceforth for that he is helpful towards his father's maintenance.
>
> (Sessions, 8 June 1637.)

Later, Mary, now a widow, may having been living with a son called R. Lackland. Both R. Lackland and George Lakeland lived in St Clement's parish close to each other.

So, by the time of the trial she must have been close to 70. We know from the pamphlet that she is poor, for the quarrels are all those of the poor – a request for the return of a 12*s* loan, the return of a needle, the loan of a shilling. We know that witchcraft was seen as a crime of the very poorest, the most desperate. We know something of St Clement's parish, and we know something of the lives of poor widows. Some of her immediate neighbours were also widows. She and they may have been given a spinning wheel by Christ's Hospital to help them earn a living. We know also that she was devout and interested in sermons.

Now let's create a picture:

Mary Lackland has emerged as the head of a little group. They and their little houses are in the way of the expansion of Christ's Hospital land. They know whether or not they have been paid fully for all the spinning they have done on the wheels paid for by the hospital. Almost immediately next door is the large house built by George Dameron, whose relative John has been involved in the transport of child apprentices. When people ask why there are no beggars in Ipswich, Mary Lackland knows. She is bright, she is intelligent and she has read her Bible. She has been listening eagerly to sermons for years. She has gathered other poor women and a few men around her for Bible readings which may have included such passages as:

> Psalm 82.
> How long will you judge unjustly,
> And show partiality to the wicked?
> Defend the poor and fatherless;
> Do justice to the afflicted and needy.
> Deliver the poor and needy;
> Free them from the hand of the wicked.
> They do not know, nor do they understand;
> They walk about in darkness;
> All the foundations of the earth are unstable.

Authority is rightly worried when the poor read such verses to each other. This group has unofficial links with other such groups in Manningtree, in Bramford and elsewhere. They discuss all the radical versions of Christianity that are now beginning to circulate. Moreover, at least one family, the Duncons on the town council, seem to be quite interested in such ideas too. They get some protection from Robert Rich, who is encouraging religious radicals in New England.

This is reflected in the trial pamphlet, in the reference to her religious nature:

> The said Mother Lakeland hath been a Professor of Religion, a constant hearer of the Word for these many years, and yet a Witch (as she confessed) for the space of near twenty years. The Devil came to her first, between sleeping and waking, and spake to her in a hollow voice, telling her that if she would serve him she should want nothing. After often solicitation she consented to him, then he stroke his claw (as she confessed) into her hands, and with her blood wrote the covenants--- Then he furnished her with three imps, two little dogs and a mole (as she confessed), which she employed in her services.
>
> (Now the subtility of Sathan is to be observd in that he did not presse her to deny God and Christ as he usethe to do to others; because she was a professour, and might have lost all his hold by pressing her too far.)

So, Mother Lackland was a devout Puritan who often went to sermons. In fact, her reputation as a devout Christian is so strong that the authors of the pamphlet have to come up with an elaborate explanation based on the extreme cunning of the Devil to explain away her known Christian beliefs.

We have learnt that in a number of cases of witchcraft there is another dimension: that of an attack on religious dissent, especially on women who were in some way proto-Quakers, and that Sir Robert Rich was actively using his influence to protect them. Mary Lackland very likely may have been a Puritan dissident, leading perhaps a small group of widows who met for religious and mutual support. There had been such a small group of women dissidents in the town for years, subjected to occasional legal harassment:

> Robert Burrage and Thomas Badston Junior both gave sureties of £10 each for good behaviour of Jane Badston for speech against Mr Sparrow.
>
> (Sessions of the Peace, 1624.)

> Thomas Boothe labourer £20 John Dyer labourer £10 and Thomas Badston fustian weaver £10 for disturbing Mr Smart in his sermon.
>
> (Sessions of the Peace, 21 July 1625.)

Abigail Jessope, ?Underwood wife of Gregory Underwood and Margery Simpson presented for absenting themselves from church by the space of 3 months to be brought before the Bailiffs.

(Sessions of the Peace, 22 Jan 1628/9.)

The body of Mathurine Chanye indicted for absenting himself from church for three months to be rendered to the Bailiffs at or before the next Sessions of Peace. He failed to appear at the session.

(Sessions of the Peace, 14 Jan 1631.)

Elizabeth Underwood and Susan Burnabie who were at the last sessions were indicted as recusants and proclamation now being made they are solemnly called to render their and every their bodies and made defaults

Henry Stott and wife Susan for absenting themselves from church for 3 months to render themselves to the Bailiffs.

(Sessions of the Peace, 1 June 1639.)

Not only is Mother Lackland a prominent female believer, but two of her accusers, Owen Reeve and John Ward, are clergymen, one of whom is of quite high standing and charged with a role in controlling other ministers. There is definite reason to believe that Mary Lackland was a highly devout woman and, given what I have demonstrated earlier about small groups of female sectarian Puritan believers, it seems quite possible that she may have gathered such a small group of women about her for Bible study, perhaps even the other neighbouring widows. If we go further, and imagine her and her little band getting in the way of property development, or perhaps becoming vocal about some other injustice, one can see a motive for targeting the woman in this way.

Time then, for another little picture, based on a speculative jump from the evidence:

Mary has started to burn up inside with a sense of moral outrage and at the injustice of the corporation. For years she has been irritating the Reverend John Ward when he walks past her house, on the way from his home in St Mary Key to his little orchard in St Clement's, by asking his opinion on difficult scriptural passages.

Finally, in the town church of St Mary Tower she has confronted the local town lecturer, Matthew Lawrence. They have had a massive public dispute. She has challenged him in this very steeple house, asking by what authority does he levy tithes on the poor? He does not rebuke the obvious corruption and injustice of the town council, which has failed to provide for widows and orphans, giving contracts for bad food and inferior clothing to their friends, profiting from unpaid labour, being behind the spiriting away of poor children.

He demands to know by what authority she, a woman of the poor, preaches. She answers that she speaks through the inspiration of the Holy Spirit. Lawrence replies that she has condemned herself; that she speaks through the inspiration of spirits which can be of many sorts. She warns him that he stands in danger of divine punishment for his persecution of the innocents and God's true saints, those like herself. There is a stunned hush.

That same week, Matthew Lawrence's son takes ill and dies. One of Mary's little group is reported as saying, 'See, how the Lord God strikes down those whose challenge the Deborah of our days. Ipswich's own prophetess, Mary Lackland, has smitten the false prophet just as Jael slew Sisera, as Esther confounded Haman.'

First amongst Widow Lackland's victims is a William Lawrence. But who was William Lawrence? The discrepancies between the trial records and the pamphlet complicate matters, but I take it to mean that William Lawrence was the child of the Mr Lawrence of Ipswich who had lent Mary Lackland 12s. So, who is this Mr Lawrence of Ipswich who needs no further explanation? I suggest that Matthew Lawrence, the new town lecturer, is the most obvious candidate. The title 'Mr' meant much more in the seventeenth century than it does today. Bacon's *Annalls* lists, every year, the people at the top of the Borough Council. 'Mr' is reserved only for bailiffs or for people that had been bailiffs in the past. Justices, guides of Christ's Hospital, or coroners did not get called 'Mr', so clearly Mr Lawrence is a very important man. Bacon makes no mention of any other person called Lawrence, important or otherwise.

Lackland's case clearly involves religious elements; she is a keen sermongoer, a constant hearer of the word. Who is paid to give the most prestigious sermons in Ipswich? Matthew Lawrence. And who gives evidence against her? John Ward, who has also been paid extra at times to give sermons. Moreover, one of the places that has just had a new pulpit added, and where the lecturer is supposed to preach from time to time, is in the Bridewell in Christ's Hospital.

So, it is at least possible that William Lawrence is a member of Matthew Lawrence's family. Matthew Lawrence lived in St Mary Key, Ipswich, close to St Clement's in the house that had previously belonged to Samuel Ward. However, unfortunately, as is the case for nearly all Ipswich parishes, there are no surviving burial registers and only patchy survivals of baptisms and marriages for the 1640s, for either St Mary Key or St Clement's. In other words, there is no simple way of knowing the full extent of Matthew Lawrence's family and whether it contained a William.

Bacon's *Annalls* and the town records tell us a little about Matthew Lawrence. He had only just been appointed in 1643:

11 August 1643. Mr Mathew Laurence shall supply the place of the Town Lecturer for one quarter of a yerre, to beginne from the time of his comming

and shall have, soe farr as in this assembly lies, £20 for his quarters salary, and £5 towards his charge of removing, and Mr Bayliffes shall effectually write to Mr Laurence to invite his comming to that place.

11 November 1644. Mr Mathew Laurence's stipend shall be enlarged to one hundred pounds yearly, payable quarterly and the year to begin at Mich: last and the payment shall be by the Treasurer without warrant And a house shall be provided for him, and £20 more shall be given him to furnish his house

(Bacon, *Annalls*)

Lawrence came from Lincolnshire, and graduated at Trinity Hall Cambridge in 1616, becoming Master of Arts in 1620. What we know of his family is fragmentary. He married Sara Moore in 1629, but she died almost immediately. He then married Grace Wirkliffe in 1631, by whom he had a daughter, Elizabeth Lawrence, born the same year. He had two further sons, Thomas and Matthew, who both died in 1636, aged 3 and 1, and two more daughters, Margaret and Jane. Grace also died, and when he moved to Ipswich he married for the third time to Judith, widow of Robert Hene and daughter of John Harrison of Sudbury. They moved into the Lecturer's House in St Mary Key with his three daughters Elizabeth, Margaret and Jane. By Judith, he is known to have had a further two daughters, Judith (1649) and Mary (1650). So, no William Lawrence is known, but infants that died early in their life often are not recorded and there is a six year gap in a career in which otherwise he and his wives seemed to have had a child per year.

Roughly at the same time, Mary Lackland also has another confrontation. This time with a Mr Beale. Perhaps the most vivid part of Mary Lackland's alleged confession relates to the curse placed on Mr Beale. It ran as follows:

Then she further confessed she sent one of her imps to one Mr Beale of Ipswich who had formerly been a suitor to her grandchild and because he would not have her she sent and burnt a new ship, that had never been at sea, that he was to go master of; and sent also to torment him and take away his life; but he is yet living, but in very great misery, and it is vainly conceived by the doctors and chirugeons that have him in hand that he consumes and rots and that half his body is rotten upon him as he is living. But since her death there is one thing that is very remarkable and to be taken notice of: That upon the very day that she was burned, a bunch of flesh, something after the form of a dog, that grew upon the thigh of the said Mr Beale, ever since the time that she first sent her imp to him, being very hard, but could never be made to break by all the means that could be used, break of itself without any means using. And another sore that at the same time she sent her imp to him rose upon the side of his belly, in the form of a fistula which ran and could not be braked for all the means that could be used, presently also began to heale and there is great hopes that he will suddenly recover again, for his sores heal apace-- He was in this misery for the space of a yeare and a halfe, and was forced to go with his head and his knees together, his misery was so great.

I suggest that we could decode and reread this charge as follows:

Mary Lackland had a beloved granddaughter who had become betrothed to a sea captain called Mr Beale, possibly a little above her station in life. For whatever reason, he rejected her at the time when he had the opportunity of a big step up in the world. This would have seriously shamed her, reduced her future marriage prospects and caused a row which was well known and much gossiped about in the neighbourhood.

Mr Beale was, however, a sick man. He had had two previous, fairly minor bouts of sickness which had, so he thought, cleared up but actually the disease was just spreading through his system. Now the tertiary stage of syphilis was affecting him and giving rise to large sores and lumps all over his body in strange shapes, even with a hard glassy surface over parts, or weeping at other times. These sores could gradually dry up and leave scars, before breaking out elsewhere. His hair was coming out in patches. The first two bouts of illness were very hard for people to recognise and diagnose, but this stage was already fairly well known and Beale would have suffered guilt and shame at the disease unless he could pass it off as some other kind of supernatural affliction. What is more, the disease would have been beginning to affect his brain as well as his mobility. In fact, he had general paralysis of the insane.

There is possibly some further information available on this Mr Beale. Neither the trial details nor the trial pamphlet gives dates for Mary Lackland's crimes, but the pamphlet does say that she became a witch twenty years ago, in other words in 1625. Martha W. McCartney's book *Virginia Immigrants and Adventurers 1607–1635* (p.121) mentions that in 1627 Stephen Beale was said to have shipped goods from London to Virginia in the *James*, and that an Edward Beale, in July 1631, was master of the ship *Gift of God* which had made a trip from Virginia to London in 1629. Given the known links between Ipswich and Virginia, and the fact that John Dameron of Ipswich was at least one local ship's captain who had made the Virginia voyage a number of times, this is perhaps not such an unlikely possible connection

Anyway, Beale is himself terribly sick, possibly with a shameful disease. His new ship has sunk, with a colossal financial loss. Is it his seamanship at fault? Is God punishing him? Rumours fly around the town, from widow to widow.

There is also another dimension to the story of the sinking ship. The other, most spectacular case of the 1645 persecution, was the charges against John Lowes, the Vicar of Brandeston. Lowes was also accused of destroying a ship, and glorying in his destructive power. Where was Lowes when he destroyed the ship? On the ramparts of Landguard Fort, the place built by Warwick that had played such an important role in a series of local confrontations from mutinies to firing on defiant Ipswich ships that did not salute the fort. Lowes had apparently sent his imp to a new vessel sailing out of Ipswich that was part of a fleet (though Stearne does not say so, this fleet out of Ipswich was likely to be the coastal coal fleet). The ship 'began tumbling up and downe with the waves, as if water had been boyled in a pot'. The striken ship sank 'making fourteen widdowes in one quarter of an houre'. Lowes, the writer is keen to make clear, when questioned by a shocked Hopkins, had no regrets but gloried in the power of his imps. The detail that both Lackland's Ipswich ship and Lowes' Ipswich ship were said to be new, makes one suspect that a similar incident lies behind this. There are two contemporary Restoration accounts, as we shall see, connecting witchcraft and Ipswich ships.

Now for another unprovable, but not unlikely, link:

Mr Beale knocks on a well-known door down by the waterfront and he speaks to a cunning man. The cunning man reassures his paying client – Mr Beale is a good captain and, far from being a lustful sinner struck with a shameful disease, he is a wholly innocent victim of the witchcraft of the very woman who had been blackening his name. The cunning man supplies him with a stoneware jug from Germany with the face of a bearded man on it, a Bellarmine. The jug is to be filled with urine and all kinds of sharp objects. Mr Beale is given precise information as to what to do, what to say and at what hour of the day. He follows all the instructions and he sees, when he leaves his house, Mary Lackland walking past.

He makes cautious approaches to the Reverend John Ward, who takes Beale to meet with Matthew Lawrence, who then approaches others on the town council. They collect other charges together. Realising that she is well thought of and known for her piety, it is necessary to destroy Mary Lackland utterly. Ancient rumours about her husband's death are dug up, tidied up and prepared. A group of lower ranking but influential people give sureties that they will testify against her.

There is something unusual in the records at this point. The usual pattern, as revealed by the depositions and the Chelmsford trials, is that the accuser who believed that the witch had harmed or killed a member of his family was the one who gave sureties for appearing as a prosecution witness. If this pattern had been followed in Mary Lackland's case, the sureties should have been drawn from the Lawrence, Alldham, Read, Beale, Holgrave or Lackland families. After all, they were best placed to bear witness to the original dispute with the witch and the subsequent strange death or disaster which had befallen them. Who, then, were the sureties in Lackland's case?

Four people gave sureties, at the 3 July Sessions of the Peace, of £10 each that they would give evidence against her at her trial. Along with

William Bull, John Ward and Stephen Johnson of Ipswich, Owen Reeve, a clerk of Colchester, heads the list. He was born around 1607, the son of John Reeve, a gentleman of Eye. It is possible that John Reeve had been considered for the lectureship of Ipswich. On 19 July 1602, Bacon had recorded that a 'Dr Reeve commended by the Treasurer to be preacher to the Towne, and the Town answered: if uppon somme continuance and stay amongst them he were liked, they would elect him'. The relationship between this Dr Reeve and Owen Reeve's father is unknown, he may have been either Thomas Reeve of Caius College Cambridge (d. 1590) or possibly John Reeve of Christ's College (d. 1609).

Owen Reeve had been to school at Eye under Mr Hall and became a student at Caius College Cambridge in 1625, receiving his MA in 1632. He had been a licensed schoolteacher at Debenham in 1635, and at the time of the trial was the minister of Fingringhoe; but the next year in 1646 was removed as 'never approved by the assembly'. His brother William was also a cleric. Reeve was still living in Ipswich in 1650, when he is recorded as having accused John Thame (Thane) of trespass (Petty Courts, 14 October 1650).

Next is John Ward, another Presbyterian. John Ward was the younger brother of the famous Samuel Ward and the rector of Saint Clement's church. While Samuel was dead at this time, Samuel Ward's widow and his son, another Samuel, were still living in the town, although his other brother Nathaniel was overseas in Aggavam or Ipswich, Massachusetts, New England.

John Ward had gone to Emmanuel College Cambridge, and received his BA in 1626 and his MA in 1630. He was originally rector at Dinnington in Suffolk, then a preacher in Bury, before becoming the rector of St Clement's through the action of John Brandling the bailiff. His estate (at death) in 1662 is thought to have been worth £400 per annum ('English Origins of New England Families 1500s–1800s', CD from Genealogical Publishing Co. Inc. See Candler Pedigree Chart of Ward Family).

He is described as a clerk in a case in the Petty Courts on 11 November 1642, when he is listed as being a surety (or mainpernor) for the appearance of Richard Alpe in court, in connection with a case for debt brought by Robert Clarke and Richard Grimston Jnr.

When his brother Samuel died, John Ward agreed to step in, and kept a regular series of lectures in St Clement's parish while no town lecture was being held, for which he was paid £20 according to a General Court held 5 December 1643. In an Act of Parliament of August 1654, entitled 'An Ordinance for ejecting Scandalous, Ignorant and insufficient Ministers and Schoolmasters', Mr Ward is listed as the representative of Ipswich on the committee.

He held property close to that of the Lacklands, and presumably Mary Lackland had constantly heard his words since he was her minister. If she was a religious dissident it would have been John Ward who would have been most affected, the person with most reason to see her as a thorn in his flesh and an attack upon his position.

William Bull had been a governor of Christ's Hospital and treasurer in 1637. Part of the job of the treasurer was to administer the operations of the town's charities. Bull's own civic career had not been straightforward as he had been summoned in 1643:

> Sessions, 5 June 1643. William Bull summoned by – for words against the Bailiffs.

And he had been one of nine men fined for leading a walkout from a council meeting:

> Court, 20 May 21 Charles (1645).
> Samuel Carnaby, Isaac Day, Symon Cumberland, Edm Bedwell, Wm Bull, Rich. Lawyer, Geo Raymond, clothier, Geo Raymond haberdasher and Jn Hammond departed the Court without licence in contempt of Court Fine 2s 6d a piece at a subsequent court upon their submissions and some reasoning shewn to the Court fine reduced to 1s each.

He may well have been related to Richard Bull, shipbuilder of Ipswich and Harwich, who owned land in St Clement's.

If we look at the rest of the witnesses against her, and Alice Denham, the suggestion of a definite pattern appears. I have tabulated it as follows, based on mentions of the men in Bacon's *Annalls of Ipswche*:

WITNESSES AGAINST ALICE DENHAM

Edward Martyn. In 1641 'Mr Retheriches gift (for loans to Godly Tradesmen for five years) of £10 a peece lent unto —, and £8 a peece to Joh: Shewter and Edw: Martin.'

William Nunn, n. 1643, 5 December, Bacon records 'Mr Cock's gift of £20 a peece, lent for 5 yeres to Steven Cole, Rob: Wade, John Parkhurst, Tho: Garwood, Willm. Nunn.'

Peter Cole. Peter Cole held several corporation offices, as alderman, chamberlain, governor of Christ's Hospital, claviger, and had held office as Treasurer in 1624.

Henry Wright. In 1638 a Henry Wright was lent £5 from Mr Tie's gift. This was a charity set up by the will of John Tye 1583 to lend money to promising young Ipswich tradesmen to give them a start.

WITNESSES AGAINST MARY LACKLAND

Owen Reeve of Colchester.

William Bull was a governor of Christ's Hospital and a treasurer in 1637.

John Ward, Rector of St Clement's.

Stephen Johnson, 'Lent money from the town charities. 2 November 1629. Lent unto Steven Johnson, £5 by the Town.'

Stephen Johnson, Henry Wright, William Nunn and Edward Martyn had all been the beneficiaries of loans to young businessmen advanced from the different charities administered by the borough. Peter Cole was a typical borough oligarch who had held the offices of alderman, chamberlain, claviger, treasurer in 1624 and governor of Christ's Hospital.

Some of these people were near neighbours. The owners of the property immediately to the north of Mary Lackland's own was, in fact, the Borough Council in the shape of Christ's Hospital, who were trying to improve it. Officers of Christ's Hospital or beneficiaries of borough charities were to give evidence against her.

Amongst those also owning neighbouring property were John Ward, the minister of St Mary Key who gave evidence against her, and Richard Grimston (the lawyer nephew of Sir Harbottle Grimston) who was an attorney in the court that convicted her. Not so far away, was property belonging to the Bull family, shipbuilders from Harwich. Richard Bull also gave evidence against her.

Why were the people who gave sureties for their appearance as witnesses against her not the relatives of her victims, but people of a different station in society connected with the elite running the town? There has to be some reason why the leaders of the community should have paid any attention to the rumours, and quarrels and neighbourhood backbiting amongst the poorest of Ipswich. What reason did they have to dig up 20-year-old crimes, and make her punishment the most extreme ever suffered by a witch in England in the whole of the 1645 witch trials? Why, of the thirty or so in the town jail and of the seven actually tried within Ipswich, was it only these two who were executed, one in such an exceptional way, when two of those found guilty with her were only given a custodial sentence?

Now, for another little leap:

Harbottle Grimston learns of the case through his Ipswich relative, Richard Grimston, and through Richard Bull, the Harwich man living close to the Lacklands. He offers the advice and support of his experts, John Stearne and Matthew Hopkins. Stearne and Hopkins are not directly involved because the Ipswich Corporation prefers to handle such matters itself, but they offer their techniques from the sidelines. Following their advice, Mary Lackland and her group are all arrested and subjected to searching, watching and swimming. Lackland and her friend hold out with great determination, but possibly one couple, James and Mary Emerson collapse, confess, and offer incriminating evidence.

The accusations made against her in the pamphlet follow the exact form of the accusations made against all witches in the depositions, and they have the same detail of a devilish version of the Solemn League and Covenant, 'with her blood wrote the covenants'. By now, the continually repeated phrase 'as she confessed' takes on a much more sinister role. Firstly, we know from the trial records that even if she had confessed, she retracted any previous confession at the trial, for she pleaded not guilty to all the charges. Secondly, we now know exactly how confessions were acquired.

The confessions provide the twelve of the council with what they needed – evidence to convict Mary Lackland, destroy her reputation, break up her followers and warn others to keep silent. Mary and James Emerson are given the most lenient sentence ever passed on a convicted witch, while Mary is given the most terrible.

Now for the final summary. Afterwards, the case won't go away. Many people, including those quite wealthy led by the Duncons, are very unsure that any kind of justice has been done and they start staying away from Matthew Lawrence's sermons and lectures in droves. For a time, the general court makes gains in its struggles with the portmen. Matthew Lawrence is very unhappy, perhaps he had not been prepared for what it really meant to burn an old woman alive. He wants to leave Ipswich, but the old guard rally support and persuade him to stay, though they have lost much ground and some of them never hold high office again. Robert Rich and his good friend Oliver Cromwell are riding high nationally, and Harbottle Grimston and his like just have to weather the storm. Robert Rich has been too late to stop the trial, but he has put a stop to other trials in the area and challenged Hopkins' methods of extracting confessions. Legislation to finance new trials remains a dead letter. No one is quite sure what to do about the Quakers, who are alternately persecuted and released.

Stearne defended both his and Hopkins' activities by saying that they were the victims of political change. Lawrence's behaviour also points to political change. The pattern of trials and borough policy points to the political dimension of witchcraft as well. Until 1645, Ipswich had not seen many trials. Immediately following the trials, the borough passed a sinister ordinance:

> For as much as there hath been much money laid out by several persons within this towne by the order and appointment of Mr Bayliffes in the searchinge, watchinge and further prosecuting of divers persons of this Towne suspected for witches and in the bringine of them to legal triall at this sessions and whereas also at the general Gaole delivery nowe lately holden at Bury it was the direction and order of the Judge and Court there in the same case that the Charge of prosecuting Witches should be a general charge it is nowe therefore ordered that the charge of searchinge, watching and prosecuting of all such persons within this town as hath been or hereafter shall bee suspected for witches and hath been or hereafter shall bee searched, watched and prosecuted by the order and direction of the bayliffes or justices of Peace of this town shall be borne by the inhabitants of this towne as a general charge and in pursuance herof and for the repayment of the monies already laid out and to be laid out in this behalf it is now further ordered that

the Churchwardens and Overseers of the severall Parishes of this town do presently collect 1 fortnight's pay according to their weekly single rates for their poor and make payment thereof immediately unto Richard Sheppard of the Tower parish who is to issue out the same again to the purpose aforesaid according as he shall receive direction by warrant under the hands of Mr Bayliffes from time to time.

This regulation is sinister, not only because it enabled the borough to pass on the costs to the wider community in the obvious expectation that there would be further such cases in the future, but because it actually arranges for the parishes to collect and hand the money into a central fund ready to be used, before any investigations have even begun. Perhaps lists had already been drawn up – this we don't know.

Other communities had passed very similar local legislation, for example after the Bury trials. All of this suggests collaboration and organisation at a much more powerful level than that which Stearne and Hopkins had at their disposal. Yet within Ipswich, in this heartland of the Puritan and Commonwealth movement, no further trials were held until the Restoration. There is definitely a series of politically based changes of policy going on.

It is difficult to assess what changes there were at the top of the corporation, but changes there were. Bacon, the contemporary historian, is a very careful reporter. There is only one year in which he does not give the names of the justices, and that year is 1645 – the year of the witch trials. There are ten leading men whose careers stop in 1645–1646, and who therefore were probably on the wrong side politically. Pemberton, one of the bailiffs that year, is one of those who do not hold high office afterwards

Men who had been at the top of the council in 1639, and became bailiffs after 1648 and before 1660, were obviously seen as reliable supporters of the Commonwealth. There were eleven men in this group, Manuel Sorrell being the best example. The Duncons, who rose to local power at just this time, even had Quaker sympathies.

So, there was clearly change of some sort at the top. Some old names vanish and some new names rise higher and faster than they might have done. Mary Lackland's case, and the subsequent end of witch trials locally, does seem to coincide with a political change in the corporation.

The year of the trial, 1645/1646, also saw the town lecturer, Matthew Lawrence, suddenly decide to leave his profitable and influential post to return to rural quiet in Lincolnshire, even though he had just been awarded the full lecturer's salary of £100 after his extended probation of two years, along with his rent-free house and access to the town library. There is no obvious career sense to his decision, as far as he gives reasons he seems to have become concerned about his position in the Ipswich community. This unexplained action on Lawrence's part is in some way linked to his sermons becoming less popular. This attempt to withdraw precipitated a mini crisis within the borough.

Bacon records the complicated negotiations which ensued as follows:

22 Charles Wednesday 10 June (1646).

Mr Laurence by letter informing the Towne of his doubtfullness in continuance at this Towne: 1. in regard of his call he hathe recieved to returne to Lincolnshire. 2. That the aire wherein he is he finds not soe suitable wth. His healthe as somme place in the upper pt. of the Towne might be. 3. The dayly lessening of the publique congregacon renders an oppinion that his ministry is not soe aceptable as hathe bein. 4. The burden of 2 sermons on the weeke dayes he findes too heavy for him, and wisheth that one sermon might be changed into the Lords day.

Hereunto this answer is declared: that they shall ever be willing to satisfie Mr Laurence in all his desires wthin the power of the Towne. 1 That if Mr Laurence shall make choise of any house wthin this Towne it shall be hiered for him. 2. All the members of this Assembly will be carefull in theire owne p'sons and wth theire families, to be present at the congregacons, and will doe what they can to p'swade others therto. 3 As to the altering of one sermon to the Lords Day, They can not answere wthout the concent of ministers and people; nevertheless they will indeavour to give him all just satisfaction that they may. 4. As touching his call, wch. Mr Laurence desires might be determined by the Councell of able and learned men: This Assemblie desires Mr Laurence to informe Mr Bayliffs what his proceedings therein are from time to time, and this assemblie will proceede according to occasuion

They agreed to a meeting in August at Cambridge, which two Lincolnshire ministers were also to attend. Clearly Ipswich council, far from taking offence at Lawrence's decision to leave, were very eager indeed to get him to stay and willing to promise all sorts of concessions. Something was clearly going on again, and yet once more we don't know precisely what.

The possibility that the child of Mr Lawrence alleged to have been killed by Mary Lackland was the child of Mr Lawrence, the town lecturer, would give one explanation for this strange behaviour. It would have been understandable if Lawrence wished to leave the scene of a family tragedy. If this tragedy was linked to a high-profile case connected to a series of trials that important national and local interests thought were flagrant miscarriages of justice, all the more reason. It is worth remembering that it would have been seen as the duty of the town lecturer as the senior religious figure in the town to attend the execution

If his audience, or if he himself, had later had doubts about the justice of what had happened, it would have been very difficult indeed for him. Promises from the leading councillors to go and encourage as many people as possible to attend his lectures strongly suggests some kind of boycott or division of opinion over Lawrence within the town. Earlier, I have quoted at length one of Lawrence's surviving sermons on government in which he encourages his listeners to see who does, and who does not, attend his sermons as a way of determining who should govern Ipswich. In the end he was to stay on in Ipswich, so somehow the crisis was smoothed over:

> 4 May 1648. The clay wall on the north of Mr Laurences house orchard shall be pulled downe and a brick wall sett up in the stead thereof.

I cannot say that we can prove beyond doubt this version of the facts, but I believe this is a credible alternative reading. Remember 'the Justices of the Peace may not always expect direct evidence, seeing all their works are workes of darknesse, and no witnesses present with them to accuse them'.

AFTERMATH

ocial catastrophes like the witch persecutions are never simply over and done with at some moment of climax. They may have been years in preparation, and they cast a long shadow into the future. We can read back from what happened next, to help illustrate and confirm the mechanisms of what we have suggested for 1645.

Local, not national, policy dominates the history of witchcraft. The period of the Civil War was one in which each region tended to follow its own patterns dependant on the fighting, the dominant group in the region, underlying sympathies and a whole range of other factors.

There is a clear Suffolk pattern of growing persecution leading up to 1645, followed by an end to trials under the Commonwealth, until the Restoration. This pattern was not replicated in other areas, such as Kent – where there was a large trial in the 1650s after the collapse of the Kentish Royalist rising in 1647 – nor in Hertfordshire. Various other counties seem to have had hardly any trials at all.

Within Suffolk and Ipswich, the period after 1645 to the end of the protectorate saw an almost complete end to witchcraft trials (there was an execution of a mother and daughter called Boram in 1655 at Bury, but little seems to be known about it). The persecution machine had been set in action, regulations had been put in place to fund it, large numbers of accused had been put on trial, and it might have looked as though with the victory of the Puritans all was set for a very dark period indeed.

Yet as we have also seen, the project was being shut down almost as fast as it started. The only possible explanation is the victory of the Independent faction over the Presbyterian faction, which in north-east Essex and south-east Suffolk meant the victory of Sir Robert Rich over Sir Harbottle Grimston and his relatives.

The Civil War years saw both the worst persecution of witches and the emergence of a rejection of the whole process of witch trials. This struggle was an internal one within the Puritan movement.

In Suffolk, witch trials returned with the king and the bishop. The key case was the famous trial of the Lowestoft witches which took place on 10 March 1664. The trial was very fully reported. In fact it is probably the best reported of any such case, and has been the subject of an excellent book, *A Trial of Witches*.

The incident that precipitated the trial took place on 10 March 1656, *Nono Caroli Secundi*, the ninth year of Charles II, with the kingdom still under the Commonwealth. The suspicion around the two accused and some of the other accusations were even older than that. This suggests that the case had been delayed because the principals were well aware that it would not have succeeded under the Commonwealth.

The case was brought by Samuel Pacey, the most important man in Lowestoft at the time. He is believed, interestingly, to have been involved in the Yarmouth accusations brought by Matthew Hopkins, and he had prior dealings with the trial judge, Hale, over a dispute between Yarmouth and Lowestoft.

The first stage in the trial was that Pacey, the father of the affected children, went to Sir Edmund Bacon of Redgrave, premier baronet of England and commander of the Suffolk militia (and therefore a trusted Royalist), as the magistrate who could issue a warrant against the witches. Sir Edmund was not the nearest, nor most obvious, magistrate for the people of Lowestoft to approach and it is a mystery why they did so. Bunn and Geis suggest that Sir John Pettus, who was a friend of Doctor Thomas Browne and closely connected with Lowestoft affairs, may have been the link. He had been part of a Royalist attack on Lowestoft in the Civil War and claimed to have served under Prince Rupert, as well as to have supported the Royalist cause financially. Pettus had considerable difficulties with his wife, who became a Catholic and ran away to a foreign nunnery with his money before finally returning to her husband. He later became MP for Dunwich (not that far from Lowestoft, on the Suffolk coast). Sir Edmund Bacon was linked to the legal dynasty which had provided Nathaniel Bacon of Ipswich, which was now also linked by marriage to the Grimstons, and headed by our old friend Harbottle Grimston at the summit of the English legal establishment.

The young Lord Cornwallis of Culford was another magistrate at the trial. He was related to the Bacons by marriage. His father was a staunch Royalist who had even followed Charles II into exile.

The presiding judge was Sir Matthew Hale. Hale was not just any old judge but was perhaps the leading Royalist judge. As a barrister, he had defended Archbishop Laud, he had been chosen as a possible lawyer to defend Charles I and it had been Hale in Parliament who had moved the motion to bring Charles II back as king.

The junior judge at the trial was Sergeant-at-Law, Sir John Keeling (or Keyling). He had been imprisoned in Windsor Castle as a Royalist for the whole of the Interregnum. It was Keeling who presided over the trial which led to the execution of Sir Henry Vane for treason (as a supporter of the Commonwealth), and who sentenced the great Puritan writer John Bunyan to prison.

During the trial, Thomas Browne of Norwich was called on as an expert witness. He was a doctor of medicine, influenced by the ideas of Paracelsus, and probably the most prominent doctor within the region. Browne was a major intellectual figure, a very learned man, and some of the books he wrote are read to this day, for his style alternates between the almost incomprehensible and the sometimes rather beautiful. In his best known book, *Religio Medici* (*The Religion of a Doctor*), he was prepared to accept the reality of witchcraft, which is why he was called as a specialist witness (although another of his books was entitled *Pseudodoxia Epidemica* and was a study of popular errors).

The long inception of the case; the importance of the members of the legal team and their closeness to the new regime; the presence of such an important medical specialist (something that had not happened in any previous trial); the care taken to take a trial transcript and print it; as well as the dramatic courtroom test that was to take place, all suggest that this was no routine, run-of-the-mill trial but was a test of the legal status of witchcraft. Those behind it were the same combination of Presbyterian gentry, lawyers, urban leaders and ministers that had formed the supporters of Hopkins and Stearne, and indeed, in some cases, they were the same people.

The first accusation shows clearly how the accused and the accuser were close neighbours, who had originally been on extremely good terms before falling out over child care:

> Dorothy Durent [Durrant] (the mother) having special occasion to go from home, and having none in the House to take care of her said Child (it then sucking) desired Amy Duny her Neighbour, to look to her child during her absence, for which she promised her to give her a Penny: but the said Dorothy Durent desired the said Amy not to Suckle her Child, and laid a great charge upon her not to do it. Upon which it was asked by the Court, why she did give that direction, she being an old Woman and not capable of giving Suck? It was answered by the said Dorothy Durent, that she very well knew that she did not give suck, but that for some years before, she had gone under the reputation of a Witch, which was one cause made her give the caution: Another was, that it was customary with old Women, that if they did look after a sucking Child, and nothing would please it but the Breast, they did use to please the Child, but it sucked nothing but Wind, which did the child hurt.

Amy took no notice of Dorothy's instructions and suckled the baby. The mother found out and there was a row in which Amy 'used many high Expressions and Threatening Speeches towards her'.

Then, almost inevitably, Dorothy Durrant's son fell sick. Dorothy Durrant was perfectly prepared to admit that she took the boy to a well-known cunning man in the nearby town of Yarmouth, who gave her advice that comes clearly from the same body of belief as that which other cunning men continued to give over the next centuries:

> A certain Person named Doctor Jacob, who lived at Yarmouth, who had the reputation in the Country, to help children that were Bewitch'd; who advis'd her to hang up the Child's Blanket in the Chimney-corner all day, and at night when she put the Child to Bed, to put it into the said blanket, and if she found any thing in it, she should not be afraid, but to throw it into the fire.

Dorothy did as she was told:

> There fell out of the same [blanket] a great Toad, which ran up and down the hearth, and she having a young youth only with her in the House, desired him to catch the Toad, and throw it into the Fire, which the youth did accordingly, and held it there with the Tongs; and as soon as it was in the Fire it made a great and horrible Noise, and after a space there was a flashing in the Fire like Gun-powder, making the noise like the discharge of a Pistol, and thereupon the Toad was no more seen nor heard.
>
> The next day there came a young Woman a Kinswoman of the said Amy, and told Dorothy, that her Aunt [meaning the said Amy] was in a most lamentable condition having her face all scorched with fire, and that she was sitting alone in her House, in her Smock without any fire. And thereupon this Deponent went into the House of the said Amy Duny to see her, and found her in the same condition as was related to her; for her face, her Leggs, and Thighs, which this Deponent saw, seemed very much scorched and burnt with Fire, at which this Deponent seemed much to wonder. And asked the said Amy how she came into that sad condition? and the said Amy replied, she might thank her for it, for that she this Deponent was the cause thereof, but that she should live to see some of her Children dead, and she upon crutches.

As far as Mrs Durrant was concerned, Amy Duny's curse came true five years later in 1661, when her daughter was taken sick.

In 1663, Amy Duny asked Samuel Pacey to sell her some herring, which he refused to do. There is something a little strange, or at least unexplained, about this because there seems no reason why someone who had fish to sell should refuse to sell it to a person. Refusal to sell fish to someone was also given as the reason why Rose Cullender attacked the reluctant saleswoman's child by magic. Perhaps they were asking to buy the fish at a special charity rate, but the report simply doesn't explain. In any case, Pacey's children became ill and a doctor, this time a genuine Doctor of Physic, declared himself puzzled by the children's symptoms, as well he might because they were vomiting pins (this is a new feature in such trials). Pacey then tried sending his children to his married sister in Yarmouth. The children's aunt at first thought the children were faking, but was then convinced. They also went into hysterical fits of fear when mice, or on one occasion a bee, appeared.

Before going to the magistrate, and on his own authority, Samuel Pacey had Amy Duny put in the stocks. With the leading townsman going after Duny, other townspeople followed his lead and began to collect more charges against another woman, Rose Cullender.

Samuel Pacey then put the case before the magistrate, Sir Edward Bacon. Bacon immediately authorised six women to search Rose Cullender. Although Rose Cullender was not subjected to the swimming test, or kept awake and watched in the way developed by Stearne and Hopkins, the searching, as is very vividly and unpleasantly recorded here, was in itself a form of assault, shaming and brutalisation:

> Coming to the House of Rose Cullender, they did acquaint her with what they were come about, and asked whether she was contented that they should search her? she did not oppose it, whereupon they began at her Head, and so stript her naked, and in the lower part of her Belly they found a thing like a Teat of an Inch long, they questioned her about it, and she said, That she had got a strain by carrying of water which caused that Excrescence. But upon narrower search, they found in her Privy Parts three more Excrescencies or Teats, but smaller than the former: This Deponent farther saith, That in the long Teat at the end thereof there was a little hole, and it appeared unto them as if it had been lately sucked, and upon the straining of it there issued out white milkie Matter.

A feature of this case is that four young girls believed themselves to be bewitched, and went into hysterical fits when they saw either of the two accused, Rose Cullender and Amy Duny. During the trial, Keeling, Cornwallis and Bacon tested the girls by having them blindfolded and then touched by the magistrates. The girls went into fits even though the witches weren't present, and the magistrates claimed that the accused women should be released as the whole thing was obviously fake:

> Several gentlemen-- Mr Sergeant Keeling, and an ingenious person who objected that the children might counterfeit this their distemper, were

unsatisfied with the evidence; upon which an experiment to see whether the afflicted children recognised blindfold Amy Duny's touch, having failed, Lord Cornwallis, Sir Edmund Bacon, Mr Sergeant Keeling, and others, openly protested 'that they did believe the whole transaction of this business was a mere imposture'. But Mr Pacy's (a dissenting minister) arguments, and those of the learned Dr Brown, of Norwich, prevailed. Sir Matthew Hale summed up against the prisoners, who were condemned to be hanged.

This intervention by influential bystanders, on the grounds of simple common sense had, as we have seen, often proved enough to rescue the accused – but not here. It sounds from the trial pamphlet as though Pacey was able to get more witnesses brought down with fresh accusations from Lowestoft. Hale was convinced, and brought in a guilty verdict and the women were executed. Though Hale had come down hard against the accused, and indeed quoted scripture to the effect that witches existed, there is some evidence that the Lord Chief Justice later regretted his judgement:

[Hale] gave in to the sottish belief of witches, a superstition that age had been much addicted to. He condemned some persons at the Assizes for the County of Suffolk, and suffered them to be put to death, who had been convicted before him of witchcraft; but it appears by the account of the trial that though he declared his belief of witches, he had some uneasiness about him, and did not sum up the evidence to the jury, a very unusual thing; and I have been told that he was afterwards much altered in his notions, and had much concern upon him for what had befallen these persons.

(From a notebook of anecdotes made by George Onslow, Speaker of the House of Commons. For some reason Ivan Bunn and Gilbert Geis, the author of A Trial of Witches in which Onslow is quoted, choose to question this story.)

As a test case given high prominence it was not very convincing, and it does seem to have been very much a last attempt to keep the old system going. The old certainties had ceased to go unchallenged, and the clergy and the lawyers were moving away from the necessary intensity of belief to convict and execute witches. Still, weird tales abounded and were widely believed.

Around this time, another headmaster of Ipswich School, Cave Beck, became fascinated by stories of witchcraft just as Argentine had been so long before. Cave Beck was not only headmaster but he was also tutor to Viscount Hereford Leicester Devereux's children in Christchurch Mansion in Ipswich, and acted as the town librarian. He was rather far from being a conventional headmaster. His main claim to any kind of fame is that he had developed an attempt at a code in which numbers replaced letters and sounds, and in which, therefore,

Sir Thomas Browne, writer and doctor of Norwich, employed as a specialist witness on the reality of witchcraft in the Lowestoft trial. (National Portrait Gallery)

it should have been possible for two people who knew the numerical code to converse, no matter what language they actually spoke. This he published in a book called *The Universal Character*, in 1657.

Largely on the basis of his interest in codes, it has been suggested that he was a Royalist agent. He accompanied his master, Leicester Devereux (who was one of the leaders of the British nobility under the Commonwealth), to the Netherlands to meet with Charles II to negotiate his return to the throne. He was also a witness to the disputed authorship of the book *Eikon Basilikon*, to prove that it had in fact been written by Charles I, and not by John Guaden (one time chaplain of Sir Robert Rich and later Bishop of Exeter), as Guaden had claimed.

Obviously a learned man, he, just like Browne, was a supporter of the reality of witchcraft. Nathaniel Fairfax, the main correspondent of the Royal Society living Suffolk, had suggested to its Secretary Oldenburg that Beck might make a good fellow correspondent, reporting back on curious incidents within the county. Beck then wrote a letter to Oldenburg. This letter was something of a test for Beck. Fairfax regularly reported medical information in great detail, especially on unusual births. Such births, whether of human babies or of animals, were called 'monsters'. They were seen as a sign of divine punishment and are another illustration of the overlap between early scientific enquiry and superstition.

Beck made the mistake of concentrating on witches as monsters, and of sending in secondhand reports of old cases, accepting Hopkins and Stearne's test case as authentic. The Royal Society, while fascinated by unusual births, had moved on from an interest in witches:

Cave Beck to Oldenburg, 943 15 August 1668 Sr.
I acknowledge my selfe much indebted to yu for yr obliging letter & present. I shall be restless till I find opportunityes of gratefull returnes. Sr. observing that yu sometimes take notice of monsters I thought it might not be unphilosophical to acquaint yu wit the greatest & worst sort of Monsters among us which are witches (for they can but apply natural agents unto patients, although with ye assistance of some more unseene & spiritual Confederate).

Beck then recounted four cases:

The following narrative I recd. from a neighbour minister of to much prudence to be imposed upon & of approved veracity not to deceive others, he assureth me that one Mr Spatches of Cookley in this County (who hath formerly invaded ye Ministerial office without permission) was by fascination brought to that passé that if he but prayed God or heard others name him reverently he was put into strange fits his body would be wrenched into many

Sir Matthew Hale. (Suffolk Record Office)

postures his legs strecht backwards to his sholders his head & backe bowed no
artificial tumbler could imitate, also the Minister with more saw him raysed
out of his seate into ye aire in a high and large roome thrown against the
opposite wall at least 9 yards distance from his seate touchd ye ground. One
woman freely confessed herselfe to have acted upon him but affirmed others
were partners in ye guilt. He told that saw that woman in his Chambr one
night with 2 women more & that woman layd (as he thought) her hand upon
his face wch in great haste he layd hold upon & bitt, and he same night that
woman was heard to shrike out 2 miles of & complained her toe was hurt,
ye neighbours cam in upon ye Cry Saw bloody clouts. Now that woman is
detained he is recovered and released of his fits, Sr if ye Royal Society desire
it I can procure a fuller story from ye patient himselfe and other Eye & ears.

This case was also recorded in 1693 by Samuel Petts (Petto), minister of the
gospel at Sudbury in Suffolk. He wrote *A faithfull narrative of the wonderful
and extraordinary fits which Mr Thomas Spatchett late of Dunwich and Cookly was
under by witchcraft*. The booklet, which was thirty-five pages long, includes a
confession from the witch but as the outraged author notes: 'notwithstanding
what could be witnessed against her, yet she was sent home; and nothing in
point of law was done against her.'

Beck's next case was a retelling of one of the Manningtree cases in the
form in which it had been recounted to Leicester Devereux of Christchurch
Mansion in Ipswich:

As also a relation from Sir Tho. Bowes & Esquire Bruce which said Esquire
make to my Lord Viscount Hereford That he saw Bowes three women accused
by a young man who was emaciated like a skeleton. He also had a threefold effect from them 1t an him as of many women scolding. 2ly a Confused
noye of div voices singing. 3ly a Noyse of many harsh and ill sounding Inst
these noyses came out of his belly but no motion of his lips was Sr. Thomas
exhorted the women to take of their charmes from man and put them into a
walled Courtyard to advise about it wh (to harken) brought word that after a
Contentious debate two of the were willing to release the young man but ye
3d refused & it w immediately ye young man ceased two of his Noyses but
continued one & shortly after dyed & all ye women were executed.

Beck's next case was up-to-date:

Sr. a man of this Towne lately come from France assureth /spectre upon ye
River about the 10th of June last in a bright night. He first took notice of a
man in a boat (as he thought) ro a ship within a stones cast of yt himself was in,
& on ye suddan ye boat vanished & ye likeness of a very tall man standing up

he called up ye master of ye ship & all his Company (they wer who agreed in
ye following description they observed ye spec upon ye water & then leasurely
draw towards ye same ship & a shape manifestly changed to ye habit of a woman
& then of ye likenesse of a horse wch went to ye shore & returned moving
upon ye water & then appeared a less beast & at last as litle as a Cat wch they
saw run quite of ye water into ye neighboring woods. The next morning they
enquired of those in ye mentiond ship who sayd they were ashore at ye time of
ye apparition but doubted they were in ill handling (as our Country phrases it)
for they had bin divers times in danger of being cast away this summer in calme
weather, a narrative of this (upon my request) was subscribed by all ye company
who saw it, but unfortunately lost by a careless messenger.

This case somewhat resembles another that appeared in an official letter from
the government officer at Harwich to his superiors:

Capt. Silas Taylor to Williamson. They tell a strange story at Ipswich of one
of their ships that was lost in the late storms; that another of the same town
passing by them and being well acquainted, they sent their remembrances
to friends; the master, Jonathan Banticke, to his parents, one Hornegild, a
passenger who had lost his ship at Scarborough Road, his love to his wife
and children, and all the other seamen to their relations. When asked the
reason, and whether their ship was leaky, or what they wanted, the first ship
replied that they had long labored to free their main-top, where sat a couple
of witches; but by all that they could do, could not remove nor get them
down, and so they were lost people. The master named the two witches to the
second ship's master and his company, insomuch that they are now in prison
at Ipswich. The story is credibly reported by the second ship, and generally
believed. Many light vessels pass by to the north, and laden ships to the south.
I hope the price of coals will fall apace.
                        (Calendar State Papers Domestic, Charles II 1667–68)

Both these stories are contemporary with the Second Dutch War, a time of
extreme tension and stress for merchant men and sailors. Beck gives one last
story which refers to a practice that continued into the nineteenth century:

I shall conclude with a story wch a Physician of our towne recovered from ye
Host of ye Queens Arms in Wollpit. That having denyed to sell 2. Of his hogs
to a neighbour woman soon after divers of ye hogs came home from ye fields
in a strange distemper & dyed, wherfore by ye advice of a travaylor then in ye
inne the next that came in those fits was held with prongs alive in ye fire till
halfe ye head was burnt & so the rest of his swine escaped but ye fasinatrix was
found dead in her house with one side of her face burnt. This and such like

undoubted stories seeme to favour ye Digbean Hypothesis, & will exercise ye
Curious among you to salve ye phaenomena besides ye service they may doe
against ye Vitiosi of ye Sadduces Invasions.

Thus wishing you all happiness, I remaine Your very affectionate & engaged
servant Cave Beck.

Beck's last sentence requires a lot of explanation: 'ye service they may doe
against ye Vitiosi of ye Sadduces Invasions'. The 'Vitiosi' must be a misspelling
of the name 'Virtuosi', a title given to members of the Royal Society. Their
approach, being based on human reason, was theologically controversial of
course in an age which relied on the Bible and authority rather than reason
and evidence. The Virtuosi of the Royal Society could not directly confront
their opponents' appeal to the authority of scripture, but they did have their
defenders who argued that reason and scripture were not opposed.

By a typical contradiction of the time, the greatest Anglican supporter of the
Royal Society (and their defender against attacks from religious opponents) was
Joseph Glanville. Glanville had, in part, taken up the cause of reason because he
believed that it was impossible to be a dissenter *and* be reasonable, as they relied
(in his view) on a blind faith that he called fanaticism.

However, Glanville also believed that it was completely reasonable to believe
in witches, and that to disbelieve in witchcraft and ghosts inevitably led to
disbelief and atheism, which he associated with the views of the Sadducees, who
were mentioned in the New Testament as Jewish thinkers who were opposed
to Christianity. His book *Saducismus Triumphatus*, published in 1681, was an
attempt to prove the existence of witchcraft and to describe its opponents as
atheists. It was initially written as a defence of witch trials in Somerset. The
appearance of the term in this letter, long before the publication of the book, is
good evidence of the controversy amongst the the elite on the subject during
the Restoration and of an organised body of support for witch trials in Suffolk
amongst a section of the non-Puritan Anglican elite during the Restoration.

Beck, therefore, had good grounds to believe that the Royal Society would
welcome such stories as part of its attempt to clear itself from charges of
disbelief. At least as far as Oldenburg was concerned, he was wrong. Beck's
mistake was to take the camouflage for the reality.

So, Beck was saying that he was collecting evidence in favour of the reality
of witchcraft to protect the Virtuosi of the Royal Society against the attacks of
those atheists who did not believe in witchcraft. The force of nature that he
thought witches used was the 'Digbeian Hypothesis'. This refers to the 'powder
of sympathy', an alchemical powder that the Catholic courtier Sir Kenelm
Digby had devised. The powder was used to anoint a weapon that had caused
a wound and so heal the wound from a distance. The weapon and the wound
were in a sympathetic relationship, so that an action on the one had an effect

at a distance on the other. Beck had also written 'for they can but apply natural agents unto patients, although with ye assistance of some more unseene & spiritual Confederate', which is to say that witches must use natural methods to commit their crimes, but were helped in them by the Devil.

Contradictory though his own ideas were, they show powerfully the effect of a new way of thinking and the way it was slowly undermining old certainties, leaving people conflicted and puzzled. His letter did not get the reception he wanted. Beck was to write a number of times more to Henry Oldenburg, promoting his universal character and fishing for an invitation to become associated with the Royal Society, without success.

Nathaniel Fairfax (1637–1690) was a very different man. He was a very detailed and accurate recorder on medical, natural history and agricultural matters, perhaps the first real researcher in a modern sense in the county. He was interested in everything from spider poison to waterclocks as an alternative to pendulum clocks. He had been a clergy man at Willisham for a year before being expelled as a Puritan, and had then studied at Leiden as a doctor. He was a friend of Sir Thomas Browne, the Norwich doctor.

He had what might be called an open mind about 'supernatural' matters, but he was far from being obsessed by them. This is what marks him out from men like Beck. His letters, too, reflect the beliefs circulating in the county at the time. For example, in his letter of 1666/67 (the variable date due to the changes in the calendar) he wrote of a marketman riding from Hadleigh to Ipswich who had seen three moons in the sky, one large and the others smaller and bloody. In his next letter of 10 April 1667, Fairfax explained that the man was in His Majesty's victualling office in Ipswich, that he had seen the moons on Monday morning, 3 December, and that once the rumours had spread some of the portmen of Ipswich had felt concerned enough to bring him to the town hall to report to the bailiffs, at which point the matter petered out. In his letter of 29 January 1667/68, he reports on his investigation of an old whitethorn in Parham Park which was believed to miraculously flower on Christmas Day like the Glastonbury Thorn. On 18 February 1667/68 he was reporting various cases of people who had had dreams which had since come true. So many of these cases were of women true dreamers (Mrs Stallon of Norwich, a Congregationalist, and Mrs Reyner of Bury, are the two named), that he thought perhaps it was an especially female power until he came upon a male example.

This seemed to suggest to him an innate, if weak, human facility to dream the future. And from this he went on to speculate about Romani fortunetelling, in what must be one of the very first accounts. The passage is interesting in itself, and interesting too as an example of a wholly new attitude, one which allowed for there being very many strange things in the world but which turned first to secular explanations, and only secondly to supernatural ones, rather than first and exclusively to supernatural causes:

Cave Beck, explaining his 'universal character' to the peoples of the world. (Suffolk Record Office)

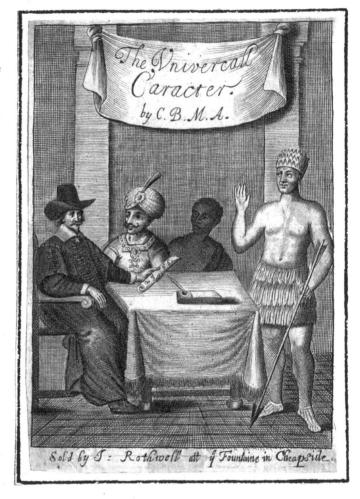

For I believe all the fortune tales of Gypsies are wrought wth no other tool thn ths, (an innate human ability to detect the future derived from the soul). That they don't work by Cheiromancy (though they seem to do so) I am more thn half sure, partly because they are altogether unacquainted with the inside & strength of tht cunning, & though they were never so deeply skilld in it, they don't face the hand, half long enough, nor half wistly enough, for the steddy passing of a judgement on't.

... besids I remember I had once a good acco[unt] possitively of an Oxf. Schollar who herding himself wth tht. Cattle, [associating himself with that people], leaving their trade, professed to his friend tht it consisted onely in determining the imagination [working out what people wanted to hear].

From true dreamers to Romani palm readers, his thoughts next moved to witches:

> Would I also referr wht is done by white witches in their blessing (not to say a good deall of tht wch is done by the black spellers.) I known an old wife in Rumborough who being threapd down [denounced in Suffolk dialect] by the neighbours tht she was a witch, denyed it bitterly, onely acknowleged tht she had an unluckie tongue & wht she spleenfully sd. Should betide a neighbour in person, Cattle, beer &c did so.

There is another reference to witchcraft in his letter of 18 March 1667/68:

> Mrs Lunden of Middleton in tht. Count kept a catt, wch it seems, used often to lye upon her lapp, but then offering to skip up, she put it by, because having layn a lttle before on the embers, she thought the the coat might be ashie, presentl;y after the maid servt. Comes & makes a larg fire intending to hang the pot on for supper, the catt fairly walks into the midst of it lyes down & burns, Mrs L. being amaz'd call in some to take her out, but they seing twas too late let her lye there till she burnt to ashes. How much of this is from nature or withchery is a Q. [question] tis a busines I se tht has taken ayre hugely in the neighbour hood.
>
> [Note: the printed version of these letters uses the letter 'y' for 'the' throughout, but I have changed this for ease of understanding.]

Witchcraft and the supernatural was as much part of the reality of Fairfax's world as it was of his colleague Beck, but his approach to it was quite different. Fairfax was interested to see what it was, Beck was interested in using it as a way to prove orthodoxy.

Another case for which we have several details, is that of Magdalen Holyday, a servant to the parson of Saxmundham, which was written down in 1685 but was referring to 1672. The details are contained in a letter written by Tobias Gilbert to Richard Baxter, who was collecting evidence for his book *The Certainty of the World of Spirits Fully Evinced*, and was probably preserved for another edition which did not appear:

> Magdalen Holyday, spinster, aged eighteen years, the daughter of poor honest persons, Phineas and Martha Holyday, of the parish of Rendham, near Framlingham (as may be seen by the register of the said parish), was servant-maid to Mr Simon Jones, minister of the parish of Saxmundham, with whom she had dwelt for the space of three years and upwards, and was esteemed by all the neighbours as a civil, well-behaved young woman.

In fact, a girl who could not be too highly praised:

... nor was any reproach ever thrown upon her, save that some few of the Gospellers (a party that sprang up in the reign of Queen Elizabeth, and doth now continue to the great division of the one Catholic Church,) would taunt her, that being handmaid to a Minister of the Church, she would frequent wakes and fairs at Whitsuntide, and saint days and holy days; but they could not throw anything in her teeth which they would, as she always went in company with her brother, aunts, or other sober people of good repute, who could keep scandal from her door. Her family did not like Oliver Cromwell, nor any of his ordinances, but were true and faithful to King Charles, of blessed memory, though they were but poor folk.

But to come to my story. It happened on Monday, in Lammas, the year 1672, about noon, as she was carrying in dinner, no one in the parlour, save the parson, his wife, and their eldest daughter, Rebecca, then about to be married to a worthy and painstaking Gospel Minister, then living at the parish of Yoxford, in the said county, that on a sudden, just as she had placed a suet dumpling on the board, she uttered a loud shriek, as if she were distraught, and stooping down, as in great pain, said she felt a pricking as of a large Pin in the upper part of her leg, but she did not think that any such thing could be there. Yet on ungartering her hose, she felt a pin had got there, within the skin, yet not drawing blood nor breaking the skin, nor making any hole or sign, and she could hardly feel the head of it with her finger, and from that time it continued tormenting her with violent and retching pains all the day and night; and this continuing and nothing assuaged, Mistress Jones, by advice of the minister, sent for the assistance of two able apothecaries (medici) then dwelling in the said town; one a chirurgeon of great repute, who had studied under the famous Hondius at Frankfort; the other a real son of Galen; who, on examining the part, and above and below at sufficient distance, both declared they could see neither 'volva, nec vestigium' of the said pin; but on her constant and confident assertion that there was a pin, though it had now time to work itself deeper into the flesh, like an insidious enemy, they made an incision, but could find none, only the maid asserted that a few days before, an old woman came to the door and begged a pin of her, and she not giving her one, the said woman muttered something, but she did not suspect her. And now it was time these noted leeches should do something for this afflicted person; for now she lies in ceaseless torment, both by night and by day, for if she slept her sleep was troubled with dreams and wicked apparitions: sometimes she saw something like a mole run into her bed, sometimes she saw a naked arm held over her, and so was this poor maid thus tormented by evil spirits in spite of all godly prayers and ringing of church bells, etc. But now the doctors took her in hand, their names, Anthony Smith, Gent., and Samuel Kingston, chirurgeon to Sir

John Rouse, of Henham, Knt., having taken down the deposition of the said Magdalen Holyday before Mr Pacey, a pious Justice of the Peace, living at Marlesford in the said county, upon oath; they then gave to the said M.H. the following medicines: Imprimis, a decoction exfuga Deomonum of southern wood, mug wort vervain, of which they formed a drink according to Heuftius Medical Epistles,' lib. xii, sect. iv, also following Variola, a physician, of great experience at the court of the Emperor. They also anointed the part with the following embrocation: Dog's grease well mixed, four ounces; bear's fat, two ounces; eight ounces of capon's grease; four and twenty slips of misletoe, cut in pieces and powdered small with gum of Venice turpentine, put close into a phial, and exposed for nine days to the sun, till it formed into a green balsam, with which the said parts were daily anointed for the space of three weeks' time, during which time, instead of amendment, the poor patient daily got worse, and vomited, not without constant shrieks or gruntling, the following substances: paring of nails, bits of spoons, pieces of brass (triangular), crooked pins, bodkins, lumps of red hair, egg-shells broken, parchment shavings, a hen's bone of the leg, one thousand two hundred worms, pieces of glass, bones like the great teeth of a horse, aluminous matter, sal petri (not thoroughly prepared), till at length relief was found, when well nigh given up, when she brought up with violent retching, 'a whole row of pins stuck on blew paper!!' After that, these sons of Aesculapius joyfully perceived that their potent drugs had wrought the designed cure they gave her comfort, that she had subdued her bitter foe, nor up to the present time has she ever been afflicted in any way; but, having married an honest, poor man, though well to do in the world, being steward to Sir John Heveningham, she has borne him four healthy children, and is likely to cover his house with more sweet olive branches from her fruitful orchard. Whether this punishment was inflicted upon her by the said old woman, an emissary of Satan, or whether it was meant wholesomely to rebuke her for frequenting wakes, may-dances, and candlemas fairs, and such like pastimes, still to me remains in much doubt. Non possum solvere nodum.

Sir, your thankful servant, T.G.
Freston Parish, nigh to Saxmondham, sent by the carrier.

PS. I hear the physicians followed up their first medicine with castory, and rad. ostrutii, and sem. dauci, on Forestius, his recommendation.

The tone of Tobias Gilbert's account is half-believing, half-mocking. It is clear that the process had become medicalised and doctors and their recipes were now centre stage. Moreover, he sums up the whole moral dilemma at the centre of witchcraft very neatly:

Whether this punishment was inflicted upon her by the said old woman, an emissary of Satan, or whether it was meant wholesomely to rebuke her for frequenting wakes, may-dances, and Candlemas fairs, and such like pastimes, still to me remains in much doubt.

The nature of the curse is fascinating, as it follows the pattern of the two Lowestoft witches very closely. Vomiting pins is not mentioned by either Stearne or Hopkins as an effect of witchcraft. There seems to be an association in thought between the pins used to determine whether or not a person was a witch, and the curse inflicted by the witch. The strange motif of pin-vomiting may start with the Lowestoft trial. That being so, it is both fascinating and frustrating to note that the bewitched girl is taken before a magistrate with the familiar name of Mr Pacey of Marlesford – Pacey of course being the name of the leading Lowestoft family in that case. The nature of the link, if any, between the two Paceys is unclear.

In 1702, Suffolk was to become the home of the Lord Chief Justice Sir John Holt who purchased Redgrave Manor, the home of the Bacon family which has appeared so many times in this story. Holt was an extremely interesting man. He had been very wild as a young student; there were rumours that he had even been a highwayman. His cases included protecting a man's right to vote and two cases that called into question the right to keep slaves in England. In one of these he decided against the theory that it was right to keep as slaves people who were not Christian.

Holt had presided over eleven witchcraft trials (further evidence for the continuing post-Commonwealth, post-Puritan Restoration persecution of witches) and dismissed them all. The following are his Suffolk cases:

In 1694, Mother Munnings was tried at Bury St Edmunds for maleficia, for casting a spell upon her landlord causing his death, having an imp in the form of a polecat and a further two imps – one black, one white. On her acquittal, the two imps were found to be a black and a white ball of wool.

Around the same time, Margaret Elnore of Ipswich was accused of accepting familiars from her grandmother (said to have been hanged for witchcraft). She was supposed to have the witch marks on her body, and she was accused of sending lice to infest her neighbours.

An anecdote about the judge was preserved in Suffolk and recorded in a book called *The Betts of Wortham*:

During a trial, the 'powerful spell' of an accused witch – some words written on a parchment – was brought into court. This the prisoner confessed had been given originally to her, to cure her child of ague, and that it had since cured many others. The judge examined the parchment, and then addressed himself to the jury thus: 'Thirty years ago', he said, 'I and some companions

The Right Honble Sr John Holt Knt
Lord CHIEF JUSTICE of the Court of KINGS BENCH
And one of their Maties most Honble Privy Council Año 1689
Printed and Sold by John King at the Globe against the Church in the Poultry

Sir John Holt. (Suffolk Record Office)

as thoughtless as myself, went to this woman's dwelling, then a public house, and after enjoying, found we had no means to discharge the reckoning. I had recourse to a stratagem. Observing a child ill of ague, I pretended I had a spell to cure it, and wrote the classic line you see on that parchment before you (14). I was discharged that demand of me, by the gratitude of this poor woman for the supposed benefit. Nature did much for the child; imagination the rest. This incident', he continued, 'but ill suits my present character and station; but to conceal it would be to aggravate the folly for which it becomes me to atone, to endanger innocence and countenance superstition.'

These cases, dismissed by Holt, seem to be the last cases of witchcraft to have been prosecuted in Suffolk. With them, witchcraft ceased to be a legal matter in Suffolk.

II

CONCLUSIONS

The witch trials will always hang, in England and America, as an albatross around the neck of the Puritans. This needs to be modified. Some writers describe the witch persecutions almost as though the populace, led astray by Puritan fanaticism, simply sleepwalked into the nightmare of the witch-hunt and did not wake up until the Restoration. Such an explanation has a considerable appeal for a certain political cast of mind and approach to religion, and has a very long lineage indeed, all the way back to the politics of the Restoration itself. How convenient to load everything on to the backs of the Commonwealth, and how it suits modern sensibilities to assume that deep religious conviction is inevitably destructive.

There is a problem for anyone looking at this period, because the word 'Puritan' itself now carries such a heavy baggage that it is almost impossible for many historians to see beyond the label to the broad, argumentative, and often highly creative, traditions that lie behind the term.

This is simply wrong. Witchcraft was in no way an exclusively Puritan belief. The pre-Christian Romans and Scandinavians believed in and punished witches. The Roman Catholic Church believed in and persecuted witches, far more viciously and in far greater numbers. The Restoration Government and its bishops did not stop persecution for religious reasons. In point of fact, in Suffolk and Norfolk there was actually a resurgence in interest in trying to promote witch trials during the Restoration.

As a village belief, witchcraft continued after the short Puritan ascendancy for another 200 years or so. All serious 'Puritan' clergy who discussed the subject pointed out that witchcraft, as an explanation for misfortune, was in contradiction to the basic Puritan theological insistence on the idea of an all-powerful God who tests the righteous and uses misfortune to cause them to humble themselves and reflect on their sins. The Puritan movement, like all major movements, included many things, and hypocrisy, self-righteousness and a repressed sexuality were amongst them. However, it had no monopoly on common human problems – contemporary secular newspapers still claim moral outrage at the behaviour of politicians who do not follow the sexual codes of the moment. It did encourage people to think, to debate, to argue and to weigh up evidence (even if some of this evidence was Biblical 'proof' texts) and to write passionately and eloquently. The pamphlet war was a very Puritan phenomenon.

Above all, such a view totally obscures the reality that it was Puritans who wrote *against* the trials, who questioned and debated what was going on; it was Puritan clergy who investigated the abuses of the trials and, in some cases, sought to protect rather than to persecute, and it was Puritan juries who threw out approximately two-thirds of the cases. The struggle was not between a Puritan and a non-Puritan approach to witchcraft. The struggle was an internal one within the Puritan movement.

On the one hand, there were the Presbyterians who wished for a State Church, to be controlled and policed by ministers appointed by town councils along Calvinist lines. They wanted no kind of social change, and had a strong opposition to ordinary men and women choosing their own religious viewpoint. On the other hand, there were the Independents – in religion they wanted to preserve what they saw as the Reformed Church, and wanted an end to the bishops as religious police. They were also suspicious of the Presbyterian Church and town councils replacing bishops in this role. As Milton said, 'New Presbyter is but old priest writ large.' They usually had a radical understanding of Luther's teaching of 'the priesthood of all believers.'

Neither the Royalist Laudians nor the Independents had any interest in persecuting witches. It was the Presbyterian town councils and the Presbyterian gentry who took the lead. We have seen how a whole underground of unofficial experts, the cunning men, could find a commercial niche exploiting the insecurities, fears and tensions of society. As tensions increased, we have seen just how easy it was to create a machine that could produce accusations, confessions and convictions which allowed people to believe that they had turned a village lynching into due process of law, while still providing the necessary scapegoat whose ceremonial death would restore peace and harmony to society.

We have seen large sections of society choose to disassociate themselves from reality, and enter a world of distortion which turns the most powerless into figures of immense otherworldly menace, in which everyday infringements of the current sexual morality or moments of bitterness and despair are turned into acts of cosmic evil, and in which those who have denied charity to those poorer than themselves become the victims rather than the victimised.

This part of the story – human stupidity, superstition and brutality – is not unfamiliar. But it is only part of the story. Just as the witchfinders had their friends in high places, and access to their own publicity machine, so too were there sections of the powerful who were appalled at what was happening and wanted to close the persecution down. There were movements trying to give a voice to the voiceless and a dignity to the ideas of the poor, including poor women. There were those working slowly round to the idea of freedom of conscience. To those opposed to this movement, the Quaker had been turned into the witch.

The people of the seventeenth century, just like us, had the ability to see through obvious fantasy by maintaining their own moral compass. Arthur Wilson's doubts about the Chelmsford trials were not only intellectual, but arose from simply seeing what was before him. Much the same seems true of Fairclough's support of Binkes. Ralph Gardiner and John Willis's attacks on events in Newcastle were similar. There were those who simply could *not* believe. Some were just anonymous juries who refused to convict in case after case. The world might, or it might not, contain witches, but clearly these women before them were innocent sacrifices accused of impossible crimes and fitted up by the totally unscrupulous. It shows a further universal conflict in the difference between those who see knowledge as something to be learnt from careful observation of what is around them (e.g. Nathaniel Fairfax), and those who see knowledge as the assembly of quotations from the past (e.g. Beck).

The story of witches in Suffolk is one of a society that fell into persecution, but also of a society that, through basic common humanity and a refusal to become intoxicated with a convenient fantasy, managed to retain a level of decency.

BIBLIOGRAPHY

NOTE ON SOURCES

Malcolm Gaskill's work *Witchfinders: A Seventeenth-Century English Tragedy* (John Murray, 2006) is absolutely essential reading for witchcraft in East Anglia, and I owe his work a debt of gratitude – even where I have come to different conclusions!

Ipswich is rich in the number of original borough documents that survive from the seventeenth century, preserved in the Ipswich branch of the Suffolk Record Office. A very large number of the records for this period have been fully transcribed, indexed and translated by the First Archivist of the borough, Vincent Redstone, and his notes have been extremely useful to me in writing this book. They are held, along with the original documents, in the Suffolk Record Office in Ipswich.

Ipswich is also very frequently mentioned in the enormous series of the Calendar of State Papers – Foreign, Domestic and Privy Council. Obviously the Domestic series is the most relevant for this study. This source has been slightly less used by local historians.

SOURCES AND FURTHER READING

Books

Argentine, Richard, *De Praestigiis et Incantationibus Daemonum et Necromanticorum* (Basel: 1563).

Bacon, Nathaniel, *Annalls of Ipswche. The Lawes, Customes and Government of the same. Collected out of ye Records Bookes and Writings of that Towne.* William H. Richardson (ed.), with a memoir by Sterling Westhorpe (Ipswich: 11 April 1644). Printed for the subscribers by S.H. Cowell.

Baxter, Richard, *The Certainty of the World of Spirits* (1690).

Bernard, Richard, *A Guide to Grand-Jury Men* (1627).

Blagrove, Joseph, *The Astrological Practise of Physick* (1671).

Bradshaw, Ellis, *The Quakers' Whitest Devil Unveiled ...* (1654).

Bugg, Francis, *Quakerism a Grand Imposture, or, the Picture of Quakerism Continued* (1715).

Bullein, Dr William, 'Bullein's Bulwark Defence against all Sickness, Sornes and Woundes that dooe daily assaulte Mankind' (1562), in *The East Anglian: or Notes and queries on subjects connected with the counties of Suffolk, Cambridge, Essex and Norfolk*, Vol XIII (1800).

Bunn, Ivan and Gilbert Geis, *A Trial of Witches. A Seventeenth-Century Witchcraft Prosecution* (Routledge, 1997).

Bunyan, John, *The Holy War ... or the Losing and Taking again of the Town of Mansoul* (1682).

Burnet, Gilbert and Osmund Airy (ed.) *Burnet's History of My Own Time* (Clarendo Press, 1900).

Burrough, Edward, *A Declaration of the Sad and Great Persecution and Martyrdom of the People of God, called Quakers, in New England, for the Worshipping of God* (1661).

Canning, Rev. Richard, *An Enquiry into the Gifts and Legacies of the Town of Ipswich* (1747).

Clarke, Samuel, *The Lives of Sundry Eminent Persons in this Later Age: In two Parts*, Part 1 'Divines' (1683).

Coldham, Peter Wilson, *Emigrants in Chains: A Social History of Forced Emigration to the Americas of Felons, Destitute Children, Political and Religious Non-conformists, Vagabonds, Beggars and other Undesirables, 1607–1776* (1992).

Cooper, Janet & C.R. Elrington (eds), *History of the County of Essex: Volume 9 – The Borough of Colchester* (1994).

Defoe, Daniel, *A Tour Thro' the Whole Island of Great Britain* (1724–1727).

Dobson, Austin, *The Diary of John Evelyn* (London: Macmillan, 1906).

Doughty, Katherine Frances, *The Betts of Wortham in Suffolk, 1480–1905* (London: John Lane, 1912)

Evans-Pritchard, E.E., *Witchcraft Oracles and Magic among the* Azande (Oxford, 1937).

Evelyn, John, William Bray (ed.) *The Diary of John Evelyn* (New York and London: M. Walter Dunn, *c*.1901).

Everitt, Alan (ed.), *Suffolk and the Great Rebellion 1640–1660* (Suffolk Records Society, 1960).

Ewen, C. L'Estrange (ed.), *Witch Hunting and Witch Trials: The Indictments for Witchcraft from the Records of 1373 Assizes Held for the Home Circuit AD 1559–1736* (1929).

Foxe, John, *Actes and Monuments* (1563).

Foxe, John, *Foxe's Book of Martyrs* (1563).

Fu-Kiau, Kimbwandende Kia Bunseki, *African Cosmology of the Bantu-Kongo* (2001).

Gale, Thomas, 'Certaine workes of Galens, called Methodus Medendi ...' (1567), in Norman Jones, *The birth of the Elizabethan Age: England in the 1560s* (Blackwell, 1993).

Gardiner, Ralph, *England's Grievance Discovered, in Relation to the Coal Trade* (London: 1655).

Gaskill, Malcolm, *Witchfinders: A Seventeenth-Century English Tragedy* (John Murray, 2006).

Gaule, John, *Select Cases of Conscience Touching Witches and Witchcraft* (1646).

Gifford, George, *A Dialogue Concerning Witches & Witchcraftes* (1593).

Glanville, Joseph, *Saducismus Triumphatus* (1681).

Gough, John, *A History of the People called Quakers from their First Rise to the Present Time* (1789).

Grimston, Sir Harbottle, *Reports of Sir George Croke ... Formerly one of the Justices of the Courts of King's Bench and Common-pleas: of such select cases as were adjudged in the said courts in the reign of Queen Elizabeth collected and written in French by Himself revised and published in English by Sir Harbottle Grimston* (London: 1715).

Hall, Joseph, *Occasional Meditations* (London: 1631).

Henning, B.D. (ed.), *The History of Parliament: the House of Commons 1660–1690* (Haynes Publishing, 1983).

Hopkins, Matthew, *The Discovery of Witches* (London, Norwich, 1647).

Hussey, Frank, *Suffolk Invasion* (Terence Dalton Ltd, 1983).

Hutchinson, Francis, *A Historical Essay Concerning Witchcraft* (1718).

Ingler, William (ed.), *Certaine Informations from severall parts of the Kingdome* (London: Henry Overton, 1643).

Jonson, Ben, *The Devil is an Ass* (1617).

Lake, Peter, *The Antichrist's Lewd Hat, Protestants Papists and Players in Post-Reformation England*, p.252 (Yale, 2002).

The Lawes against Witches, and Conjuration: And Some brief Notes and Observations for the Discovery of Witches. Being very useful for these Times, wherein the Devil reignes and prevailes over the Soules of poor Creatures, in drawing them to that crying Sin of Witchcraft. Also, The Confession of Mother Lakeland, who was arraigned and condemned for a Witch, at Ipswich in Suffolke (Printed in London for RW, 1645).

Lawrence, Mr Matthew, *The Use and Practice of Faith, Delivered in the Public Lectures at Ipswich by the Late Eminent and Faithful Servant of his Lord* (1657).

McCartney, Martha W., *Virginia Immigrants and Adventurers: A Biographical Dictionary, 1607–1635*, p.121 (2007).

MacCulloch, Diarmuid (ed.), *Letters from Redgrave Hall: The Bacon Family 1370–1704*, pp.50–73 (Forby Vocabulary of East Anglia: 1830).

More, Sir Thomas, *A Dialogue Concerning Heresies* (1529).

Notestein, Wallace, *A History of Witchcraft in England from 1558–1718* (Washington: 1911).

Partridge, Charles, *East Anglian Miscellany*, Vol. 9, p.293 (1934)

Petts, Samuel (Petto), *A Faithfull Narrative of the Wonderful and Extraordinary Fits which Mr Thomas Spatchett Late of Dunwich and Cookly was Under by Witchcraft* (1693).

Powell, William Stevens, *John Pory, 1572–1636: The Life and Letters of a Man of Many Parts* (University of North Carolina Press, 1977).

Reyce, Richard, *Suffolk in the XVII Century: The Breviary of Suffolk*, 1618 (London: Lord Francis Hervey, 1902).

Rivett-Carnac J.H. (ed.), 'Witchcraft: The Rev. John Lowes' in *The East Anglian: Notes & Queries* (1896).

Sir Nicholas Bacon Collection of English Court and Manorial Documents, item 4552, University of Chicago Library.

Stearne, John, *A Confirmation and Discoverie of Witchcraft* (London: 1648).

Stubbes, Philip, *The Anatomie of Abuses* (1583).

Summers, Montague, *The Werewolf in Lore and Legend* (1933).

Ward, Nathaniel, *The Simple Cobler of Aggavam* (1647).

Ward, Samuel, *Balme from Gilead: To Recover Conscience*, Thomas Gataker (ed.) (London: 1616).

Ward, Samuel, *Jethro's Justice of the Peace*, Nathaniel Ward (ed.) (London: 1618).

Ward, Samuel, *The Wonders of the Lodestone* (Suffolk Record Offices, 1640).

Ward, Samuel, *Woe to Drunkards. A Sermon* (London: 1622).

Webb, John, *Poor Relief in Elizabethan Ipswich* (Suffolk Records Society, 1966).

Webb, John, *The Town Finances of Elizabethan Ipswich: Select Treasurers' and Chamberlains' Accounts* (Suffolk Records Society, 1996).

Whalley, Henry, *The True Informer: Containing a perfect collection of the proceedings in Parliament and true Information from the Armies* (1645–1646).

White, Rev. C.H. Evelyn, *The Great Domesday Book of Ipswich* (1885).

Whitehead, George, *The Christian Progess of George Whitehead that Ancient Servant & Minister of Jesus Christ*.

Willard, Thomas, 'Pimping for the Fairy Queen: Some Cozeners in Shakespeare's England', in Albrecht Classen and Connie Scarborough (eds), *Crime and Punishment in the Middle Ages and Early Modern Age* (Berlin: Walter de Gruyter, 2012).

Williams, Roger, *The Bloudy Tenet of Persecution, for Cause of Conscience, Discussed, in a Conference betweene Truth and Peace. Who in all Tender Affection Present to the High Court of Parliament*, I (1644).

Wilson, Arthur, 'Observations of God's Providence in the Tract of my Life' (as published in the critical edition of *The Inconstant Lady*).

Winship, Michael P., *The Times and Trials of Anne Hutchinson: Puritans Divided* (Kansas: University Press of Kansas, 2005).

Wodderspoon, John, *Memorials of the Ancient Town of Ipswich* (Ipswich: F. Pawsey, 1850).

Other

Calendar of State Papers – Foreign, Domestic, Privy Council.

Clarendon Manuscripts, Letter 2624, Bodlian Library.

The Commonplace Book of William Davenport of Bramhall. (Published on www.earlystuartlibels.net), Chester City Record Office MS CR 63/2/19, fols. 70v–71r.

'English Origins of New England Families, 1500s–1800s', CD from Genealogical Publishing Co. Inc. (see Candler Pedigree Chart of Ward Family).

'Mr Fysher's Accompt for the Fortifications and the Accompt of Joseph Pemberton of the moneys received and laid out by him about the fortifications', Ipswich Borough Archives.

Philosophical Transactions of the Royal Society.

Sessions of the Peace.